COMMODORE

REIGART BOLIVAR LOWRY

WILLIAM F. MCCLINTOCK, JR.

Print ISBN: 978-1-09837-324-5

eBook ISBN: 978-1-09837-325-2

CONTENTS

INTRODUCTION

THIS BIOGRAPHY OF REIGART BOLIVAR LOWRY IS THREE books in one. The story centers on the struggle of the most senior Captains in the United States Navy against political influence within their service. This attempt at the use of influence was the culmination of several years of political corruption within the Republican administration of Ulysses S. Grant. Reigart spoke out against the President and his Cabinet only to be put on their enemy list and to become the victim of their dirty tricks.

During this struggle in the last years of his life, Reigart met with men whom he had served with and served under during every important phase of his naval service. During his years in the Navy, 1840-1880, Reigart was on the scene during nearly every important event that took place. His first sea duty was in China during the Opium War. After graduating from the first class at Annapolis, Reigart joined the Home Squadron to fight in the Mexican War. When Commodore Matthew Perry opened Japan, Reigart was there. A few years later, he witnessed the first firing on Fort Sumter and then took part on every important front in the Civil War.

Therefore, this book is not only a story about the struggle of a man against political influence and corruption, but it is also a story about the man himself and about the Navy in which he served.

1.
YOUR OBEDIENT SERVANT

"…REPUBLICAN THIEVES HAVE TAKEN EVERYTHING IN SIGHT. They even stole the Presidency in 1876, but they could not take Congress from us. Open corruption, right up to the office of the President, has undermined the American government. As your obedient servant, I have served my country for thirty-eight years. I pledge to continue serving it until my dying day. You can do your part by electing a Democratic Congress in 1878. Help put the United States back on the road to recovery. Thank you."

Captain Reigart Bolivar Lowry stepped down from the podium amidst tumultuous applause. He had been stumping for Democratic Congressional candidates throughout the 1878 campaign. Democrats liked him. He was one of the few high-ranking officers of the armed forces who would speak out for them. The nation's political and military leadership had been predominantly Republican following the Civil War. Captain Lowry was an impressive figure, and though he had not seen active duty in over three years, he often wore his dress uniform to speaking engagements.

The fact that he spoke out was one of the reasons that he had not seen active duty for so long. Reigart had served faithfully as a professional naval officer for thirty-eight years. He had performed with distinction in the Mexican and Civil Wars. By 1878, he had become one of the most senior Captains in the United States Navy.

Reigart had been proud to be a part of the Navy as long as it had remained a strictly professional service. He had always looked down on the Army because of the political influences that were a part of that service. Beginning in 1869, when Ulysses S. Grant became President of the United States, corruption and politics permeated every part of the government. The Navy was no exception. Secretary of the Navy, George M. Robeson, introduced these elements to the Navy.

Reigart could not tolerate corruption. He felt compelled to speak out. He openly and loudly criticized both his Commander-in-Chief and his Secretary of Navy. He published a magazine on board a naval vessel in which he wrote biting satires. During the election campaign of 1876, Reigart vigorously campaigned against Rutherford B. Hayes. He was a forceful speaker and left a good impression wherever he went. He swayed many people with his efforts. When the election was contested and Hayes won, even though the Democrat, Samuel J. Tilden, had more popular votes, Reigart was bitterly disappointed. His candidate, Tilden, even had more electoral votes before the votes were recounted. Hayes, like Grant, had been a general in the Army. Reigart felt that Hayes's election had been fixed like everything else had been for the past eight years.

As a result of his own behavior, it did not come as much of a surprise to Reigart that he had not had a command for the past three years. He had been blacklisted. There had even been some talk of having him tried for treason. What had begun for Reigart as a brilliant career had in recent years turned into disaster. He would have it no other way. He refused to kowtow to his commanders just to obtain a command.

Following the speech, Reigart left the podium and slipped away before anyone noticed. He did not like politics, and he hated it when people made a fuss over his speeches. He was not speaking to be admired but because he felt it was his duty to his fellow countrymen. As he walked down the back streets of Erie, Pennsylvania, he was alone. Though most of his fellow naval officers agreed with him, they would not take the risk of speaking out or being associated with him. Going home was no big relief to his loneliness. Working himself up to a high pitch at political rallies and lack of duty for three years had made him unbearable at home. Reigart drank heavily. His problems led him to drink even more. His temper was short. He constantly yelled at everyone within hearing range. His wife and children did not look forward to his coming home.

Financial difficulties plagued him. As a Captain, Reigart had made $4,500 per year while on active duty. Now, waiting orders, he made only $2,800 per year. Bess, his wife, enjoyed spending money and had always had it in the past. Her wild spending and his lack of active duty had put the Lowrys into financial trouble. Bills could not be met, and Secretary of Navy Robeson had used this fact to discipline Reigart. Even though she was partly at fault, Bess blamed Reigart for all their financial problems.

As he approached home, Reigart wondered whether to go directly in or whether to stop at the local pub. Somehow stopping at the bar made going home a little easier, but this time he decided to go straight home. As he entered the house, his wife asked, "Ricard, where have you been?"

He told her he had been to the political rally. She did not like it when he went to these rallies. They made him tense and irritable and got him too excited. She called him Ricard, which was a shortened version of Ricardo, her nickname for Reigart. Reigart called her Bess, short for Elizabeth, her middle name.

When Reigart saw that Bess was going to nag him about the rally, he went straight to the liquor cabinet. This did not do any good, however, because she began to nag him about his drinking. This aggravated the situation, and he drank more just to spite her. Bess often tried to hide the liquor when Reigart had had too much, but he always seemed to find it.

Bess was particularly concerned about the impression Reigart was making on their children. They were at vulnerable ages, running between eight and fifteen years old. The children had become torn between their parents. Ricardo, Marion, and Robert usually sided with their father while Walter almost always sided with his mother.

Reigart claimed that alcohol was necessary to ease the pain of his various ailments. His health was failing him. He really was in pain, but, of course, alcohol aggravated rather than cured his diseases. He suffered from rheumatism, diabetes, and gout. If one of these diseases was not bothering him, another one was.

Finally, Bess told him, "Ricard, I think that it is best that you leave Erie. Your behavior has become a constant strain on the children and me. Perhaps if you left for a while, we could work things out later."

Reigart was stunned. While these had not been the happiest years of his life, he had thought that his wife would stand behind him until his work had been done. Disillusioned not only by his family, but also by his Navy and by his country, Reigart decided to leave the United States.

He did not even stay until after the 1878 election. Without his wife and children behind him, he no longer had his drive. The fight had seemed so frustrating. Now he wondered whether it had all been worth it. Within a couple of weeks, Reigart packed up and moved to St. Catharines, Ontario, in Canada. He got himself a room in a boarding house along the shore of Lake Ontario.

Reigart hoped that he could clear his head of all his problems by going to Canada. He did not know how long he would be there. He would stay until either his family or his Navy asked him to come back. The tensions that had existed at home were no longer with him, but Reigart was a lonely, washed-up man. He continued to drink and became isolated from the world.

2.
CATHERINE ELIZABETH COURTRIGHT LOWRY

◦ ◉ ◦

ONE COLD MORNING IN NOVEMBER 1879, REIGART LAY IN BED half asleep, half awake. Someone was knocking at the door, but he was trying to ignore it. It was too cold to get up from under his warm blankets, and he had a headache from drinking too much the night before. Even though he had been in St. Catharines for nearly a year and a half, he knew no one and hoped the person would just go away.

The knocking persisted, so he finally got up, cursing whoever it was all the way across the room. Opening the door, he found a boy there holding a telegram for him. Reigart snatched it from the boy and slammed the door in his face. Staggering back across the living room, Reigart slumped into one of his easy chairs. He had a good mind to get back under those nice warm blankets, but it would take too much energy to get out of the chair and back into bed. He did not feel like reading anything with the headache he had, but his curiosity finally got the best of him.

Ripping open the envelope, he pulled out the telegram. When he saw Erie, Pennsylvania, in the heading, his heart skipped a beat. He wondered whether it was good news or bad news. The telegram was from a lawyer. He was notifying Reigart that Catherine Elizabeth Courtright Lowry had divorced him on November 8, 1879. Reigart read the telegram two or three times. Even though he had been separated from his wife for a year and a half, he had always hoped for reconciliation. He should have expected it, but Reigart could not accept the fact that his marriage of twenty-two years was over. This fact just would not sink in.

As he sat there, he began to think about Bess and his marriage to her. He had been assigned to the *Michigan* in Erie, Pennsylvania, when he met her. He reported to the *Michigan* in August 1857, knowing that sailing on Lake Erie could be nothing like the ocean voyages to which he had become accustomed. Much to his regret, also, Reigart found that the *Michigan* spent most of its time stationed in Erie. In the winter when the lake froze over, the *Michigan* could not leave dockside for several months.

In desperation, Reigart roamed the town looking for something to do. One day, shortly after his arrival in Erie, Reigart was walking through a park when he noticed a girl sitting alone on a bench. She was very pretty and petite, being only a little over five feet tall. Nineteen years old, Bess was twelve years Reigart's junior. It was love at first sight, and the Reverend James Abercombie of St. Paul's Episcopal Church married them at the Milton and Hannah Courtright home less than two months later, on October sixth.

Reigart had married into a prominent family. Bess's father, Milton Courtright, was a canal and railroad builder. He later introduced rapid transit to New York City and became the first President of the elevated railroad there. He built the Canada Southern Railway, later renamed the Michigan Central Railway, and became its first President. Milton had become one of the most wealthy and prominent citizens of Erie.

Reigart hit it off with Milton. Milton was only sixteen years older than his new son-in-law and the men became great friends. Reigart was interested in Milton's railroad building, but, even more, he liked to talk to Milton about canal building. For his part, Milton enjoyed talking with someone who understood canals. At the time of Reigart and Bess's marriage,

Milton was working on the Chesapeake and Albemarle Canal. Reigart had saved up some money, and when Milton asked him to become a partner, Reigart jumped at the chance. Now that he had a stake in the canal, Reigart studied the charts of the area until he knew every river, creek, inlet, and bay anywhere within fifty miles of the canal. Reigart's divorce from Bess was terrible, but it also cost him a wonderful and close friendship with Milton.

The fact of his divorce was beginning to sink in. It was all over. His depression began to deepen. The fact that he had a terrible hangover came back to him. He staggered into the kitchen, got a bottle of bourbon, and returned to his easy chair. He thought that maybe a few drinks would make him feel better.

As he gulped his first mouthful of bourbon, he began thinking about Bess again. The first few months of marriage were among the happiest times of Reigart's life. At about the same time as his marriage, the *Michigan* had gone into dry dock for seven months because Lake Erie had frozen over. Reigart had welcomed this opportunity to become acquainted with his new wife and family. These seven months would be the longest they would be together for many years to come.

Reigart's orders to report to the *Cyane* at Norfolk, Virginia, came as a terrible shock to the couple. Reigart reluctantly went, but his heart was not in it. He had become used to the easy life in Erie and all the pleasures of marriage. As he sat there, slumped in his chair in St. Catharines, Ontario, he had to crack a smile as he thought of what he had done to get back to his wife. Reigart told his new commanding officer that his wife was sick and that he had to get back to her side. He must have been convincing because his commander fell for it hook, line, and sinker. Reigart returned to Erie after being away for only one month, and miraculously, his wife's health soon improved.

Reigart's good fortune did not last forever, however, and within a few months he became assigned to a ship that was scheduled to go to South America. This time, he was away from his wife for eight months. He was "condemned" by a medical survey as unfit for service when he returned. As on previous voyages, Reigart had suffered from rheumatism and had to be confined to a hospital in Norfolk. Before returning to Erie, he visited the Chesapeake and Albemarle Canal to review his investment. The Courtrights were happy to welcome Reigart back to Erie. Bess had missed her husband and Milton wanted to hear about the canal. Reigart spent many evenings with Milton going over the charts of the canal. Bess seemed happy that her husband got along so well with her father.

Reigart's life with his wife and in-laws was again interrupted after about five months when he became reassigned. He was relieved from this assignment because he had not completely recovered from his illnesses, and within a month, he again returned to Erie.

When he was well, Reigart was assigned to the ship he would be on when the Civil War began. He would not see Bess again for over two and a half years. They corresponded, of course, but even that had to be sporadic because of the difficulties of the war. This period was a lonely one, for both parties. Reigart missed Bess, but he was kept so busy during the war that he had little time to think about her. At night when things settled down, he would think about her and write to her. During this time, Bess, too, tried to keep busy. She and Reigart had moved to Philadelphia just before the war. There, she joined social circles where she found other women in similar situations. Whenever one of the women received a letter, it was cause for a meeting. A letter from one husband would often have news about several other husbands.

As Reigart took another swig of bourbon, he recalled the spending spree Bess went on when he came home in 1863. He felt bitter as he remembered how she blamed him for their financial difficulties. Spending money came naturally to Bess. She went to New York about once a month to buy clothes, often spending hundreds of dollars. Money had never been a problem for Bess. Her father had become wealthy from building railroads and canals. Bess always bought the best, whether in clothing, food, or any other merchandise, though she spent more on herself than on other members of her family. Just before Reigart returned from the Civil War, Bess went to New York on one of her wildest shopping sprees. She went to several of the finest shops in the city, including Mme. Anastasie Gigon-Russel, Couturiere de Paris, where she bought a gray silk dress for $250.00!

When Reigart arrived in New York, Bess was waiting for him on the dock. Bess had arranged for a hotel for the night and had a coach waiting to take them there. They had a lot to catch up on. They retired early that evening. The couple returned to Philadelphia the next morning where they began to resume their regular home life at 132 S. 18th Street. Reigart was completely free from naval duties for his first month home. He and Bess got right into the social whirl of Philadelphia, going to parties and social events nearly every night. Reigart, the returning war hero, was always the hit of the party.

By this time, Reigart had consumed most of his bourbon and was feeling no pain. As thoughts of his marriage flashed past him, he thought that his wife had not really had it all that bad, at least until the last year or two. At home, though Bess did all the shopping, she never lifted a finger inside the kitchen. She had cooks, maids, and servants do all the household work.

The Lowrys ate and drank well. Liquor was a common commodity around the Lowry household. Reigart favored bourbon and brandy, and usually had a drink in his hand. Whenever a guest arrived, he was immediately offered a drink. At the dinner table, there was always a selection of wines, Claret and Catawba being the favorites. The food was always good. The most popular entree was chicken croquettes, and ice cream and cakes often topped off the meal as dessert.

Reigart remembered how thrilled Bess was when she met President Abraham Lincoln. Reigart had been on special assignment in Washington for several months. During this time, he attended several White House receptions. Lincoln enjoyed talking to men who had seen action, and he talked with Reigart on several occasions. At one of these receptions, Lincoln asked Reigart if he would take a runaway slave into his house for a while. Reigart consented. The slave was a big man, but nice and gentle. At a future reception, the President met Bess who was petite as well as being Reigart's junior by twelve years. She was only twenty-five years old. On meeting her, Lincoln remarked, "Ma'am, if I had known that you were so young and so small, I never would have let that big black man in your house." Lincoln was charmed by Bess and invited her to dance at this and following receptions.

Reigart thought about his children. This was the saddest part of his divorce. He was devoted to his children. He had missed them terribly during the past year and a half. Now this notice of his divorce made him wonder if he would ever see them again. His oldest son had been born in 1864, only nine months and three days after his return north! He was named Ricardo St. Philip Lowry. Ricardo was Bess's nickname for Reigart, and St. Philip was the name of a fort in New Orleans that Reigart had battled two years before.

The Lowrys would have eight children during their marriage, all born between 1864 and the early 1870s. Two died in infancy; two (Courtie and Lilly) would die in their early childhood. Robert Oliver would die at Yale while he was a student there. Ricardo, Walter, and Marion would be the only children to live full lives.

Bess often went with Reigart when he traveled. She could not go on the same boat but followed on a passenger vessel. Bess took Walter with her on one of these trips when he was just a little baby. Bess got terribly seasick on this voyage and got to the point where she felt that life was not worth living. The nurse came in and said, "The baby is so sick that I am afraid he is going to die."

To which Bess replied, "It's the best thing that could happen to him." She later claimed that she only said this because she was so miserable.

While the Lowrys lived in New London after the Civil War, Reigart's executive officer, Robert D. Mauly often came to the house for a meal or a drink. He was single, but he enjoyed the company of the Lowry children, becoming an honorary "uncle" to them. He was especially fond of Lilly, a cute, darling little girl. She had Bright's disease and would die at a young age. Bob Mauly used to write her affectionate little notes. Lilly would send him bouquets by her father, and Bob would put them in water in his cabin. When he visited, Bob went for walks in the garden with Lillie when the weather was suitable. Lillie died at about six years of age, but this man had made her happy during much of her life by doing these little things for her. It was a small sacrifice, but one which most men, especially a hardened naval officer, would not have made.

In 1868, the Lowrys took a long overdue vacation in Europe. They spent a year there. They traveled all over Western Europe. They spent time in Italy, in Baden-Baden, Germany, and in Interlaken, Switzerland. They went sightseeing and gift shopping. In Interlaken, they bought several clocks, including a cuckoo clock. The last seven months of their visit was spent in Paris, France. Their daughter, Marion, was born during the stay in Paris.

In later years, Reigart and Bess spent more time together, but at the same time, President Grant and Secretary Robeson had appeared on the scene. The strain had been too much.

News of the divorce sent Reigart on a drinking binge. He thought his world had come to an end. Everything he had worked for and believed in had gone against him. His depression hit a low ebb when Christmas came a few weeks later. He did not think that anything else bad could happen.

3.
WE NEED YOUR HELP

———•●○●•———

REIGART DID NOTHING BUT DRINK FOR THE NEXT TWO months. The new year came and went, but he did not know or care that it was now 1880. The only thing that he knew for sure was where he kept his bourbon. His apartment was a total wreck. He had not cleaned it or even made his bed for two months.

He could not remember when the last time was that he washed or shaved. His clothes were filthy. He had worn just about everything that he owned and had run out of clean clothes long ago.

As he sat in his easy chair, he spotted something on the floor over by the door. He went over to see what it was and discovered that it was another telegram. He did not know how long that it had been lying there, but it could not have been more than a few days. Reigart chuckled to himself as he thought how the boy who delivered it must have been afraid to knock. This time the boy just slid it under the door.

Reigart wondered why he should even bother opening the telegram. The last one had shattered him so that he hesitated for a minute. It might contain something from the Navy Department, he thought, so he finally decided to see what it said. He tore it open. It was from Sam Franklin, a boyhood friend and a fellow Navy captain.

The telegram read, "Jouett has gone to Congress for a promotion. We need your help to stop him."

Reigart knew right away what this meant. One of his fellow officers was trying to use political influence for personal advancement. He was enraged. He knew that he and his fellow captains had a fight on their hands, and he welcomed it. This was just what he needed.

The telegram brought him back to his senses and started to sober him. Putting his bottle of bourbon away, Reigart put a pot of coffee on the stove. He had a lot of work to do, and he set out doing it. He began cleaning the house, eating some good solid food, and drinking cup after cup of coffee. Soaking in the tub, he began to map out his strategy as layer after layer of dirt soaked off. He trimmed his beard and waxed his mustache.

When Reigart looked in the mirror, he noticed that he was beginning to look presentable. Reigart went out to hire some help to fix up his room and wash his clothes. Before long he had several women busily working. He was all over the place ordering them around. It was just like old times, except instead of sailors, he had cleaning ladies and washerwomen hustling to and fro.

He gave one washerwoman his old uniforms. He had not worn them since he had moved to Canada in 1878. He asked her to clean and press the uniforms because he wanted them in especially good shape.

While the women worked, Reigart began to prepare to return to the United States. He knew that he would be much more effective if he could meet with his fellow captains and work with them personally.

Within a couple of days, Reigart was ready to leave. When he boarded the train for New York, he was no longer the man he had been a week before, a pitiful, lonely, drunken bum. He was now an officer and a gentleman. He now had a cause and a purpose in life. Wearing his dress uniform, he looked impressive, and he turned many an admiring head on his way to New York. New York seemed to be the best place to go. Several of his fellow captains were there, and he could use the Brooklyn Navy Yard as a base of operations.

This Jim Jouett case meant a lot to Reigart. The position at stake was Commodore. These captains had all grown up in the days when the naval hero everyone looked up to was Commodore Oliver Hazard Perry. The Commodores of the early nineteenth century were much admired men. They had gained fame and wealth, and many a boy growing up in the 1830s and 1840s had dreamed of someday becoming a commodore.

Reigart could remember the thrill when he served under Commodore Matthew Calbraith Perry during the Mexican War and on the Japan Expedition. Matthew Perry was Oliver Perry's younger brother, and just to serve on the same ship with him was an honor.

The official ranks of the Navy were small throughout the nine-teenth century. When Reigart joined the Navy in 1840, the highest avail-able rank was Captain. The senior Captain in squadron was afforded with the honorary title of "Commodore." Besides Captain, the only other ranks in 1840 were Commander, Lieutenant, Master, Passed Midshipman, and Midshipman. To achieve the higher ranks, a man would have to be a faith-ful and loyal servant to his country for many years. Until the 1850s, there had been no retirement system and so mobility at the top was limited. This permeated all the way down to lower ranks. It was not unusual for a man to be in the service for over twenty years before he would become a Lieutenant.

During the Civil War, the official ranks had been expanded some-what, but they remained limited. In 1862, the ranks of Rear Admiral, Commodore, and Lieutenant Commander were added. In 1866, the posi-tions of Admiral and Vice Admiral were created.

Even with these changes, the ranks remained small. The law allowed for one Admiral, one Vice Admiral, ten Rear Admirals, twenty-five Commodores, fifty Captains, ninety Commanders, eighty Lieutenant

Commanders, 180 Lieutenants, sixty Masters, and 160 Ensigns (which had replaced Passed Midshipmen).

Reigart had dreamed of becoming a commodore all his life. It was still a much-coveted rank. He had served his country for forty years and had worked long and hard for the chance of becoming Commodore Reigart Bolivar Lowry.

By the beginning of 1880, Reigart was the third most senior Captain. That meant that there were only two men ahead of him before he would be promoted. Every man knew his number. It was published in the Navy Register every year, and it was omnipresent. Whenever two men of the same rank met, each knew who was senior and who was junior, and each behaved accordingly. Reigart was number three and Jim Jouett was number seventeen on the list of captains.

These numbers had originally been assigned upon graduation from Annapolis. Until 1855, the only way anyone moved up the list was when someone died or retired. Then everyone below that person moved up one number. Since there was no retirement system, death was the most common reason for change. In 1855, Congress passed a Naval Retiring Act that set up a retirement procedure and allowed a Naval Retiring Board to force the retirement of some officers. This thinned the ranks a little, but all the remaining officers retained their relative positions.

Following the Civil War, a Board was set up to review all the officers in the Navy. The Board gave its recommendations to Secretary of Navy, Gideon Welles, who made the final determination in each case whether a man's relative position should be changed. Secretary Welles refused to act in a way that would lower a man's number, but the law of 1866 had created a number of new openings. Therefore, Welles was able to make minor readjustments of the relative positions of some men. Of the seventeen captains now involved in the Jouett case, most had been advanced over ten to fifteen of their seniors.

Jim Jouett had been advanced over the heads of nine of his seniors during this review. Now, he was claiming that his name was on a list of men who were not favored by the Navy Department. Now, fifteen years after the Civil War, he was trying to be advanced over the heads of sixteen more of his seniors.

Reigart and all the other captains had worked as hard as or harder than Jim Jouett to get to their present positions. Even with the changes in 1866, the list of seventeen senior captains looked like a partial list of the Classes of 1846 and 1847 at Annapolis. All but one of the men had graduated in one of these classes, and they were still in pretty much the same order in which they had graduated some thirty-three or thirty-four years before. Every one of the men had joined the Navy in either 1840 or 1841.

Jim Jouett was a Republican and his family had wealth and influence. He was now trying to use his influence to receive a political promotion in the now more permissive government. This is what irked Reigart the most. He had fought politics from without when he had battled with Grant and Robeson. Now he had to fight it from within, and this hurt him much more deeply.

Jim Jouett was a great storyteller, and he had built himself into a hero. His one claim to fame, however, had some loopholes in it as far as Reigart was concerned. It was Reigart's impression that if it were not for the incompetence and bungling of Jouett and his men that they would not have gotten themselves into the trouble that they became so famous getting out of. Reigart planned to argue his version before Congress if he had to.

4.
MAJESTIC SAILING VESSELS LINED THE PIERS

REIGART WAS GLAD SAM FRANKLIN HAD WIRED HIM AND looked forward to seeing his old friend. While Sam was number six on the Captain's list, Reigart had not seen his old friend for nearly twenty-five years. He and Sam had grown up together in Philadelphia during the 1830s. On the day that he had decided to join the Navy, Reigart had been with Sam and another boy, now number fourteen on the Captain's list, Bill Truxton.

Reigart had gotten up early that morning. As he dressed, he noticed the aroma of coffee in the air. This meant that his mother was already up and preparing breakfast. Reigart knew that he had gotten up too late. On Saturday mornings when he arose before his mother, he was able to slip out of the house and be on his way. When his mother was up, she made him eat breakfast before he left the house.

Henrietta Wager Lowry was strict. She had to be. For thirteen years, she had had to raise five sons on her own. Her husband had died just prior to Reigart's own birth. Henrietta heard Reigart getting up, and by the time he came downstairs, his breakfast was almost ready. While his mother cooked, Reigart went over to the living room window. Pulling the drapery aside, he looked out over Rittenhouse Square. The Lowrys lived on the northwest corner of this park in a fashionable area of Philadelphia. A light snow from Thursday's snowfall covered the park. Wondering what the temperature was outside, Reigart touched the back of his hand to the glass in the window. It was very cold. Other than the snow and the cold, it was a beautiful day. Reigart looked up and down the street and saw houses much like his own—three-story brownstones with bay windows jutting out from the second and third floors. There was little activity in the streets as it was still early.

"Reigart," his mother called, "your breakfast is ready."

He hurried to the table and began to gobble it down.

"Reigart, don't eat so fast," Henrietta cautioned. "You have all day ahead of you. What are your plans that you are in such a hurry?"

Between mouthfuls, Reigart answered, "I'm going down to the docks with Peter Wager, Mother."

Reigart loved to go down to the Philadelphia docks on Saturday mornings. The adventure surrounding the great three-masted sailing vessels that sailed in and out of this port captured the imagination of the young boy. Henrietta understood. Her boy was a dreamer. He wanted to be a sailor someday. Though he was her youngest boy, he was the most ambitious, and she knew that he had the most promise of becoming successful.

Peter Wager was Reigart's first cousin. Henrietta was glad that Reigart and Peter were friends, but she was concerned because Peter was a little on the wild side. He got into fights more than a sixteen-year-old boy should, and more than once, he had been caught with alcohol on his breath. Nevertheless, a day down at the docks could not lead to any trouble and so Henrietta put these thoughts out of her head.

When Reigart finished his breakfast, he rose from the table and went to the coat closet. He put on his coat, gloves, and scarf, and then reached to the top of the closet for his broad-brimmed hat which would give no protection to his ears on this wintry day. As Reigart left the house, his mother handed him a bag containing several sandwiches that she had prepared for Peter and him since she knew that they would be gone all day.

"Be home in time for supper," Henrietta called after him. She knew he would be. Though he was only thirteen, he was mature and independent and could take care of himself. Tucking the sandwiches inside his coat, Reigart was on his way.

Peter lived only a couple of blocks away on 18th Street. As Reigart approached his house, he saw Peter sitting out front waiting for him. Reigart apologized saying, "I'm sorry that I'm a few minutes late, Peter. My mother made me eat breakfast."

"That's okay, Reigart," Peter answered. "I've only been out here a few minutes. Let's get going. It's cold out this morning. Maybe we'll warm up once we get moving."

The boys liked to walk down Chestnut Street on their way to the docks. It went straight through to the Delaware River and was rather picturesque as well. They had over a mile ahead of them on this cold November morning. It was still early, and a breeze made it a little nippy out. Reigart's ears were cold, and the wind was cutting through his trousers, making his legs numb. He began walking more briskly to try to get warmer.

There were few people up at this hour, and Chestnut Street was lonely on this Saturday morning. Occasionally, a carriage rattled over the cobblestones in the roadbed. Adjoining three-story brick houses lined both sides of the street. The combination of brick sidewalks and the brick houses gave a reddish hue to the entire street. There was a tree in front of every fifth or sixth house that added a bit of green to this part of Philadelphia. A horse was tied to one of these trees. Peter and Reigart stopped to rest and pet its nose.

From behind, Reigart heard someone calling his name. It was Sam Franklin, a friend from school. When Sam caught up, he asked, "Are you fellows going down to the docks?"

"Yes, we are," Reigart answered. "Why don't you join us? You know my cousin Peter, don't you?"

"Yes, I've seen him at school," Sam acknowledged.

The boys passed in front of Independence Hall where the Declaration of Independence and the Constitution had been debated and approved by the Continental Congress and the Constitutional Convention. Reigart was a patriotic boy, and he often paused in front of this building to contemplate the great events which had taken place in there.

From Independence Hall, the boys could see the masts of the larger ships in the Delaware River. In a few minutes they arrived at the docks. Reigart saw a steamboat steaming into port and recognized it as the *Robert Morris* that had been steaming up and down the Delaware River as long as he could remember. He marveled at the technology and ingenuity that was used in this and other steamers that came into Philadelphia and wondered why so many ships still relied on sail power.

The boys did not see any of their friends at this part of the dock, so they began walking down toward the Navy Yard. The scene along the Delaware River was romantic. Majestic sailing vessels lined the piers. Steamboats and barges plied up and down the river. Onshore, sailors and seamen scurried to and fro while ladies and gentlemen strolled among the quaint little shops that lined the wharves. On the docks were piles of cargo in boxes, barrels, and numerous other containers.

The boys took their time as they walked down the docks. They occasionally stopped, sat down, and took in the activity that was going on around them. Reigart could sit all day and watch the water and the boats. It seemed as if there was always something happening. There were eight or ten boats of one kind or another plying up or down the river at any given moment. Reigart knew the names of most of them.

The boys reached the Navy Yard at about noon. By this time, Bill Truxton had joined them. Bill's grandfather was Thomas Truxton, one of the country's first Commodores. Bill had inherited his grandfather's love for the sea. Reigart had never been down as far as the Navy Yard before and he was curious about all the activity going on there. The boys found a spot where they could all sit down on the pier and lean up against some barrels. As they watched the goings on, Reigart remembered his sandwiches. He pulled them out and passed them around. There were plenty for all since Henrietta always made too many for Reigart and Peter.

After awhile, Reigart noticed several young boys wearing uniforms. He wondered aloud, "Who could those boys be? They seem to be too young to be in the Navy. They're only about our age."

No one seemed to know the answer, so when Reigart saw a naval officer walk by, he asked him who the boys were.

Lieutenant William Chauvenet responded that the boys were in the Navy in a training program. They were midshipmen training to become officers in a new program the Navy was offering. The Navy took boys in their teenage years but preferred boys fourteen to sixteen. This fact disappointed Reigart who was only thirteen at the time. Lieutenant Chauvenet invited the boys to look around and to talk to the midshipmen.

The boys wanted to learn about the program, and when Lieutenant Chauvenet invited them on board a ship, they were quick to accept. While he took them on a tour of the ship, Lieutenant Chauvenet explained the program in more detail and told the boys how to apply. He told them that they were fortunate because the Navy was going to open schools in New York, Boston, and Norfolk and was looking for qualified students.

The four boys thanked Lieutenant Chauvenet and went on their ways home. They all wanted to ask their parents for permission to apply to the program. Henrietta Lowry's first reaction was that Reigart was so young. He was only thirteen and she expressed this concern to him. He assured her that many boys his age were in the program, hedging a little bit on this point. Henrietta Lowry, while having reservations, knew how much this meant to her son. She also knew that the Navy would give guidance and discipline to him and that it would provide the male leadership he had never had since his father had died before his birth.

Reigart had to apply for the program through a Senator or Congressman. His mother suggested that he write to Senator James Buchanan who was a friend of the family.

Reigart went to his room and began to write the letter. He put down his name, Reigart Bolivar Lowry. He had been named Reigart after his uncle, Adam Reigart, Jr. His middle name, Bolivar, came from the fact that his father was a friend of Simon Bolivar. Reigart's father had been the United States' first diplomatic representative to South America.

Reigart next wrote his address: 1908 Rittenhouse Square, Philadelphia, Pennsylvania. As he started to write the date of his birth, July 14, 1826, he hesitated. He remembered both Lieutenant Chauvenet's and his mother's comments about his age. He wrote July 14, 1823, adding three years to his age with the stroke of a pen.

Reigart wrote that his birthplace was La Guayra, Venezuela, where his father had been serving as Ambassador to South America. He wrote a few paragraphs about why he wanted to join the program and sent the letter off. The next several weeks were the longest weeks of his life. He kept wondering whether he would be accepted. When his acceptance came, he was the happiest boy in the world. He had been appointed to the program as Midshipman Reigart Lowry.

Peter Wager was also accepted, but Sam Franklin and Bill Truxton were not permitted to apply for a year by their parents. They both applied the next year and were accepted into the program at that time. Now forty years later, three of these four boys had been drawn together to fight a common cause.

When Reigart's train arrived from St. Catharines, Canada, he wondered when he would see these men. Sam Franklin was in New York, and Reigart intended to look him up as soon as he was settled. Reigart found a room at a place called the Coleman House. He was ready and raring to fight Jim Jouett's bid for promotion.

5.

IT SMELLED LIKE RUM, TAR, BEAN SOUP, AND TOBACCO COMBINED

———•○•———

ONCE REIGART HAD SETTLED IN, HE WENT TO THE NAVY YARD at Brooklyn to look up his old friend, Sam Franklin. Reigart had no trouble finding Sam and they met with a warm, firm handshake. Both men had aged considerably in the twenty-five years since they had seen each other, but they both recognized each other readily. Both men were now fifty-three years old, and it had been more than forty years since they had met Lieutenant Chauvenet that day in Philadelphia.

"Have you reached all sixteen of the captains senior to Jouett?" Reigart inquired of Sam.

"Yes, and all are anxious to help," Sam answered. "They are located in several cities along the east coast, but they have agreed to meet in Washington during the first week in March."

"Well, Sam," Reigart added, "You know that I will do anything to help."

"We know, Reigart," Sam continued. "We all feel pretty badly that we didn't stand behind you when you spoke out against Grant and Robeson.

We want you to be our chairman, and we promise we'll stand behind you from this point on. We've learned our lesson. If we had stood behind you before, this Jouett thing would never have happened."

Reigart felt pleased that his fellow captains had honored him in this way. He had been disappointed when none of them had followed his lead against Grant and Robeson, but he understood. They did not want to lose everything the way that he had. In any case, that was water under the bridge, and if they were to stop Jouett, the sixteen senior captains would have to work together as a unit.

Reigart turned to Sam and asked, "Where do we start?"

"Most of the men here in New York spend their free time at the New York Club," Sam commented. "I think that you should start there. I'll show you where it is."

They arrived at the club a short while later. Reigart was impressed. It was posh and exclusive. Near the entrance was a large reading room where several men were reading the paper. The club had meeting rooms, dining rooms, and exercise rooms with athletic equipment. In one of the lounges, Sam and Reigart found two of the men they were looking for, Stephen P. Quackenbush and Earl English, numbers one and two on the captains list, respectively.

They had both joined the Navy in the same training program as Reigart just a couple of months before him, and they both graduated with him from Annapolis in the class of 1846. Earl English became Reigart's best friend during the first several years of his career, but Stephen Quackenbush was the first person Reigart met when he reported to his first command.

Reigart Lowry and Peter Wager had finally received their first orders in March 1840. "Report to the Receiving Ship at New York." They were so excited they could hardly contain themselves. Reigart had run down to the Philadelphia Navy Yard to tell Lieutenant Chauvenet who was pleased to hear the news. They only had a couple of weeks to prepare to leave.

Reigart's and Peter's families were all at the train station to see the boys off. It was a happy and a sad occasion. It was a proud moment, but the boys would be gone for a long time. They were leaving boys, but they would come back men. Reigart insisted on sitting by a window. He had never been on a train before, and he did not want to miss a thing. Even though all he saw was flat farmland and an occasional forest, Reigart found the trip exciting. He wondered what New York would be like. After several hours, the train pulled into the Hoboken, New Jersey station.

The boys made their way down to the Hoboken Ferry that would take them across Hudson River to New York. As they crossed the river, Reigart noticed a large ship lying in the harbor of New York's battery, and called it to Peter's attention. "Hey Peter," he shouted, "Look over here. Isn't that a beautiful ship? I would give anything if our ship would only be half as nice."

Peter agreed, and the boys were getting excited with anticipation about their new life. When they reached Manhattan, the boys knew that they had to get across the island and take another ferry to Brooklyn. It was a gorgeous day, so they decided to walk rather than hire a carriage. They picked up their bags and began their trek. New York was a busier city than Philadelphia. The streets were more crowded, and everyone seemed to be in a hurry.

When the boys arrived at South Street, they could not believe their eyes. What they saw was a forest of masts. Philadelphia was nothing like this. The wharves were filled with goods and men, and as the rest of New York, the area was busy. They wanted to stay awhile but Reigart thought that they should find the Navy Yard. He asked a passerby how to get there and learned that he could see the yard right across the East River. They got on the Brooklyn Ferry, crossed the East River, and wandered down to the New York Navy Yard at Brooklyn.

The Navy Yard, too, was busy. Sailors hustled about and oxen-drawn wagons passed by. Cannon balls were heaped everywhere. They saw a couple of naval vessels at the docks and came across an immense dry dock. Across the East River, they could see the line of ships that were docked along South Street with the city of New York in the background.

Reigart stopped a sailor and asked, "Where can we find the Receiving Ship?"

The sailor replied, "Sir, the Receiving Ship is called the *North Carolina*. It is out in the harbor. You have to take a launch to get to it."

"Where do we catch the launch?" inquired Reigart.

"It leaves from right over there," the sailor replied, pointing to a spot only a couple of hundred yards away. "One just left, and it will be about an hour before the next one leaves.

Reigart thanked the sailor and turning to Peter, said, "Why don't we sit down on the dock and relax. It has been a busy day."

Peter agreed, commenting, "I wish we could see the *North Carolina*. I wonder what it looks like."

"Me, too," added Reigart.

The launch was right on time. Reigart and Peter introduced themselves and were told to board the launch. As it rounded the tip of Manhattan Island, the operator announced, "Right up ahead is the *North Carolina*, your new home."

Reigart and Peter looked at each other with astonishment. It was the very same ship they had seen from the Hoboken Ferry several hours before. The *North Carolina* was a huge ship with three large masts. Three flags flew above it, one at the bow, one at the stern, and one atop the rear mast. A large platform floated on the water where the launch would come in. Two stairways rose from the platform to the ship. Two white stripes ran the length of the ship, interrupted by square holes out of which cannons could be fired.

Landing on the float and looking up at the mighty guns above him, Reigart commented, "I sure am glad we are coming peaceably."

When he reached the top of the stairs, Reigart announced, "Reigart Lowry reporting for duty, sir."

Peter piped in, "Peter Wager reporting for duty, sir."

"Mister Lowry. Mister Wager. Mister Quackenbush will show you to your quarters," the officer replied.

Mister Lowry? Mister Wager? Mister Quackenbush? Sir? Reigart had never been called Mister before. It felt good, but he felt a little bit uneasy. Mister Quackenbush was Stephen Platt Quackenbush a boy about a year older than Reigart who had joined the program just a couple of months before. Stephen took Reigart and Peter below and showed them where to put their gear. Stephen told the boys that they were free to roam about the ship and that they should not hesitate to ask questions of anyone.

Reigart soon returned to the top deck where he watched groups of seamen sitting in circles, telling stories, and playing checkers. Leaning against one of the massive masts, he watched the goings on. He noticed how proper and handsome the officers looked in their fancy uniforms with their swords hanging at their sides. While he stood there, another boy approached.

"Hello, my name is Earl English," the boy said. "You must be new. I don't believe I've seen you here before."

"I've just arrived today," Reigart said.

"Well, in that case, let me show you around the ship," Earl offered. Earl was also in the training program and, like Stephen Quackenbush, had joined a couple of months earlier.

Earl knew right where to take Reigart. Their first stop was the ship's wheel. This was a great thrill for Reigart because to any boy his age, the ship's wheel was the whole ship itself. Here was the center of control. All around were compasses and other navigational aids. Reigart stood behind the wheel and imagined himself steering the mighty vessel.

Earl then took Reigart down the wooden plank stairs to the gun deck. This deck was almost barren except for the row of cannon along each side. It was kept clear so that battle operations could be handled most effectively and efficiently during the chaos of battle. There were ropes and pulleys all around the cannons that were used to move them back and forth and to hold them in place while they were being fired. Reigart stood behind one of the cannons and looked down its sight, trying to imagine what it would be like to stand behind one of these guns in the heat of battle.

As Earl showed Reigart around the rest of the ship, Reigart noticed the peculiar odor that prevailed. It smelled like rum, tar, bean soup, and tobacco combined. He liked this smell, and he was beginning to know that he would like life aboard a ship.

It was nearly suppertime, so Earl took Reigart to the mess deck. At supper, Reigart began to meet more of his fellow midshipmen and the other men on the ship. After dinner, Reigart joined Earl and many of the other boys who gathered around the older sailors to hear them tell stories. Reigart hung on every word. A few of these men had been in the Navy during the War of 1812, and they loved to tell of the Battle of Lake Erie and of the heroism of Commodore Oliver Hazard Perry. Reigart dreamed about becoming a commodore someday himself. Little did he imagine that Stephen Quackenbush, Earl English, and he would ever be numbers one, two, and three on the captains' list, next in line to become commodore.

After a few hours of stories, it became time to go to bed and time for Reigart to learn about the hammock. Each man slept in a hammock that was suspended from the ceiling of the gun decks. All the boys watched Reigart and Peter as they made their first attempts to get into their hammocks. When Reigart finally got into his hammock, he found that it was not as comfortable as the bed he was used to at home. He was so excited that he would not have slept well that night anyway.

Reigart settled into the routine on the ship. Up at the crack of dawn, he went through inspection, ate breakfast, and swabbed the decks. Later, he and the boys would practice with the armament. Most importantly, Reigart attended classes, the primary purpose of the program. He wore his dress uniform to class: light-colored pants, a white shirt with a big, wide bowtie, and a blue coat opened at the front with tails in the back. Brass buttons with anchors on them lined his lapels. This was all topped off with a full-brimmed hat.

Reigart showed up six days a week at Lieutenant James Harmon Ward's classes. Ward was a distinguished looking man, an excellent teacher, and well liked by the boys. He was stocky, his hair was always combed very neatly and parted on the right, and a mustache and mutton chop whiskers adorned his full face. Professor Ward wore his Lieutenant's uniform to class. His specialty was navigation, but he had to give the boys all their general education. Reigart got along well with James Ward. A love and respect grew between these two men as often grows between a professor and his students. Professors have their followings, and James Ward had a large one. But, among all his students, Reigart became one of his favorites.

Reigart, never a strong student in Philadelphia, never missed a class on the *North Carolina*. Ward gave him inspiration. Between classes, Reigart discussed various subject matters with Ward to try to relate what he had learned in class to what it was really like on the open seas. James Ward admitted that much of what he taught was theory, and it would have little meaning to his students until they took their first cruise. Reigart became a strong believer that experience was the best teacher and began to get anxious to go to sea.

One afternoon, Stephen, Earl, and Reigart were relaxing on the top deck when James Ward approached. Their sea orders had finally arrived. All three of them would be going to China. Stephen and Reigart had been assigned to the *Boston* and Earl had been assigned to the *Constellation*. Reigart was disappointed that his friend Earl was assigned to a different ship, but they were in the same squadron.

6.
MINOR GUARDIAN OF THE HEIR APPARENT, PRESIDENT OF THE BOARD OF WAR, MEMBER OF THE CENSORATE, GOVERNOR OF THE PROVINCES OF KWANGTUNG AND KWANGZE

⸻ • ◎ • ⸻

"YOU KNOW, THIS JOUETT THING REALLY BOTHERS ME," Reigart said, sipping his bourbon between thoughts. "If he consummates this outrage, the Navy will never be the same again. There is a lot more at stake than the numbers of sixteen captains on a list."

Stephen and Earl nodded agreement, and Earl continued, "If Jouett is successful, then every man in the Navy will try to use political influence. The professionalism of the Navy will be gone forever."

Stephen piped in, "What do you propose we do, Reigart?"

After a little thought, Reigart said, "We must be organized. If we split up as a group, we do not have a chance. This meeting in Washington is good, but we must go there prepared. I think that as the three senior captains, we will have to provide the leadership."

Stephen interrupted, "Though Earl and I are senior to you, Reigart, you are the boss during this Jouett affair. What do you want us to do?"

"Read through old newspapers, correspondence, government publications," Reigart began. "See what you can find with relation to promotions, especially with respect to the Naval Review Board of 1866. Also see what you can find on Jouett's record. For that matter, we should compile the records of all sixteen senior captains. Placed next to Jouett's record, these would show that he is no more deserving than the rest."

"That sounds like a good start, Reigart," Stephen responded. "I'll go to the Naval Library to look through government records and reports, and you, Earl, can go to the public library to study the newspapers."

Earl chimed in, "There's no time like the present. I'm on my way."

Stephen and Reigart continued to map out a strategy after Earl had gone. Before long, their conversation had shifted to the good old days. They had both been assigned to the *Boston* after their training on the *North Carolina*. The *Boston* and the *Constellation* were going to China to protect American interests during the Opium War. This was a great opportunity for these boys because China was a place that few Americans had visited by 1840. The purpose of the expedition was two-fold: to protect American merchants, and to prevent the smuggling of opium under cover of the American flag.

The day the *Boston* went to sea was an exciting one for Reigart. His only other ocean voyage had been when he had come to the United States from South America when he was only a few months old. Reigart stood by the side of the ship as the *Boston* left the harbor. He noticed a slight roll as it got out to sea. However, he had been told stories about this roll, and it was not nearly as bad as he had imagined. His ship was a large one and took the waves quite well. Reigart kind of enjoyed the roll. Whenever he was not performing his duties, Reigart would go to the side of the ship to see how far out the *Boston* had come. Before long, he could hardly see the shore.

When the *Boston* crossed the equator some weeks later, there were ceremonies that always occurred during the event. The men put on an especially good show to impress Reigart, Stephen, and the other boys who were crossing the equator for the first time. The god of the sea, Neptune, was honored, and silly little skits were performed to celebrate the event. Reigart enjoyed those little skits, as he enjoyed everything about the sea. He loved the smell of salt water, and while the sea was vast and lonely, he found it soothing and comforting. During much of his free time, Reigart would stand on the deck against the rail. He would look out over the sea and enjoy the spray of the salt water against his face. These times were spent thinking about the Navy, about the ship, and about his family back in Philadelphia.

Young Reigart made a favorable impression on his fellow sailors during the voyage to China. He was active and always ready to lend a helping hand. He was all over the boat, making himself conspicuous and available for any task his superiors might assign him. Never satisfied to be idle, he preferred to be busy, hurrying to finish one job so that he could get on to the next. Each new activity was an adventure, and he mastered every job he tried. Having an inquisitive mind when there was something that he did not understand, Reigart would study it until he had full comprehension of it.

During this voyage and during his stay on the *North Carolina*, the authority that was vested in the officers of the ship awed Reigart. These men seemed to be all-powerful and omniscient. Reigart's heart jumped every time an officer approached. When officers spoke, Reigart obeyed. He wondered how they came by those traits, whether they came through experience or whether they merely came with the position. He also noticed when his friends became officers that they changed. They no longer mixed with their old friends and they behaved differently toward them. Reigart always assured himself and his friends that when he was promoted, he would not change like this.

One afternoon, after Reigart had been on the *Boston* for about six months, Commander Long called Reigart aside. Reigart wondered what this man might want with him. He did not have to wait long. Commander Long looked young Reigart squarely in the eye and said,

"Midshipman Lowry, I thought that you might like to see this letter that I'm sending to the department. This is not normal procedure, but your conduct and enthusiasm has been so great that I'm going to make an exception in this case. Keep up the good work."

Reigart looked at the letter which certified that he had served with Commander Long for six months and that his conduct, morally and officially, had been strictly correct in every respect. Long took great pleasure in recommending young Reigart as a promising young officer. Reigart was pleased. He had tried his hardest and he had enjoyed every moment of it. Seeing this letter made him proud of himself. He knew now that he would be successful as a naval officer.

The entire cruise, however, was not pleasurable for Reigart. During the three-year voyage to the Far East, he spent nearly one hundred and fifty days in the infirmary with various diseases that were common at that time due to changes in climatic conditions. Though active and hardy, Reigart was young and unused to being on board a naval vessel during a long voyage. One affliction he suffered during the trip was rheumatism that would trouble him for the rest of his life. Another disease he contracted and was treated for was one which most midshipmen caught during their maiden voyage after making stops at various ports of call. The older, more experienced men would take the younger men ashore and show them how to have a good time. As a result of these good times, Reigart was treated for gonorrhea three times during the voyage.

The squadron arrived in China after a journey of nearly one and a half years. Upon arrival, Reigart saw many new and strange things. Here was a whole people and culture that was unfamiliar to him, and he was anxious to observe them. The small boats that lay in all the harbors and in which many Chinese people made their homes fascinated him.

The historical events in which Reigart was playing a part made him proud. Upon arrival in China, the expedition served two purposes. First and foremost, the mission's responsibility was to protect American interests and merchants. Commodore Lawrence Kearney, the expedition leader, received several letters from American citizens when he first arrived. They described outrages inflicted upon them by the Chinese and demanded redress.

Included was one report that told of an American being killed by the Chinese. Kearney took moves to correct these matters. Sailing up the Whampoa River, where no American ship of war had ever before traveled, Kearney demanded that his message be sent directly to Viceroy Ke, Minor Guardian of the Heir Apparent, President of the Board of War, Member of the Censorate, and Governor of the Provinces of Kwangtung and Kwangze.

As Reigart observed these events, he felt excited knowing that he was among the first Americans ever to see this part of China. During these events, the Chinese were hospitable, and they apologized for all actions that had wrongly been taken against Americans. One afternoon as the ships were preparing to leave Canton, Reigart noticed an important looking Chinese man approaching the ships. This man turned out to be a representative from Viceroy Ke who had come to pay a parting call and his compliments. Reigart watched the small ceremony with fascination.

The other responsibility of the mission was to protect the American name. This meant ensuring that no vessels of other nations were smuggling opium into China under cover of the American flag and ensuring that Americans themselves were not smuggling opium. When the squadron reached Macao, in March of 1842, the Opium War had been going on for nearly two years. The British had possession of Hong Kong, Amoy, Ning-Po, Ting-Hai, and Chu-Hai. Upon arrival, Commodore Kearney informed the Chinese that the United States would not tolerate any opium trade under the American flag. He kept his word most emphatically the next May when he seized the American schooner, *Ariel*, a notorious opium smuggler. Participating in the seizure was exciting to young Reigart. Even though it was a relatively routine capture, it was the first time he was ever involved in such an event.

Great Britain and China signed a peace treaty on August 27, 1842, opening five Chinese ports to the British. Recognizing the significance of this event, Commodore Kearney dispatched Vice-Consul Delano to Washington, D.C., with a copy of the treaty, sent copies overland by mail, and sent the *Boston* to the west coast of Mexico with copies in triplicate. Delaying his own return voyage, Kearney remained in Hong Kong to help open China to other nations besides England, including the United States. He established a close rapport with the Chinese and set the stage for Caleb Cushing to conclude America's first treaty with China in 1844.

While Reigart had enjoyed his stay in China, he was glad to hear that the *Boston* was returning home. It had been a few years since he had seen his family and friends, and he began to feel homesick for the first time in his naval career. He had been fine while the voyage had been necessary, but now that he was heading home, Reigart just wished that it would not take several months for the return. This seemed like unnecessarily wasted time. While the voyage headed out, there was something to look forward to, but now there was no purpose in the voyage, other than to return home. The ship, *Boston*, returned to the city of Boston via Cape Horn in August 1843. A few days later, Reigart was granted a three-month leave of absence which he spent at his home in Philadelphia.

He had much to tell his mother, brothers, and friends for at the age of seventeen, he had completed his first trip around the world. Reigart's brothers wanted to hear all about China. While some Chinese products were sold in America, little was known of China or the Chinese except what was available in books and newspapers. Reigart had an audience wherever he went. Reigart's family friends came from near and from far to hear his tales. He told them what the Chinese looked like and what some of their habits were. Among his favorite stories was to tell about the small feet of the Chinese women. It was a sign of class, he explained, and many young girls had their feet bound at an early age to prevent them from growing. He also told of the way that many Chinese lived in small boats just off the Chinese shore. Reigart was acquiring a trait necessary to successful sailors—to be able to tell a story.

Reigart's mother, who had not seen him since he left for the Navy several years before wanted to hear everything about Professor Ward, Reigart's friends, and his health. She was especially anxious to hear about his health since she had learned that he had spent much time in the sick bay. Reigart tried to make light of these health problems and assured her that he was typical of all the young boys on their first cruise. Also typical, although he did not tell his mother about it, was the fact that he had been admitted to the sick bay three times for treatment of gonorrhea following a couple of port calls.

Although he had missed his family, Reigart began to get restless after being home for a couple of months. He was delighted when orders arrived to report to the *Princeton* that was about to become commissioned. Reigart's memories of the USS *Princeton*, a terrifically modern ship, would be among the most vivid of his colorful naval career.

7.
THE PEACEMAKER

—•◦•—

REIGART'S FRIENDSHIP WITH STEPHEN HAD GROWN ON board the *Boston*. They spent a lot of time together on the ship and had usually gone on shore leaves together. They used to meet Earl English on these shore leaves who was on board the *Boston's* sister-ship, the *Constellation*. The three of them would explore the backstreets of the Chinese towns they visited.

When the *Boston* returned, Reigart went home to Philadelphia and Stephen went home to New York. Earl lived in New Jersey and had returned there earlier when the *Constellation* had come back to the United States. Soon after Reigart received orders to report to the *Princeton* in Philadelphia, he received a letter from Earl English. Earl had also been assigned to the *Princeton*. Reigart answered Earl's letter and told him that he was welcome to stay at Reigart's house if he wanted to come down to Philadelphia early. Earl was anxious to see his friend again and accepted the invitation. He told Reigart that he would arrive about a week before they had to report.

When Reigart learned that his new ship was being completed in the Philadelphia Navy Yard, he decided to go down to see it. He had not been down to the docks since he had returned to Philadelphia, and he jumped at the chance. He wandered down his old favorite route—Chestnut St.—until he got to the Delaware River. Then watching the ships and checking out the merchant shop windows, he walked on down toward the Navy Yard. As he approached the yard, he remembered that day nearly four years before when he had met Lieutenant Chauvenet. This time he toured the yard as a midshipman himself, and he felt proud.

Learning which vessel was the *Princeton*, Reigart went over to it. At first glance he thought that it was a beautiful, trim, three-masted ship, but there was something about it that was different. He noticed that there was a large smokestack just behind the foremast. Reigart's curiosity was aroused. He could see that this was not just any ordinary ship. Besides the smokestack, there seemed to be basic design differences that Reigart could sense, though some were subtle.

As Reigart studied the vessel, an officer approached who had noticed the young midshipman studying the *Princeton*. The officer turned out to be Captain Robert F. Stockton who had designed and supervised the construction of the *Princeton*. Captain Stockton was pleased to learn that he would be Reigart's commanding officer. He invited Reigart aboard to show him some of the vessel's attributes. Reigart was attentive. He wanted to learn about this vessel that he could tell was revolutionary in many ways.

As they walked around the vessel, Reigart noticed that Stockton was a modern officer who was not afraid to innovate. Reigart knew that while steam power had existed for several decades—he had seen the steamer, *Robert Morris*, plying up and down the Delaware River all his life—that the Navy had made little use of it. Captain Stockton told him that as a sailing vessel, the *Princeton* was equal to any ship of her class. With her auxiliary power of steam, she would make greater speed than any seagoing vessel previously built.

Captain Stockton pointed out to Reigart the advantages that the *Princeton* had as a steam vessel over sailing vessels. She would go in and out of ports without regard to the direction of the wind or the thickness of the ice. She could withstand the severest gale in safety. Even if her masts were destroyed, she still had her steam power to fall back on. Captain Stockton took Reigart below to show him the steam engines, explaining that they were safe from shot since they were below the water level.

Reigart was fascinated by the tour. He was impressed when Captain Stockton showed him the vessel's armament. Armed with two 225-pound wrought-iron guns and twelve 42-pound carronades, all of which could be used at once on either side of the ship, the *Princeton* was able to throw a greater weight of metal at one broadside than most frigates. The big guns could be fired with almost incredible effect and with a certainty previously unknown. The two large guns were named the "Oregon" and the "Peacemaker." Captain Stockton told Reigart that the two guns were similar but that he had made a few design changes on the "Peacemaker." This latter gun fired a 12-inch, 225-pound ball, and weighed 27,334 pounds.

When Earl arrived in Philadelphia the next week, Reigart could not wait to take his friend down to see the *Princeton*. When they got there, Reigart introduced Earl to Captain Stockton and asked the captain if he could show Earl around. Captain Stockton assured Reigart that it was all right. Reigart was anxious to give a good tour since Earl had been the one who showed him around the *North Carolina*. He remembered everything Captain Stockton had told him, and Earl was impressed by both the boat and by his friend's knowledge about it.

The boys reported the next week, along with the rest of their shipmates. At first, the ship and its armament were tested. Wanting to see these large guns being fired one day, Reigart went to the side of the vessel to observe. Through his telescope he saw a target that had been set up on shore equivalent to a 74-gun ship.

When target practice began, Reigart calculated that the *Princeton* was about one-third of a mile from the shore. He heard a resounding boom as the "Peacemaker" was fired for the first time and seconds later, he saw the shell shatter the intense mass of the timber target—fifty-seven inches thick—tearing it away and splintering it for several feet on either side, covering the whole surface of the ground one hundred square yards with fragments of wood and iron. Reigart had never seen anything like this and was duly impressed. A short while later, Reigart noticed that the gun was about to be tested again. He noticed that the *Princeton* was out a little further, perhaps a half a mile from the shore. Reigart sighted the target through his telescope. The first shot was a direct hit. Another shot was fired and struck the same horizontal plank. Reigart could hardly believe his eyes when he saw this accuracy, but he had seen nothing yet. Four more shots were fired in succession and they all hit that same horizontal plank one half mile away. The conversation among the men and boys on the *Princeton* that night centered around one topic, the "Peacemaker."

The innovations on the *Princeton*, including these two marvelous guns, made the vessel a showpiece of the United States Navy. As such, she was sent to Washington, D.C., to be observed by various members of the government. On February 20, 1844, most Congressmen, some Senators, and a few reporters boarded the *Princeton* for an afternoon cruise and a demonstration of the ship's powerful armament. This was an exciting day for Reigart; he had never seen so many dignitaries in one place at one time. He and the other seamen were in their full-dress uniforms, and they looked very smart and proper. As Reigart watched the guests come aboard, he was impressed. The men wore high top hats and dress tails. Most of the Congressmen wore black tails and black pants, but an occasional dapper Senator would come aboard with checked pants and a fitted, herringbone frock coat.

Reigart mingled with the Congressmen and Senators and talked with many of them. These were men he had read about in newspapers, and he felt thrilled to be able to meet and talk with them. He was anxious to answer their questions and to tell them about the attributes of the vessel. He took many of them on the same kind of tour that Captain Stockton had given him and he had given Earl English some months before. The Congressmen had read reports about the "Peacemaker" and they were especially interested in hearing about it. Reigart described how it worked in vivid detail, and he loved to talk about the test when six shots from the "Peacemaker" struck the same horizontal plank from one-half mile away during target practice. Many of these Congressmen had been curious about the gun before, but after hearing Reigart's descriptions about it, they were more anxious than ever to see a demonstration.

When Reigart was introduced to one Senator, he was surprised to learn that he was James Buchanan from Pennsylvania. Reigart had never met his Senator before. He had much to thank Senator Buchanan for since the Senator had appointed him to the naval training program. Senator Buchanan was glad to meet Reigart and to learn that Reigart was doing so well and enjoying himself so much. He remembered Reigart's letter of application because he had been so impressed by the young boy's desire to serve his country. While Reigart and his Senator chatted, the ship got underway. Reigart noticed that the gun was about to be fired and invited his Senator over to watch it from a more favorable point of view.

Captain Stockton had mounted the "Peacemaker" and announced, "Now, gentlemen of the House of Representatives, fellow citizens, and shipmates, we are going to give a salute to the wisdom of the mighty republic, in Congress assembled. Stand firm, and you will see how it feels!" The guns were fired in rapid succession. The ship shook and the distant hills reverberated with each thunderous discharge. The instantaneous combustion of forty pounds of gunpowder used in firing the "Peacemaker" closed the round of thirty-six guns and enveloped the deck of the ship in smoke.

Reigart could see that the dignitaries were impressed by this show, and he listened intently as Captain Stockton's voice shouted high in the commotion: "It's nothing but honest gunpowder, gentlemen; it has a strong smell of the Declaration of Independence, but it is none the worse for that. That's the kind of music when negotiations fail. It has a little of the ring of an earthquake, but it tells handsomely on salt water."

Reigart was observing the reaction to the gun from all the guests on board. He heard one of the reporters ask Mr. Speaker Jones what the main question was before the House. The Speaker promptly rejoined, "The main question was the Navy, and that it had been carried by the casting vote of the "Peacemaker.""

In due time, the statesmen and seamen were called to dinner. Reigart and the other sailors directed the guests to the middle deck that extended the entire length of the vessel. The seamen had been instructed to mingle with the Congressmen. Reigart knew how important this was since the primary purpose of the visit to Washington, D.C., was to get more funds for the Navy from Congress. As the meal progressed, Reigart thought that he had never seen such a feast, and he proceeded to stuff himself. The menu consisted of duck, chicken, turkey, ham, beef à la mode, and partridge; ice cream, apples, oranges, raisins, and almonds; champagne, sherry, and cognac. Reigart never saw such a meal in the regular mess, and he could not imagine when he would get another one like it. Captain Stockton was a man of means, and this magnificent feast was drawn from his private resources.

The ship passed below Alexandria as far as George Washington's Mount Vernon residence where it turned around. Several experimental shots were fired from the "Peacemaker" during the return trip, sending solid balls, weighing 225 pounds each, skimming over the water for several miles. The *Princeton* returned to Washington by three o'clock. It had been a great trip for all, but Reigart was looking forward even more to a visit that was scheduled for the following week by the President and his Cabinet. Little did he suspect that this following visit would end so tragically.

8.
I HAVE THE ASSENT OF CONGRESS, AND I'LL GO AHEAD

———•◉•———

STEPHEN, EARL, AND REIGART HAD AGREED TO HOLD THEIR next meeting about the Jouett case the following week at the New York Club. Reigart arrived early to see who else might be around. Heading for the same lounge where he had met them before, Reigart came across Sam Franklin who was chatting with Captain John H. Upshur, number four on the list, right after Reigart.

"Well, if it isn't the senior member of the class of 1847," Reigart commented, referring to the fact that numbers one through three on the list were from the class of 1846.

"How do you do, Reigart. It's been a long time since we've seen each other," John answered.

Reigart joined the men in drink and discussion as they waited for Stephen and Earl. Reigart had met John Upshur's father before he knew John. John's father, Abel Upshur, had been Secretary of the Navy and then Secretary of State under President John Tyler. Upshur had come with President Tyler to witness the firing of the "Peacemaker" on board the *Princeton* on its second Washington outing on February 28, 1844.

Reigart watched as President Tyler, his Cabinet, and many Congressmen and other distinguished gentlemen boarded the *Princeton* for the second excursion. The men were again dressed properly in their tails and top hats. One difference Reigart noticed this time was that many of the gentlemen had elegant ladies hanging on their arms. The women were pretty in their bonnets and their full-length dresses that were tight around the waist but very full at the bottom with many layers of petticoats beneath them. Senator Buchanan approached Reigart and asked him if he would like to meet the President and some of his Cabinet members. Reigart told him that he would be thrilled.

The first Cabinet officer whom they came across was Secretary of State Abel Upshur who until recently had been Secretary of the Navy. Reigart was familiar with the name since he had received orders under Upshur's signature. Secretary Upshur enjoyed seeing the young up-and-coming officer, and he told Reigart how pleased he was to be on the *Princeton*. As Secretary of the Navy, Upshur had tried to innovate and reform the Navy, and he thought that the *Princeton* would show the government the advantages of its various innovations.

Leaving Secretary of State Upshur, Reigart and his Senator next came across Secretary of War, William Wilkins, and Secretary of the Navy, Thomas Gilmer, who were engaging in a lively conversation. Secretary Gilmer had only held his office for ten days at this time and was happy to meet his young officers. Finally, Reigart met his President and Commander-in-Chief, John Tyler. It was a brief meeting since so many others also wanted to shake the President's hand, but Reigart was thrilled just to be able to do that.

It was a beautiful, bright day, and the sun blazed without a cloud in the sky. The crowd of guests seemed gay and joyous, and watched with great interest as the "Peacemaker" was fired several times. When the public's curiosity seemed satisfied, Captain Stockton invited everyone below for some food and some drink. Reigart looked on as many guests proposed toasts and was happy to see that everyone seemed merry. He watched as Captain Stockton rose to propose a toast to the President.

As Stockton rose, Reigart noticed an officer approach the captain and inform him that some persons wanted the "Peacemaker" discharged once more. Captain Stockton shook his head and dismissed the officer saying, "No more guns tonight." While Captain Stockton was expounding about his toast, the young officer returned with a message from Secretary of the Navy Gilmer. Gilmer expressed his desire to see the "Peacemaker" fired one more time. Considering this message equivalent to an order, Captain Stockton immediately went onto the deck to respond to it. Everyone followed. Reigart, who had seen the gun fired numerous times before, still liked to watch it and edged his way up to a position where he could favorably view the event. He noticed Secretary of State Upshur in front of him and Secretaries Wilkins and Gilmer were right next to him.

Before firing the "Peacemaker" for the last time, Captain Stockton decided to take a vote: "All those in favor of another fire will say aye." The air resounded with "Aye!"

"All those opposed to another fire will say no." Not a voice. "The ayes have it," said the captain. "I have the assent of Congress, and I'll go ahead." Right at this point, Reigart overheard Secretary Wilkins say to his colleague, Secretary Gilmer, "Though Secretary of War, I don't like this firing and believe that I shall run!"

As Secretary Wilkins ran back, Captain Stockton placed himself on the breach of the gun, aimed, and fired. Feeling a sensible shock, stunned, and enveloped in a cloud of smoke, Reigart at first could not account for his sensations. As the smoke cleared, Stockton, alone, retained possession of his faculties. All the hair had been burned off his head and face, but he was deeply conscious of the appalling disaster. Calmly but clearly, his voice pealed over the elements of confusion. He gave a few brief orders, recalling his men to a sense of duty. He turned to leave the sad scene, and physically exhausted, fell into the arms of his men who carried him to his bed.

Reigart tried to get up to help, but he realized he had been struck on his left side and could not. Earl English came to help him but Reigart, seeing many who were hurt worse than he, asked Earl to help the others first. As he looked around, Reigart began to see what had happened. An explosion had blown off the lower part of the gun. He saw two sailors removing a section that was lying on the chest of a newspaper correspondent. Looking in front of him, Reigart saw that Secretary of State Upshur had a bad cut over his eye and that his legs were bleeding. Upshur's clothes had been literally torn from his body. He died in a very few minutes.

Right next to Reigart, Secretary of the Navy Gilmer, under whose official direction the gun had been tested again, was also gravely injured. Reigart had to move over a little while a mattress was placed under Mr. Gilmer, but before any medical assistance could be obtained, Gilmer had also passed away. Secretary Wilkins who had been standing with Secretary Gilmer had been saved by his own wit. On his other side, Reigart could see Mr. Maxcy who had both arms and one of his legs cut off, and pieces of flesh hung from his limbs in a truly frightful manner. He died shortly afterwards. Mr. Gardiner (one of whose daughters subsequently married President Tyler) and Commodore Kennan lingered about a half an hour, but they did not seem for a single moment to be conscious of their fate. A servant of the President, a Negro boy about fifteen years old, was also killed.

More than a dozen others on board, including Reigart, received minor injuries from the tremendous explosion. On the deck side, Mr. Tyson was the only person who stood his ground. A piece of the gun, weighing about two pounds, had passed through his top hat—about two inches from his skull—and had fallen by his side. President Tyler was saved by the slightest stroke of luck, being called back from where he stood just a moment before! As Reigart saw Miss Woodbury, the beautiful and accomplished daughter of the Senator from New Hampshire, pass by with her whole face sprinkled with blood, he thought that it was miraculous that all the numerous ladies on board escaped death.

A Board of Naval Inquiry cleared everyone from blame for this tragic incident saying, "the occurrence in question was one of those that sometimes takes place notwithstanding the exercise of the utmost human care and precaution combined with thorough skill and science."

Reigart recovered quickly, and within a few days he returned to his regular duties. Two weeks after the explosion, a sad and disheartened crew returned to Philadelphia. Reigart was glad to be home. Even though he had only been away for a short while, it was comforting to return home after his terrible experience on board the *Princeton*. Repairs had to be made to the vessel, and for the remaining part of 1844, the *Princeton* stayed in or around Philadelphia.

During the fall, Reigart, who had always been interested in history and current events, began to become interested in politics. Although he was only eighteen years old and unable to vote for President until the next election, Reigart followed the campaign closely in the papers. The explosion of the "Peacemaker" had had some effect on presidential politics. Secretary of State Upshur had been working on the annexation of Texas, and his successor, John Calhoun, took on the job of completing it. Calhoun's strong stand for making Texas a slave state, however irritated Northerners, and Texas became part of the North-South debate concerning slavery. The issue was thrown into the presidential election of 1844 for a decision. John Polk, the Democrat, based most of his campaign on annexation. His opponent, Henry Clay, a Whig, avoided the issue. Because of its connection with slavery, Clay did not want to alienate his Northern supporters. Reigart, though not old enough to vote, had already decided to become a Democrat since his personal values seemed to coincide more closely with those of that party. He liked Polk and was happy when the Democrat won.

John K. Polk's victory seemed to be a clear mandate to Tyler and Calhoun, so they submitted the annexation resolution to the lame duck Congress. President Tyler signed the measure on March 1, 1845, three days before Polk's inauguration. Reigart followed these events with great interest and when he heard that President Tyler had selected Captain Stockton and the *Princeton* to be bearer of the resolution to the government of Texas, Reigart could hardly believe his ears. He really felt that he was being a part of American history when the *Princeton* sailed to Galveston where the delicate and important duties were performed. The routine duties and voyages during the next several months seemed dull in comparison.

The annexation which Secretary Upshur had so wanted to accomplish, and which had seemed threatened by his death, had come to pass. Reigart thought back on these events as he talked and drank with John Upshur. Stephen Quackenbush and Earl English arrived together, and they joined the three captains at their table in a corner of the lounge.

"These meetings seem to be growing," observed Reigart. "We now have five of the six most senior captains in our presence. Tell me, Stephen and Earl, have you made any progress?"

Stephen began, "I have been checking the government documents relating to the Naval Review Board. Jim Jouett was moved from number 31 on the list of Lieutenant Commanders to number 62 on the list of Commanders. Since there were eighty Commanders, his move was forty-nine numbers, thirty-one on the Lieutenant Commander list and eighteen on the Commander list."

Reigart interrupted, "Did you notice how many seniors he passed? Some of that growth came from expansion of the size of the ranks."

"Yes," continued Stephen. "I checked the register carefully. Jim Jouett was advanced over nine of his seniors."

"My God!" exclaimed Sam Franklin. "He was advanced over nine of his seniors, and now he thinks he should be advanced over sixteen more. That's twenty-five men. Who does he think he is?"

"If you heard him tell it, you'd think he was God," quipped Reigart.

The men had a good laugh and ordered another round of drinks.

Reigart brought the meeting back to order by thanking Stephen and asking Earl if he had had any luck.

"As a matter of fact, I have," Earl replied. "I remembered reading some articles in the newspapers about ten years ago about the Naval Review Board. I have gone through piles of newspapers since I saw you last week, and I'm proud to announce that I have found it."

There was a round of applause for Captain English.

"Go on," urged Reigart.

9.
REPORT TO ANNAPOLIS, MARYLAND FOR SPECIAL TRAINING

—•◉•—

EARL BEGAN TO EXPLAIN HIS FINDINGS. "SECRETARY Robeson—pardon the reference, Reigart—issued a statement in his first annual report in 1869 condemning the handling of promotions by the Naval Review Board and Secretary Gideon Welles. In retrospect, it is easy to see why now. He wanted to be able to promote his friends and the law did not permit it. Welles responded to the charges, but Robeson leaked Welles's answers out in a way which was very unfair to Secretary Welles."

"That's not surprising," commented Reigart a little bitterly. The others remained silent. They knew how Reigart felt.

Earl broke the uneasy silence by continuing, "Well, Gideon Welles wrote a long, detailed reply and not only sent a copy to Robeson but one to the press as well. It is one of the best defenses of the Naval Review Board I have ever seen."

"I remember that," chimed in John Upshur.

"So do I," echoed the others.

"Very good, Earl," congratulated Reigart. "You and Stephen have done a fine job. We still need a little bit more before we meet in Washington in March. Sam, see if you can trace down the actual text of the laws that define the naval ranks and promotion procedures. And John, see if you can start gathering some biographical information on all seventeen of the senior captains.

As the men broke up, having agreed to meet again in the third week of February, Stephen Quackenbush reflected, "If Jouett is successful, it will mean a little to us, but what will it mean to the men now at Annapolis? What chance will they have?" Stephen's question needed no answer. These men all knew how serious the situation was. All five of these men had graduated from Annapolis about thirty-five years before. The school had been designed to add professionalism to the service, but a lot of good that would do if politics prevailed.

Reigart had received his orders for Annapolis just after he had left the *Princeton*. His new orders read, "Report to Annapolis, MD, for special training." On the surface this did not sound especially exciting, but Reigart knew that there was more to this new assignment than what appeared in the orders.

The Naval School at Annapolis opened its doors for the first time on October 10, 1845. It had become apparent that the Navy needed better-educated officers to keep up with the rapid advances in science and technology that were beginning to take place in the maritime world. Before 1845, only a few select seamen received even the most rudimentary instruction in unfavorable conditions on board receiving ships such as the *North Carolina*.

It had taken many years and many struggles to get the naval school into operation, but the necessary influence finally came in the form of President Polk's new Secretary of the Navy, George Bancroft. He had become secretary in 1845, and by the time he left the office eighteen months later, Annapolis was entering its second year and had been a great success. Instead of going to Congress as his unsuccessful predecessors had, Bancroft decided that the best way to begin the naval school was to use the resources already at hand. The Navy had some teachers on its payroll and had funds enough to pay for them. Bancroft tactfully removed several teachers from the payroll, keeping only those he thought necessary. With the money he saved, he financed the other needs of the school.

For land and buildings, Bancroft acquired Fort Severn at Annapolis from the Army department. He then obtained the able Commander Franklin Buchanan to be Superintendent of the school. Reigart's old teacher and friend, Lt. James Ward, became Executive Officer and an instructor at the school. Lieutenant Chauvenet was brought in to teach mathematics and navigation. A surgeon doubled as an instructor in chemistry, and a Chaplin doubled as an instructor in English. In all, eight qualified men made up the faculty of the naval school in 1845.

At a few minutes before eleven o'clock on the morning of October 10, 1845, Reigart arrived in one of the classrooms where he found fifty other young men assembled for the opening ceremonies. He spotted Earl English talking to Stephen Quackenbush and went over to join them. Peter Wager soon came into the room and joined his friends.

Many of the boys who had joined the Navy's training program in 1840 and who had served with Reigart, Peter, Stephen, and Earl on the *North Carolina* were in the room. Everyone had had interesting experiences, and each enjoyed relating his stories to the others. Most of the boys had not had assignments as exciting as those of Reigart, Stephen, and Earl.

Of the fifty boys who came on this first day, thirty-six had joined the Navy in 1840 as had Reigart, and the remainder had joined in 1841. The boys who had joined in 1840, such as Reigart, Peter, Stephen, and Earl, were ready for promotion, and most of them would graduate the next spring. The school was designed so that the students would go to classes for a year, after which they would serve a probationary term of six months at sea. Following this, they would complete a full term of three years of sea service. Returning to school, they would study for a year prior to examination and graduation. There was, however, much confusion in the early years, and as a result, the first few classes did not follow this format. The midshipmen who entered in Reigart's year, 1840, (forty-seven in all) graduated in 1846, 1847, and 1848.

When all the midshipmen had assembled, Commander Buchanan entered the room. Reigart rose with the rest of the boys and sat on Buchanan's command. Commander Buchanan read the rules and then delivered a brief address about complying with all laws, orders, and regulations. He concluded by reading a letter from Secretary Bancroft and then declared the school officially open.

Following the opening ceremonies, Reigart and his classmates decided to become acquainted with their new campus. As they walked around the grounds, they saw that there were no new buildings; all the buildings were those that had been constructed and left by the Army when it had used the grounds as Fort Severn. The campus was small, encompassing only nine acres surrounded by a stone wall. Reigart found that his barracks doubled as a classroom during the days. The poor conditions and the small size of the naval school by today's standards did not bother Reigart. He was proud to be a part of the first class at Annapolis.

School met from October until the last week in June. In his year there, Reigart studied algebra, geometry, plane and spherical trigonometry, nautical astronomy, navigation, descriptive astronomy, mechanics, optics, magnetism, electricity, ordnance, gunnery, the use of steam, history, composition of the French language, infantry drill, and fencing. The school had a system of merits and demerits. Merits and final grades determined one's rank in class. The professors reported to the Superintendent each week, and roll calls were taken in all classes. The midshipmen had one vacation of two weeks at Christmas time during which Reigart went home to Philadelphia. The academy was not all work, however. Soon after Christmas vacation, the naval school had its first ball that was numerously attended by ladies and gentlemen from various parts of the Union. Reigart served on the dance committee; he helped decorate, arrange for the refreshments, and prepare the invitation list. Friends and relatives were invited as well as prominent citizens and government officials from Baltimore and Washington. The dance was a great success.

For Reigart, it was a refreshing break from his studies—both the preparations and the dance itself. At the dance, Reigart was seen dancing with many of the young ladies. This dapper young man was very handsome and quite popular among the women. He had supported and pushed the idea for a dance from the beginning for he knew that it would be a great personal success as well as a great success for the new school.

On July 11, 1846, just three days before his twentieth birthday, Reigart graduated in the first class at Annapolis and became a Passed Midshipman. This was a big moment for Reigart and for his family who were proud of him. He was no longer a boy or a "middie," but now he was a man. He had completed the program he had applied for in 1840, and with the addition of the naval school it was a far better program now than he had even hoped for.

Reigart was proud of himself. He had received his first promotion, the first step on the ladder to becoming a commodore. He often thought about naval ranks, and especially so on this day of his promotion. Midshipman was the lowest rank of officer (like the rank of ensign today). When a midshipman had passed certain qualifications, as had Reigart, he would become a Passed Midshipman. As he looked back on his year at Annapolis, Reigart had mixed feelings. He never was an enthusiastic student when it came to subjects like reading, writing and arithmetic. When it came to subjects like navigation, nautical astronomy and gunnery, however, Reigart was a top student. He had especially enjoyed James Harmon Ward's classes, and his friendship with Ward had grown even more during the year at Annapolis. He had also enjoyed Lieutenant Chauvenet's classes.

Reigart made many friends during this year. He would come across many of these friends in years to come.

The training Reigart had gone through during the first six years of his service had left a lasting impression. He would later become a teacher himself and be responsible for some of the Navy's future training programs. All the men involved in the Jouett case had valued their training. It was one of the reasons for the Navy's high degree of professionalism which was what they were fighting to preserve as they prepared for their next meeting.

10.
MEXICO HAS INVADED OUR TERRITORY AND SHED AMERICAN BLOOD ON AMERICAN SOIL

———•◉•———

REIGART SHOWED UP EARLY AT THE NEW YORK CLUB FOR THE next meeting. It was the third week in February, and there was only a short time left before the meeting of all sixteen captains. Reigart showed up early to see if he could find any more of the captains before the meeting began. As luck would have it, he found three more of the captains with whom he had not talked about the Jouett Case before. Captains John Charles Philip DeKrafft (number nine on the list), John Lee Davis (number twelve), and William Kennon Mayo (number sixteen) were having a lively discussion when Reigart approached.

"Well, hello, Reigart," John DeKrafft greeted. "We were just talking about this ghastly Jouett affair. Has there been any progress?"

"No," responded Reigart. "We are about to have a meeting, and I hope you men can join."

"That's what we're here for," piped up Bill Mayo, the junior member of the contingent. "Sam Franklin told us that you have been meeting here."

Reigart brought the men up to date as far as the information that had been gathered so far. As he explained the details, the other men began to arrive. Now that they had eight members present, their corner table in the New York Club lounge was becoming crowded. Reigart did not want to change tables, though, because this table and this corner of the lounge had become a part of the Jouett cause.

Reigart began the meeting by asking, "Sam, did you have any luck tracing the laws concerning naval ranks and commissions?"

"Yes," Sam answered. "I have copies of all of the laws and tables and charts showing the size of each rank and the changes in these sizes throughout the years."

"What about you, John?" Reigart asked, looking over toward John Upshur. "Have you been able to compile biographical information about Jouett and the rest of us?"

John smiled and said, "I sure have. I found complete records of all seventeen men in the Hammersley's Record of Living Officers of the US Navy. The biographies are about a page long for each man. They show that Jouett is no different from the rest of us."

"That's great," congratulated Reigart. "If we use Hammersley's biographies, we can't be accused of bias. If we wrote the biographies ourselves, Jouett would claim that we wrote them to our advantage."

"Do you think that Jouett knows that we are organized?" inquired John Davis.

"That arrogant bastard," Earl English exclaimed. "He doesn't even know we exist. Why, he thinks that the whole universe revolves around him. We are just flies that he is trying to swish off with his tail."

Reigart nodded his head. He agreed wholeheartedly. Ever since he had known Jim Jouett, it had seemed as if Jouett's nose was stuck up in the air. "You know," added Reigart thoughtfully, "This whole Jouett case could turn into a real mudslinging affair if we are not careful. We must remember to remain above that level if we are to maintain the integrity of the Navy."

Stephen Quackenbush, the senior member of the captains continued, "Yes, we must remember that we are fighting for more than ourselves and our fellow naval officers. The future of the country is at stake. We must keep in mind that the purpose of the Navy is to protect and defend the United States."

Earl English interrupted here and added, "Yes, and if it ever comes to a point where the Navy is needed to fight for our country, we want professional officers and not a bunch of politicians leading us. We have all fought in two wars and know how important this is."

Indeed, they had. The Navy had played a key role in both the Mexican War and the Civil War. For all these men, the first action they had seen had been in Mexico.

Annexation of Texas by the United States in 1845, in which Reigart had taken such an interest, had strained diplomatic relations between the United States and Mexico. Mexico never acknowledged that Texas had seceded, and in the early part of 1846, there were boundary disputes and indemnity claims made by the United States government. In May, some Mexicans crossed the Rio Grande River and killed or wounded sixteen of General Zachary Taylor's men on what they claimed was Mexican soil. President Polk told the nation that Mexico had "invaded our territory and shed American blood on American soil." He declared war, and Congress approved it by overwhelming majorities on May 13, 1846.

The war was only a couple of months old when Reigart graduated from Annapolis. Three days after his graduation, on his twentieth birthday, he was ordered to go to New York and report to Commander Josiah Tattnall for duty on board the USS *Spitfire*. The *Spitfire* and the *Vixen*, both side-wheelers, were being built in New York for Mexico when the war broke out, so the United States commandeered them for her own Navy. Commodore Matthew Calbraith Perry, younger brother of Oliver Hazard

Perry, took command of the *Vixen* when it was finished and began his voyage to Mexico. Reigart's ship, the *Spitfire*, was completed shortly afterward and followed.

At the beginning of the hostilities, Mexico had no Navy on the high seas, and the United States was ill equipped to carry on warfare in enemy waters. The American vessels were under the command of Commodore David Conner. His entire squadron by the end of 1846 consisted of only ten ships carrying a total of seventeen guns. All but three of these vessels had deep drafts and were, therefore, incapable of river warfare for that reason. As a result, the function of the Navy during the Mexican War was to blockade the ports and to convoy troops. By the time that Reigart arrived on the *Spitfire* in November 1846, little had been done. Commodore Conner had bungled an attack on Alvarado, and Commodore Perry had come back with a successful operation against Tobasco. John DeKrafft had seen his first action during this first attack against Alvarado.

Soon after Reigart's arrival, he learned that his vessel was going to be involved in an attack on the city of Tampico, about two hundred miles north of Vera Cruz. John Mayo, on the *Sloop of St. Mary's* would be in the same attack. Reigart had learned that Tampico was the most important city and port in northeastern Mexico and that it would make a good base for an attack on Vera Cruz. Reigart was prepared to participate in his first battle. As the flotilla under Conner approached Tampico city, ready to batter it into submission, Reigart noticed that the city looked empty. This feeling was verified when he learned that the city had been evacuated. The city council promptly surrendered, which was the only thing it could do under the circumstances. Upon naval occupation of the city, General Taylor's troops began to assemble in Tampico from Monterey in preparation for the attack on Vera Cruz. In the meantime, the *Spitfire* cruised up and down the Tamaulipas River Valley destroying all the public property that could be found.

Plans for an attack on Vera Cruz were being formulated in late 1846. Vera Cruz was Mexico's only important commercial city, and it was a gateway to Mexico City. There were about 1,000 two-story, square, flat-roofed, stone houses there. The population was about 5,000. The city was surrounded by a stone wall, 3,124 yards in circumference and was defended by nine bastions capable of supporting one hundred guns. It was small, but regularly laid out, well-paved, and well-lighted. Situated on an arid plain, it was surrounded by sand hills and intervening clusters of thick chaparral. The harbor was insecure, and anchorage afforded little protection during a "Norther."

But the pride of the Republic was not the city but its famous fortress of San Juan de Ulúa. Construction began on the fortress in 1582, and the Spanish spent $40,000,000 on it. It was built on an island in front of the city about a thousand yards from the shore. With its foundations laid in the sea, it was built of soft coral, while its walls and exposed points were built of harder stone. Capable of holding three hundred and seventy guns, it held only one hundred and thirty-five in 1847.

Reigart learned that the attack on Vera Cruz would be a joint Army-Navy operation. His job would be to help attach surfboats to the *Spitfire*, which would haul some of them to the landing site and then his vessel would cover the landing.

The troops were loaded, and the squadron got under way by 11:00 a.m. on March 7, 1847. Reigart noticed that it was a bright, beautiful day with a smooth sea and a gentle breeze. He felt a twinge of excitement as the soldiers' bayonets flashed in the sunlight. He knew that the next few weeks would be filled with action.

In about three hours, the frigates and transports dropped anchor opposite the Isla de Sacrificios, south of Vera Cruz. Sixty-five immense surfboats, each capable of holding one hundred men, were hauled to the gangways of the ships. By 4:00 p.m. when the surfboats were loaded with 4,500 men, they drew abreast of each other in a single line that Reigart felt was nearly a mile long. As the surfboats began to land, the *Spitfire*, along with the *Vixen* and five gunboats, moved in to cover the landing. Reigart went to man his station and prepare for action. The first division under Brigadier General William Worth was ready to land.

Reigart heard the *Massachusetts* fire the signal for landing, and almost simultaneously, the flotilla of surfboats got under way. Amid the hearty cheer of those who were left behind, Reigart watched as the soldiers neared the shore. He and his comrades were covering the landing and were watching for the enemy. He saw the first boats touch ground, and the foremost men in each sprang into waist deep water and dashed up the sandy beach followed by their comrades. As they landed, Reigart noticed through his telescope that they were meeting no resistance. The first division completed its landing with speed and effectiveness. Reigart began to prepare for the second landing that soon followed under Major General Robert Patterson. Reigart watched again in amazement at the smoothness of the operation. The reserve, under Brigadier General David Twiggs landed next, and by 10:00 p.m., the transports had landed the last troop.

Though this had been an exciting day for Reigart, he was glad that it was over. It had been a long and exhausting day. It had started early in the morning when all was made ready. It had not ended until the last troop was ashore late that night. Reigart was impressed by the facility and precision with which the landing was accomplished. The necessary arrangements had been made with such skill and forethought that nearly 12,000 men were disembarked without confusion, disturbance, or a solitary accident. Reigart did not know it, but he and the others on board had just witnessed the largest US naval amphibious operation ever accomplished prior to the North African invasion of 1942!

Within four days, the occupation was complete. Reigart often watched the events on shore through his telescope. He could see that the men were busy throwing up temporary fortifications, erecting batteries, planting mortars, landing supplies, and beating off the light troops of the enemy.

Twelve days after the landing, Reigart heard the news that Commodore Perry had replaced Commodore Conner of command of the Home Squadron that Conner had commanded for three years. Pressures from Washington, age, and poor health were all against Conner. He had wanted to stay in command until the hostilities with Mexico were completed, but the Secretary of the Navy disagreed with Conner since the length of the war was so uncertain. Conner's term was up, and the Home Squadron needed a change in leadership. Reigart was excited to be serving under Perry, brother of his boyhood hero.

By permission of General Winfield Scott, one of Perry's first actions was to establish a marine battery under direction of Captain John H. Aulick. This unit would support the Army artillery under Captain Robert E. Lee, and it played an important role in the demolition of the city. Reigart wished that he could go ashore as part of this unit, but he was needed on his ship. Two friends, his cousin Peter Wager and John Lee Davis, had been selected to be in this unit. He watched the unit with great interest and pride since they were part of his service. On March 22, nearly two weeks after the landing, both the marine battery and the flotilla of schooners and steam gunboats began shelling the city continuously. The ships continued firing all night and until 9:00 a.m. the next morning, when Perry called them off since they were within range of the guns of San Juan de Ulúa. The Army continued battering the city, and the marine battery continued until it ran out of ammunition on March 24. On March 25, Reigart saw his first heavy action. The fleet moved in to attack San Juan de Ulúa, and Reigart's commander, Josiah Tattnall, moved the *Spitfire* within 800 yards of the fortress where the little gunboat hammered at the fortress for half an hour.

That evening, fighting the enemy had to cease for a short time while the Navy fought a "Norther." It was one of the worst storms ever to hit this area. Fierce waves broke over the decks of the ships. Reigart, who had been in storms before, felt that they were nothing compared to this one. He felt seasick for the first time in his life. By morning, twenty-three vessels had gone aground.

The battle against Vera Cruz, however, had already been won. On March 27, just eighteen days after the landing, the Mexicans surrendered their forts, armaments, munitions, garrisons, and arms. The Castle of San Juan de Ulúa had fallen for the fourth time in its 325-year history. Vera Cruz, which had been considered one of the strongest fortifications in North America, had fallen, at a cost of only fourteen killed and fifty-nine wounded.

Reigart went ashore a couple of days later with other naval officers to survey the damage. Entering the city, he saw the terrible effects of the shells on the city. As he looked around, he could scarcely see a building that had escaped damage by the artillery. Some of the houses had been destroyed by fire, others by shells. Roofs were crushed, walls had collapsed, and the stones that had been used in construction of these dwellings lay in confused heaps, mingled with broken shells and dead carcasses of horses and mules. Reigart noticed an intolerable stench that pervaded the place that would require incessant efforts of the Army to subdue. Upon his return, Reigart gave a vivid report to the officers and men on the *Spitfire* on the effects of their work.

The target after Vera Cruz was Alvarado. Commodore Perry arrived there with his fleet just a few days after the surrender of Vera Cruz, but the highly active Lieutenant Charles G. Hunter commanding the *Scourge* had arrived a few days earlier and left nothing to be done. Even though Hunter had captured Alvarado, he was immediately arrested and dismissed from the squadron for disobedience of orders.

After Vera Cruz and Alvarado, Perry fitted out an expedition to occupy Tuxpan. After some delay at the Isla de Lobos, and another "Norther," arrangements went ahead for a landing on April 18. The *Mississippi*, carrying Perry's flag, anchored off the bar of the river near the town. He and many of the crew of the *Mississippi* went to other ships with lower drafts. Perry himself hoisted his flag on the *Spitfire* that would lead the other vessels. The steamers took down their masts and lightened themselves in any way they could so that they could cross the bar to enter the river. Then the steamers, each with a gunboat in tow, started across the bar. They had not gone far when the *Spitfire* was hit by a volley of musketry that came from the high grass along the bank. Reigart who had been conferring with the other officers on the boat felt a burning sensation in his left arm. He had been struck.

Also hit were Commander Tattnall and two other officers. Reigart's injury was only a flesh wound, but it put him out of action for the rest of this expedition.

A short while later, while the ships proceeded up the river, two forts on the right bank opened fire on the squadron. Reigart, now below deck, could hear the steamers return the fire of the enemy, and looking out of the ship he could see Marines landing and storming the forts, driving the enemy out. Soon, as the squadron moved up the river, Reigart heard the vessels being assailed by fire from another fort and from troops posted in the chaparral. The fort soon fell, and simultaneously, a division of Marines entered the town and took possession of it, while the enemy fled in every direction. Commodore Perry demolished the forts and returned down the river, leaving the *Albany* and the gunboat *Reefer* to garrison the place.

Tobasco was the only Mexican port left uncaptured, and Perry wanted its speedy reduction. By sunset of June 14, 1847, the flotilla had arrived at Seven Palms, a noted landmark below Tobasco. Within two days, the men and boats were ready.

As the flotilla moved up the river, the enemy opened heavy fire from a concealed breastwork called Calmera. The flotilla promptly returned a raking fire of grape, canister, and musketry along the bank and into the chaparral that checked that of the enemy. Reigart, now healed, was an active and eager participant. He made himself conspicuous and was at the forefront of the action, helping his men to fire shells into the enemy.

In the meantime, Commodore Perry prepared to land with two hundred and twenty Marines and nine hundred seamen. Standing erect in his barge, he shouted, "Three cheers and land!" The hurrahs burst forth from over a thousand manly voices, and the rowers impelled the numerous boats toward the right bank. Reigart again wished that he could be among the landing party, but all the men on the *Spitfire* were needed to give cover to it. As the men landed, the enemy left the battery and retreated toward the city. The naval and marine forces, led by the gallant commodore in person, gave chase for several miles over a narrow trail.

By early afternoon, Perry and his troops had sighted Hidalgo's Works at Acachapan that surrendered with little resistance. The steamers had proceeded up the river, captured Fort Iturbide, and raised the American flag over it by the time Perry and his troops arrived there by foot. The next morning, Reigart watched as the flag of the United States was raised over Tobasco and as the mud walls of Fort Iturbide were mined and blown up.

Five days later, Commodore Perry ordered Reigart to report for duty on the *Mississippi*. Mexico was just entering its rainy season and the swamps all abounded with mosquitoes. With the rainy season and the mosquitoes came the dreaded *vomito* or yellow fever. It struck Reigart and most of the crew on the *Mississippi* in late July. He first felt very weak and collapsed one afternoon. He began to run a high fever and became jaundiced. He felt terrible. The disease had spread quickly and most of the men on the *Mississippi* were soon suffering from it. The *Mississippi* sailed to Pensacola, Florida, where its two hundred patients convalesced quickly.

Following his recovery, Reigart spent a three-month leave of absence at his home in Philadelphia. As usual, he had much to tell his mother and friends. He had participated in nearly every major naval action of the Mexican War and was considered a war hero by his fellow Philadelphians. He told his friends about the important role the Navy had played in the war—transporting troops, covering landings, and blockading ports. He especially liked to tell of Commodore Matthew Calbraith Perry who had commanded the sixteen vessels of the Home Squadron, the largest number of American vessels ever assembled up to that time. Reigart now had his own Commodore Perry with whom he had served.

11.

THE ATLANTIC, THE PACIFIC, THE ARCTIC, AND THE BALTIC

———•◉•———

"YOU KNOW, EARL, I AGREE WITH YOU," REIGART COMMENTED, "but a naval officer has to be prepared for peace as well as for war. Some of the accomplishments we made in the decade between the Mexican and Civil Wars were as significant as some of our wartime contributions."

During the decade following the Mexican War, the Navy promoted and protected American commerce in three major ways. Ships were sent around the world to support American interest and promote good will; the Navy entered a public-private venture with Mail Steamers; and an expedition was sent to Japan to open channels of trade. Reigart played a part in each of those three activities.

His first assignment was on the *Allegheny* that left Norfolk, Virginia, in February 1848 for Rio de Janeiro. Sam Franklin was also on the *Allegheny*. During the next few months, the *Allegheny* divided its time among the ports Rio de Janeiro, Montevideo, and Buenos Aires. Reigart enjoyed his time in South America. He had been born there but had never been able to spend much time there before. He enjoyed traveling and liked to see as many different places as possible, meet the people and study their culture.

Because of this, Reigart was happy to hear that upon leaving South America, his vessel was going to spend some time in the Mediterranean Sea where he would visit European countries. Stopping at Lisbon, Portugal, the *Allegheny* proceeded to go through the Strait of Gibraltar and into the Mediterranean. The next few months were spent on the west coast of Italy and in Toulon, France. Reigart enjoyed most of his visit to Europe except from April 10, to May 12, 1849, when he was back in the sick bay for his rheumatism. During this time, Reigart was made Master of the *Allegheny* which pleased him very much. This was the final step before becoming Lieutenant and was the highest non-commissioned rank. Later in May, the *Allegheny* began its return trip, stopping at Tunis, Malta, and Gibraltar. While in Malta, Reigart joined the Masons of Malta. Returning to Washington, D.C., on the first of August, the *Allegheny* proceeded down to the mouth of the Mississippi River to become part of the home squadron. Its duties as a ship of good will were over. The vessel was back in Washington by mid-October and at the end of October, having served on the *Allegheny* for twenty months, Reigart was detached from the vessel and given a leave of absence.

The second way that the Navy became involved in promoting American interests was through the Mail Steamers. These Mail Steamers were a joint public-private venture. The vessels were built, owned, and operated by private companies with the guidance and supervision of Commodore Matthew C. Perry and were designed so that they could readily be converted into war steamers in time of emergency. These were a forerunner to the merchant marine.

The United States government subsidized the steamer lines for carrying the mail, and the Navy provided some of the crews. Of these Mail Steamers, those of the Collins Line became the nation's favorites. Vessels from the Collins Line sailed between New York and Liverpool, making the trip in ten to twelve days. Its first four vessels were named after bodies of water—the *Atlantic*, the *Pacific*, the *Arctic*, and the *Baltic*.

Of these, the *Arctic* and the *Baltic* were the fastest; they both could make the trip in less than ten days. On April 13, 1850, Reigart received orders to report as Watch Officer on the US Mail Steamer, *Atlantic*. Six months later, he was transferred over to the Mail Steamer, *Arctic*, for another six-month duty. This duty was staid compared to what Reigart was used to on naval vessels, but it was a refreshing break, and it gave him an opportunity to be on the sea which he enjoyed.

As a promoter of commerce, the Navy had yet one more important function to serve during this decade of Reigart's career. Throughout the ages, men of all nations have been lured by the mysteries of the East. An explorer searching for a shorter route to the Orient had discovered America. Much of the exploration of America was done in search of a northwest passage. Victory in the Mexican War had given the United States two major seaports on the Pacific coast—San Francisco and San Diego. This, combined with the acquisition of two other major seaports through the settlement of the Oregon question—Seattle and Portland, gave the United States a renewed interest in Pacific trade and its new neighbor to the west—Japan.

Many people made proposals to President Millard Fillmore and Secretary of State Daniel Webster for expeditions to Japan. Early in May 1851, just prior to assuming command of the East India Squadron, Commodore John H. Aulick again made a proposal. This time the idea was accepted, and as Aulick had suggested it and was going there anyway, he was selected as the American Officer to carry it out. Three vessels would make up his squadron—the *Susquehanna*, the *Plymouth*, and the *Saratoga*.

When Reigart had been detached from the Mail Steamer, *Arctic*, he had been reassigned to the USS *Susquehanna*. Just before Commodore Aulick left, however, Reigart was again reassigned, but this time he was to report to the *Plymouth* which was part of the same squadron. Reigart was happy to be back on naval vessels. He felt more at home on them since that was what he had been trained for.

In the meantime, Commodore Aulick had left on the *Susquehanna* ahead of the other vessels. Going by way of Rio de Janeiro and Madeira, he arrived in Hong Kong in July 1852. There, he began to organize his squadron and to prepare for a visit to Japan. While making these plans, an astonished Commodore Aulick received a curt order from the Secretary of the Navy, dated November 18, 1851, directing him to hand over his command to Franklin Buchanan, Reigart's old naval school superintendent, and not to leave the China Seas until his permanent successor should arrive. The Navy demanded prompt and full explanation to charges that Aulick had taken his son on board a national vessel as a passenger and that he had entertained the premier of Brazil and told him that he had entertained him at his own private expense. These seem to be minor charges for the punishment that was inflicted upon Aulick, the relief of his command. He was cleared ten years later. No one knew how or why this happened or who was responsible. Some people thought that Perry might have been behind it since he received the command. Perry was cleared of this charge, and a recent biographer, Samuel Eliot Morrison, even goes so far as to say that Perry did not want the command. What would have happened had Aulick remained in command is anyone's guess, but looking at it in retrospect, he probably would not have done as well as Perry.

Meanwhile, the *Plymouth*, with Reigart on board, had started for Hong Kong in August, sailing by way of the Rio de Janeiro and Madeira and arriving in Batavia (Jakarta, Indonesia) on January 27, 1852. Reigart was looking forward to going to China again. He had been there ten years before and had found it awfully interesting. He wanted even more to see Japan since no Americans, except a few shipwrecked ones, had ever been there. The *Plymouth* went to Haiphong, Indochina where Reigart transferred to the *Saratoga*, the third ship in the East India Squadron. He had now been on all three! While Reigart was on the *Saratoga*, he went to many of the Chinese ports he had visited a decade before and many new ones. Most of the time, his vessel was stationed in Hong Kong, and it made its trips from there to Macao, Canton, Amoy, Port Haddington, Whampoa, Blenheim Beach, Cun Sing Mun Harbor, and St. John's Harbor.

In the meantime, Commodore Matthew Calbraith Perry was selected as Aulick's replacement. Perry was a logical choice as he had extensive experience in military and diplomatic affairs. The government invested extraordinary diplomatic and naval powers in Perry for this mission. Difficulties arose and delays resulted, but Perry finally set out on his old boat from the Mexican War, the *Mississippi*, on November 24, 1852. The *Powhattan* and the *Allegheny* followed later.

Reigart saw a familiar ship come into Hong Kong Harbor in April 1853. It was his old ship, the *Mississippi*, with Commodore Perry aboard. Reigart knew that Commodore Perry would be disappointed that the *Susquehanna* and Franklin Buchanan were not in Hong Kong. Buchanan had gone on to Shanghai a fortnight before. Perry was surprised, disappointed, and upset. The *Susquehanna* was to be his flagship, and his arrival had been expected. He sent the *Plymouth* on to Shanghai to tell Commander Buchanan to remain there until he arrived. Upon his arrival, Perry performed many of the routine and administrative duties of a fleet commander. Among these was to appoint Reigart as regular Watch Officer on board the *Saratoga*.

In May, Commodore Perry assembled all his ships in Shanghai and began preparations for his visit to Japan. His ships made a couple of visits to the Lew Chew Islands (Okinawa) just south of Japan. Perry had been promised thirteen vessels for his expedition, but he still had only four— Aulick's original three, the *Susquehanna*, the *Plymouth*, and the *Saratoga*— and the vessel Perry had brought, the *Mississippi*. He could not wait any longer, so he prepared to enter Japan early on July 8, 1853.

12.
LORD OF THE FORBIDDEN INTERIOR

—●○●—

THE FOUR VESSELS ENTERED EDO (TOKYO) BAY AND anchored off the city of Uraga. The beauty of the bay struck Reigart. All the mountains seemed to come down almost to the waters edge. As the haze lifted, he could see majestic Mount Fuji in the distance. The bay was horseshoe shaped, and Reigart could see villages and towns scattered all along the shoreline.

Perry's steam frigates were the first vessels of their kind to be seen in Japan, and their arrival caused a great deal of excitement. The intelligent Japanese were interested in this development, whereas the ignorant peasants supposed that the foreign barbarians had succeeded in imprisoning volcanoes in their ships or else felt that it was a mirage caused by the breath of clams. In any case, the arrival of these vessels caused a great deal of consternation among the Japanese hierarchy. Japanese guard boats immediately came out to greet the ships and send them away.

Commodore Perry had studied the oriental mind, and he decided to use his knowledge to obtain the best results. He knew that in the Orient, when one wanted to get a message to a high-ranking official, he could never see him but would have to do business with someone at a much lower level. Therefore, when the Vice-Governor of Uraga came aboard, he was permitted to speak to a Lieutenant (Lt. John Contee); and when the Governor came, a committee of captains met with him. In the meantime, Perry remained locked in his cabin and did not allow anyone to see him. Only upon arrangements for the receipt of the proposals by a direct representative of the Emperor did Commodore Perry, who had become known as "Lord of the Forbidden Interior," consent to be revealed.

The pomp and pageantry of his first appearance was also designed to strike the oriental mind. Reigart looked over toward the shore as the big "black ships" moved in so that their guns bore on the pavilion where the President's messages would be received. He saw several thousand Japanese soldiers lining the entire shore. The infantry, with white scarves around their foreheads, stood at attention with muskets resting on their left shoulders. A few cavalrymen stood in front of the infantry, holding their horses in place. Reigart felt that even the horses looked impressive. They wore fancy saddles and had either red or gray fringed material all around them. Off to the side, he could see archers holding their bows and wearing very strange hats that looked like large flat disks sitting on their heads.

Reigart had been one of the officers who were selected to go ashore. In all, from the four ships, nearly four hundred men would land. Reigart got into his landing craft, and a few minutes later he became one of the first Americans ever to step on Japanese soil. The men in his boat landed quickly and joined the line of Marines and sailors who had landed just ahead of them. Reigart, as an officer, stood two paces in front of the enlisted men. The men all wore blue pants, white shirts, blue caps, and held a musket with a bayonet attached. Reigart and the other officers wore white pants, blue coats, blue hats, and had swords hanging at their sides.

A few hundred men lined the shore, and a handful of officers formed a corridor through which the commodore would walk when he landed. Two brass bands stood at the far end of the line of officers. Hearing a thirteen-gun salute, Reigart knew that Commodore Perry was about to enter his barge. Reigart saw that two immense "jet-black" Negroes, who were armed to the teeth as bodyguards, flanked the commodore. Immediately in front of Perry, two ship's boys bore the gold mounted rosewood box that contained the precious documents inscribed on vellum. The box itself was lined with blue velvet and was closed by seals of solid gold. After a short ceremony, Perry gave assurances that he would be back for a reply the next spring, probably with more vessels.

Leaving Japan, the fleet came across a severe cyclone that was about a thousand miles in diameter and only moved at about three miles per hour. The *Saratoga* entered the Southwest quarter of the storm and was heading right for its vortex. The farther out the ship got, the wilder the sea got. Reigart knew that this storm was going to be far worse than that "Norther" he had experienced at Vera Cruz. Waves constantly broke over the ship and the decks became flooded. Reigart and his men removed most of the canvas, and all hands were on deck. Reigart held on for dear life to lifelines that went around the boat.

The officers were all summoned to the captain's cabin. Reigart moved cautiously along the lifeline to the cabin. The First Lieutenant had tried to give orders on the deck, but his roaring voice could not be heard six inches from his lips. The orders were given in the cabin, and the officers relayed them individually to the men. As Reigart moved out to give the instructions to his men, a gigantic wave struck the head of the vessel on the starboard side with such force that Reigart thought the ship would break in two.

The main topsail could not be taken down, and this presented a great danger. All efforts were made, but they had to be abandoned. As the wind blew into it, it sometimes caused the yardarms to dip into the frothy sea. As Reigart inched along the lifeline, the air was as black as pitch and full of flying scud. The wind scooped off the tops of the waves and sent them hissing through the rigging with the force of chain shot.

The ship was being rapidly driven toward the Paracels where she would be driven onto the rocks. The crew desperately tried to turn her around, but without her sails, this was a hopeless task. She became more unmanageable as time went on, and something had to be done. With a good deal of persuasion and some force, more than one hundred men, including Reigart and the other officers, went into the fore rigging to form a sort of human sail. These men hung in mid-air for over a half an hour while the ship jerked and writhed beneath them. It was a miracle that every one of them was not thrown into the sea. Finally, Reigart noticed that the ship was responding. In a few minutes, it became evident that the storm was passing. Within a few hours, it was safe to raise the sails again and continue to China. Miraculously, not a life was lost, though boats were missing and anything that had been on the deck was now gone.

Reigart was transferred back to the _Susquehanna_ shortly after this and then to the _Powhatan_ when it arrived with the _Vandalia_. The next several months were spent by Reigart hopping from port to port, rarely staying in one place for more than a month. The _Powhatan_ visited many parts of China, including Hong Kong, Cun Sing Mun, Macao, Canton, and Whampoa. During that period, Reigart was again afflicted with rheumatism.

Near the end of January, the squadron again assembled and headed back to Japan. On February 14, 1854, Perry and his fleet arrived in Edo Bay to continue negotiations of the treaty he had presented to the Japanese the previous July. This time, he brought with him four more ships, making eight in all—one-fourth of the United States Navy.

On March 8, Perry landed at Yokohama with five hundred armed men and a glittering staff of officers in full uniform. Reigart was again fortunate enough to be selected to land. While the negotiations were going on, Reigart watched the presents for the emperor being sent ashore and helped set them up. There was a railway track three hundred and sixty-nine feet in circumference on which a one-quarter scale locomotive with a tender and a passenger car operated daily to the great interest and delight of the

Japanese people. A mile-long telegraph line also fascinated the Japanese. Included among the other gifts were stoves, clocks, maps, books, and machinery of all kinds.

A treaty signed on March 31st conceded little to the Americans, but it opened the door for future negotiations. The Japanese agreed to treat shipwrecked Marines kindly; it gave permission to Americans to buy fuel, water, and other provisions; and it specified that the ports of Shimoda and Hakodato as places where foreign ships might anchor for repairs or refuge from storms. The Japanese refused to trade for goods other than ship's needs, but other privileges would come soon.

For three months following the treaty, the fleet sailed between the newly opened ports of Shimoda and Hakodato. Reigart ended up in the infirmary once again during this period for his rheumatism. At the end of June, the *Powhatan* left Japan for China. While on the Chinese coast, as during the rest of the expedition, the seamen collected information in many fields. They charted the coastlines, and artists made drawings of the local plants, animals, fish, and birds. They explored the geology of each area and studied the customs of the local peoples. The expedition, therefore, not only played a valuable role in the opening of Japan to the West, but it also contributed to many scientific fields. While the *Powhatan* sailed along the Chinese coast, Commodore Perry left for the United States, leaving Captain Joel Abbot in charge of the *Macedonian, Powhatan,* and *Vandalia.*

During 1855, Reigart's ship made one final trip to Japan and then went back to China. Reigart enjoyed the Orient, but he was getting anxious to get back to the United States since he had been away for several years. September 14, 1855, was an especially happy day for Reigart. It was the day he finally received his promotion to Lieutenant. He was twenty-nine years old. This was a big step toward Reigart's goal of someday becoming a commodore like the two Perrys he so admired.

On November 1st, the *Powhatan* finally left Hong Kong for home, making short stops in Singapore, Mauritius, and the Cape of Good Hope.

Reigart again got that feeling of homesickness. The expedition was over, and he just wanted to get home The *Powhatan* reached Norfolk, Virginia, on February 14, 1856, almost five years after Reigart had left on the expedition.

Reigart went home to Philadelphia where his mother and brothers were happy to see him and to listen to his stories. Upon his return home, Reigart learned some startling news. His cousin, Peter Wager, had been forcefully retired from the Navy. Until 1855, the Navy had had no retirement system. Because of this, some men who had fought in the War of 1812 remained in the Navy during the 1850s. Naval officers never retired, so promotions came slowly. Therefore, in 1855, the Congress created the Naval Retiring Board to administer a new retirement program.

Peter had been one of about two hundred naval officers who were among the first to become retired by the Board. Peter was only thirty-two years old, and he was deeply hurt by the retirement. He had intended to make the Navy his career, but now all that was changed. Peter would spend the next two years fighting the Naval Retiring Board's action, but to no avail.

While Reigart felt sorry for Peter, he knew why the Navy had acted in the way it had. Peter had always been a little on the wild side ever since he was a boy. Joining the Navy had not stopped him. Peter often returned late from shore leaves, and even then, he would return drunk and abusive.

The charges against Peter were severe, though a little trumped up. A major charge of Peter falling asleep during a watch was probably untrue. Much of the evidence was hearsay. One witness against Peter said that he had heard about Peter's reputation. What made matters worse was that he had only heard these rumors from men who had already testified. Therefore, not only were they hearsay but also added no new information.

Peter's defense was sad. He denied any wrongdoing with relation to sleeping while on watch. On the other hand, he did not challenge the other charges. In each case, he admitted that he had behaved as charged, and in each case, he pointed out that this was only one instance. Unfortunately, there were so many of these "only one instances" that his defense could not be effective.

A typical example of Peter's behavior occurred when he showed up to a new ship in an intoxicated state. Peter claimed that he was sick from exhaustion, but it was obvious that he was not. The ship became wrecked ten days later, and Peter was sent ashore in an open boat with four others to get help. When he returned from shore, he again claimed sickness due to exhaustion. He never should have been allowed to go ashore on this duty. He immediately got drunk, even though he had the important duty to send a rescue ship to his wrecked vessel.

Though saddened by Peter's problem, Reigart was glad to be home. He had quite a past behind him already. Sixteen of his twenty-nine years had been spent in the Navy. He had done a lot and had seen a lot. He had just spent five years on the Perry Expedition and had completed his second circumnavigation of the earth.

Of the seventeen captains involved with the Jouett case, only two, besides Reigart, had been on the Perry Expedition. These were Edward Y. McCauley (number eight on the list) and John Upshur. John had agreed with Reigart that the peacetime duties of the Navy were as important as the wartime duties. As the eight men sat around the table, the meeting seemed to be just about over.

Reigart asked, "Does anyone know how much of a fight we are going to have in the Senate?"

Sam answered, "It's going to be close. Jouett has the votes if they were to act today. It's mostly partisan—Republicans for Jouett and Democrats against him, but he has a few Democrats on his side. They seem to be the swing votes."

"All right," Reigart went on, "we must present a good case. Sam, would you compile all the information that has been gathered by Stephen, Earl, John, and yourself and put it into some sort of memorandum form. We'll present it to all of the captains in Washington next week for their approval."

"I sure will," assured Sam.

"Is there any other business?" inquired Reigart. When he got no response, he added, "I'm going to be in Washington by March 1. I'll be staying at Willard's Hotel if anyone wants to contact me. We'll hold our meetings on Saturday and Sunday, March 6 and 7 at Willard's. I have reserved a suite of rooms, and we will meet there."

At that, the meeting adjourned.

13.
THE WATER WITCH

---•◦•---

REIGART GOT UP EARLY ON MONDAY MORNING, MARCH 1. HE wanted to get an early start on his trip to Washington. As he crossed the Hudson River on the Hoboken Ferry, Reigart remembered how the *North Carolina* used to sit in the harbor off the battery. Reigart had served on the *North Carolina* for a second time in 1856. This time, he was the teacher instead of the pupil. He taught on both the *North Carolina* and the *Ontario* during 1856. This was his first attempt at teaching, and it would serve as an important training ground later in his career. He enjoyed this period. He liked the young boys whom he trained; some of them reminded Reigart of himself when he had entered the Navy in its training program.

Reigart had been disappointed when he was transferred from the *North Carolina*. This was when he was sent to the *Michigan* on Lake Erie. Had he not married Bess during this duty, Reigart would have been totally bored. The *Michigan* spent most of its time on Erie and was the only naval vessel there.

It was while he was on the *Michigan* that Reigart first met Jim Jouett. Jouett had become assigned to the *Michigan* in 1858. Reigart remembered him well. Jouett was quite a talker. Most sailors' language was salty, but Jim Jouett's conversation was sprinkled with a little more salt than most. About every other word out of his mouth was "damn" or "damned." Worst of all, he bragged. He made it sound like he had been assigned some of the most daring and glamorous duty that was available. He even made the *Michigan* duty sound good.

Reigart had to chuckle to himself as he thought of Jim Jouett. An assignment on the *Michigan* was the least desired assignment in the Navy. To get it once was a terrible blow. Jim Jouett got this duty three times and spent nearly five years on the *Michigan*. He had it in 1862 during the Civil War. He even had command of it from 1868-1870. Reigart thought to himself that maybe Jim Jouett does deserve a promotion, not because of his great heroism but because of all the suffering he went through on the *Michigan*.

Both Reigart and Jim Jouett got called away from Erie when an international incident arose in South America. Jonathan Young (number fifteen on the captain's list) had also been called to serve in this instance. Reigart was assigned to the *Preble*. Again, he was to participate in a diplomatic role of the Navy. He learned that in 1855, a Paraguayan fort had fired on the United States gunboat, *Water Witch*. This had forcibly prevented it from continuing to explore the La Plata River and its tributaries which the vessel had been doing for years with the permission of the Paraguayan government. The shot had killed the man on duty at the wheel, and American attempts to gain redress had been steadily repulsed by Lopez, the autocratic ruler of Paraguay. The United States government finally decided to use a show of force, and late in the year of 1858, the largest American squadron ever assembled, nineteen naval vessels carrying two hundred guns and twenty-five hundred men, gathered in the La Plata River under command of Flag Officer W. B. Shubrick.

The flagship, *Sabine*, could not ascend the river, so Commodore Shubrick switched his flag to the *Fulton*. Reigart watched as the commodore, his staff, Judge Bowlin, and his secretary, the *Sabine's* brass band, the barge's crew, and a few Marines went over to the *Fulton*. He knew that the men who were not transferred would have given six months pay to have gone along. The fleet sailed from Montevideo on December 30, passing Buenos Aires the next day and stopping at Rosario, Argentina, on January 4, 1859. Rosario, as Reigart noticed, was a pretty Spanish town on the western bank of the river, about four hundred miles from the ocean. He watched as the *Sabine's* band got off to play for the people and wished he could be part of it when he saw the townspeople reciprocate by giving refreshments to the band.

The fleet moved on up to a point just above Rosario where they would be ready to act against Paraguay if necessary. Reigart had heard terrible things about Dictator Lopez, and it had been rumored that he would give the fleet a warm reception in the form of gunpowder and grapeshot. Everything was made ready in case there was a need to fight.

Reigart did not know what to expect when he watched Commodore Shubrick and Mr. Bowlin, the special commissioner of the United States go up the river toward Asuncion in the *Fulton* and the *Water Witch*. On all the vessels, the decks were cleared for action, the guns loaded, and all preparations were made to meet the enemy. As the *Fulton* advanced up the river, she suddenly found herself under the guns of Fort Huniato that was situated on the east bank of the river and had been appropriately named the Gibraltar of Paraguay.

Anchoring about five hundred yards away, Shubrick sent in a boat with Captain Percival Drayton and Lieutenant William Murdaugh who found that Lopez suddenly held no hostile feelings toward the United States, especially since he had heard of the large fleet anchored below his city. Lopez extended a satisfactory apology to Bowlin and Shubrick for the firing upon the *Water Witch*, and his government paid an indemnity on the spot for the family of the man who had been killed.

The other ships came into Asuncion a couple of days later when Reigart saw this large and beautiful city for the first time. He saw that it was on the east bank of the Paraguay River and was well fortified. Again, he noticed crowds of people on the banks who had come to see the ships and listen to the band. Commodore Shubrick invited Reigart and many of the other officers to come and witness the signing of the treaty. The next day, each nation gave the other a twenty-one-gun salute. That night, the deck of the *Fulton* was opened, and throngs of people went on board where a dance was held.

Seeing all the women at the dance made Reigart want to get home to his wife, but the Navy was in no hurry to leave Paraguay. The *Preble* remained there until the end of March, at which time it started its return voyage to the United States. Reigart returned to Gosport Navy Yard in Norfolk, Virginia, late in May and within a week he was detached and sent to a naval hospital. There, Reigart was "condemned" by a medical survey as unfit for service. As on other voyages, his rheumatism and other related diseases were bothering him again. By the time he got home, he had been away for nearly a year.

Thoughts of Jouett had brought these old events back to Reigart. It had been during this period that Reigart had had his greatest contact with him. Reigart arrived in Washington in the late afternoon and set himself up at Willard's Hotel.

Reigart had a busy week ahead of him. First, he drafted a personal letter that he had printed up for distribution to all the Senators. He decided that he would see every Senator he possibly could and hand deliver the letter. Reigart knew many of the Senators; he had campaigned for some of them in the last couple of elections. These men would at least listen to him. They were mostly Democrats and were mostly against Jouett. Reigart did not want to take any chances. In any case, as Sam had pointed out, the Democrats were the swing vote. The Democrats controlled Congress, and if they were all against Jouett, there would have been no concern.

He saw many Senators during the next week. Most of them were sympathetic, and he began to feel good about the Jouett case. He mailed or hand delivered his letters to all the Republican Senators. During one of his visits, Reigart came across former Senator Benjamin F. Butler. Ben just happened to be in town visiting friends. Reigart had met Ben during the Civil War, and the two men had become great friends. Reigart wanted to talk to Ben because he was not sure where Ben stood, and he knew that Ben still had influence in the Senate.

Ben Butler had been a Major General during the Civil War. Reigart had to handle Ben carefully, though. Ben had been a politically appointed general. If there ever was a politician, Ben was it. Reigart knew that if he could enlist Ben's support, Jouett would never get his confirmation. While Ben and Reigart were political enemies, they respected each other.

When Reigart entered Ben's hotel room, Ben greeted him with, "Hello, Reigart. I bet I know what you want."

"Is that any way to greet a friend you haven't seen in several years?" Reigart retorted.

"No, of course not, how have you been?" Ben asked.

"Fine," Reigart answered, "and you're right about knowing what I want. I'm not going to beg. I just want you to know our side."

The men talked for quite a long time. Throughout the conversation, Ben would not commit himself. As Reigart left, Ben said apologetically, "Reigart, you know I want to help, and I'll do what I can. But don't get your hopes up. There's a lot of pressure from the Navy Department and the President on this one."

Reigart thanked Ben and returned to his hotel room. The captains all arrived at Reigart's suite on Saturday afternoon. Reigart had set up a bar. The men all had drinks and began socializing. Every one of these men had known each other for years. Except for one, all had attended one of the first two classes at Annapolis. During the thirty-nine or forty years these men had been in the Navy, their paths had crossed many times.

After a few hours of socializing, Reigart called the men to order. "Let me call the roll to make sure that everyone is here. So that I will not slight anyone, I will call the names in order of seniority. Just raise your hand if you are here:

1. Stephen P. Quackenbush

2. Earl English

3. Reigart B. Lowry

4. John H. Upshur

5. Francis A. Roe

6. Samuel R. Franklin

7. William D. Whiting

8. Edward Y. McCauley

9. John C. P. DeKrafft

10. Oscar C. Badger

11. Stephen B. Luce

12. John L. Davis

13. Alexander A. Semmes

14. William T. Truxton

15. Jonathan Young

16. William K. Mayo

All present and accounted for."

Reigart brought the men up to date. He told them about the meetings in New York and his activities in Washington during the past week. Sam had prepared a pamphlet as he promised and Reigart presented it to the men. Sam had done a good job. He presented Jouett's position within context of the laws governing naval ranks. He showed that Jouett had been given better and not worse treatment than most. He then included the text of Gideon Welles's brilliant defense of the present rankings. Finally, he gave the Hammersley biography of all seventeen men involved, the sixteen senior captains and Captain Jouett.

Rough copies of the pamphlet were distributed. Reigart then adjourned the meeting until 2:00 p.m. on Sunday, asking the men to come prepared to discuss the pamphlet.

When the men arrived the next day, Reigart again called the meeting to order. The men liked the pamphlet. There were a few minor errors in the biographies, but the group decided not to correct them. By even changing a comma or period, they risked the charge of changing the biographies to fit their own convenience. The errors were only a wrong name of a ship here or there. The men unanimously approved the pamphlet. Reigart asked Sam to put that day's date, March 7, 1880, on the pamphlet and get it printed. Reigart would arrange for delivery of the pamphlet to the Senators.

"There is no time to lose," warned Reigart. "I have found out that the Senate is going to vote on Jouett's confirmation in the next couple of weeks. Write the Senators. See them. Do whatever you can. We must stop Jouett, but it's not going to be easy. I have found out the President and Secretary of the Navy may be pushing Jouett."

14.
I AM NOT GOING
IN TO INAUGURATE
CIVIL WAR

REIGART FELT CONFIDENT THAT THE CAPTAINS HAD DONE all that they could. He had been glad to find that the men were able to unite. He only wished that they had been able to unite against Grant and Robeson. The only thing he could do now was to go back to New York and wait.

He moved back into Coleman House, and since he thought he would be in New York for a while, he took out a membership in the New York Club. One day, about two weeks later, he sat reading a newspaper in the reading room of the club. He heard a commotion, and looking up, he saw Sam Franklin rushing across the room, all smiles.

"What's up, Sam?" Reigart queried.

"Three great pieces of news," Sam responded.

"Three?"

"Yes. First, the Senate tabled Jouett's confirmation. It won't even come up for a vote!" shouted Sam.

Reigart let out a yelp. Everyone in the staid room looked at these two men. They had never seen such behavior in the reading room before. When he calmed down, Reigart asked, "What else makes you so happy?"

"Stephen and Earl have been made Commodores!" exclaimed Sam. "You're now number one on the captain's list."

Reigart could hardly believe his ears. He had been waiting all his life to become a commodore, and now he was next in line. As soon as the next opening occurred, he would receive his promotion. Reigart and Sam adjourned to the bar to celebrate the great news.

Within a few weeks, Reigart received a notice from the Navy Department to come to Washington for examinations prior to promotion. This was no routine matter, and Reigart knew that his promotion must be near. Following his medical exam, Reigart reported to the Naval Examining Board on the afternoon of April 12, 1880. Irish-born Vice Admiral Stephen C. Rowan was President of the board. Reigart was so glad that Rowan was there. He knew that he would have no trouble with Rowan as head of the board. Reigart had served under Rowan during the Civil War, and the men had become great friends. Reigart had been with Rowan nineteen years before, to the day, when the Civil War had begun.

Reigart had been made executive officer of the *Pawnee*, making him second in command to then Commander Stephen Rowan. This had pleased Reigart, as it was the most important position he had yet held.

The year 1860 was another presidential election year, and, as usual, Reigart followed the campaign closely. As a Democrat, he favored Stephen A. Douglas, and he was disappointed when Abraham Lincoln won the election. But Reigart always supported his President after the election, even when the President was from a different party. His animosity with Grant did not come from the fact that Grant was Republican but from corruption in his administration.

South Carolina seceded from the Union in 1860, following Lincoln's election, but a small garrison of Union troops remained in Charleston

Harbor at Fort Sumter. From reading the daily newspapers, Reigart could tell that there was trouble ahead, and when the *Pawnee* was ordered to Charleston, South Carolina on April 9, 1861, he knew that this was no routine trip.

Southerners had begun to fortify their harbor at Charleston, aiming their guns toward the federal Fort Sumter. In March 1861, Captain Gustavus Vasa Fox, who later became Assistant Secretary of the Navy, presented President Lincoln with a plan for the relief of Fort Sumter, where Major Robert Anderson and a handful of troops were stationed and were in dire need of supplies.

On March 28, the President directed Captain Fox to fit out a relief expedition as soon as possible. The *Powhatan* was the only vessel then on the Atlantic coast that was suitable for Fox's plan because it could carry many troops and because boats could be easily launched from it. Secretary of the Navy Gideon Welles acted promptly and issued orders to have sailors ready and to prepare the *Pawnee*, the *Harriet Lane*, the *Pocahontas*, and the *Powhatan* for the expedition.

The *Powhatan* sailed from New York on April 6, but as she was leaving the port, her commander received orders from President Lincoln detaching her from the Sumter relief expedition and placing her under the command of Lieutenant David B. Porter. The president issued this order without being aware that it would affect the Sumter expedition and without informing Captain Fox, who did not learn of the order until after he arrived at Fort Sumter.

The *Pawnee*, with Commander Stephen Rowan and Lieutenant Reigart Lowry on board, left Norfolk on April 9 and proceeded to Charleston. The *Pawnee's* instructions were to wait for the *Powhatan* ten miles east of the lighthouse at Charleston. Upon arrival at this designated spot, Reigart noticed that the *Powhatan* was nowhere in sight. Reigart conferred with Commander Rowan, and the two men decided that they had better wait for it. Later that evening, Reigart saw two boats approaching the

Pawnee. In them were Gus Fox from the *Baltic* (a converted Collins Mail Steamer) and Captain John Faunce from the *Harriet Lane* who conferred with Commander Rowan. Reigart listened as these men asked Rowan to stand in toward the bar with the other ships. He knew Stephen Rowan's answer as they had discussed the matter earlier. Rowan's orders required him to stay right where he was until the *Powhatan* arrived, so he told Fox, "I'm not going in to inaugurate civil war."

These last words disturbed Reigart. It had looked like there might be a civil war ever since Abraham Lincoln's election, but just now, hearing those two words coming from his commander's mouth and seeing the other ship go in to the bar, Reigart realized the seriousness of the situation. Reigart could not sleep, so he went to get his telescope to try to look for the fort, the other ships, and the city of Charleston. It was dark, and he could just barely make out the black forms of the other ships a few miles in front of him. As he looked toward the shore, he could see some lights on in the city of Charleston even though it was the middle of the night. He tried to locate Fort Sumter, but it was so dark out that he could not make out the fort.

As he looked for the fort, a bright flash lit up the sky right above it. For this one brief instant, Reigart could clearly see the small brick fort in the middle of Charleston Harbor. The flash was followed seconds later by a resounding boom.

Reigart turned to tell Commander Rowan that war had begun, but Rowan, aware of it, was already preparing to take the *Pawnee* in. As Reigart looked back toward the city, he could now hear heavy gunfire and distinctly see smoke and fire from both Fort Sumter and the shore batteries. Reigart saw Captain Fox coming out to inform Commander Rowan of the situation, but the Pawnee was already going in, orders or no orders. Reigart noticed the change in his commander's attitude as Rowan hailed Fox, asking for a pilot and now declaring his intention of going into the harbor and sharing the fate of his brethren of the Army. Fox told Rowan that the government could not accept any such sacrifice. Without the *Powhatan*, it would be suicide for the other ships to enter the harbor.

Reigart felt frustrated as he watched the Union soldiers being bombarded. His fellow soldiers were fighting for their lives within sight of the vessels, and there was nothing he could do but watch. As the sun rose, Reigart could see that over forty guns were firing on Fort Sumter. Before long, a thick cloud cover moved in and the sea became rough. Even heavy rain did not drive the sailors from the deck of the *Pawnee*. They lined the rails, watching the bombardment throughout the day.

Meanwhile, Reigart and Commander Rowan stood on the deck watching the activity through their telescopes. Reigart saw the shells exploding all around the fort, and noticed flames and smoke rising from within it. He could not help but wonder what was happing to the men inside the fort. At about noon, he noticed that the firing from the fort slackened. Reigart knew that this meant that their ammunition was running low. The *Powhatan* had still not shown up, and so going in to help the fort was still out of the question.

All firing from the fort ceased that evening, and fire from the Southern forts slackened. With this lull in the action, Reigart took the opportunity to go to bed. He had had hardly any sleep the previous night, and he was exhausted. Resumption of heavy firing at dawn awakened Reigart who found Captain Rowan coming up to the bridge at the same time as he. At about one thirty, the American flag could no longer be seen flying above the fort. Reigart wondered what had happened to it. In a short while Reigart saw, through his telescope, a small boat going out to Fort Sumter. Reigart became confused when he saw the American flag raised again. Apparently, it had just been shot down before. In the meantime, the men in the small boat had landed, and a short time later, the American flag came back down, and a white flag was raised over the fort. Reigart's heart sank. He never thought that the men in the fort had a chance, but he had hoped that they did. There had been no loss of life during the engagement.

The federal troops were evacuated the next day and were brought to the Union ships which were still lying outside the harbor. Reigart and Stephen Rowan had witnessed the beginning of the Civil War, and the North had lost the first battle.

Fox returned to Washington, a disappointed man. He rightly blamed the President for the failure of the mission. The President had signed the orders redirecting the *Powhatan*, not knowing the full implication of what he was doing. Secretary of State William Seward had slipped the order to the President with several other papers he had asked the President to sign. Lincoln had only been President for a couple of weeks and had not yet learned the power of his signature. He learned his lesson quickly, though. When he found out that Sumter had fallen because of a paper he had signed, he was furious. From then on, he always read what he signed, and he left all Navy business to the Navy Department.

Less than a week after Fort Sumter fell, President Abraham Lincoln announced that the Union Navy would blockade the southern ports. Looking at a map, Reigart could see the president's strategy. With a blockade on the Atlantic coast and on the Gulf coast, with control of the Mississippi River on the West, and with a strong front on land with the Army to the North, the Union forces could surround and gradually strangle the South.

Once Fort Sumter had fallen, defense of Washington became the paramount concern of the North. Washington bordered Virginia, a slave state that was expected to secede. From all parts of the country, troops flooded into Washington. A Potomac flotilla was formed to keep enemy vessels away from Washington and to protect it on the Potomac side.

At first, the Potomac flotilla consisted of only five vessels, commanded by Reigart's old friend and teacher, James Harmon Ward. One of the ships in the flotilla was the *Pawnee* with Stephen Rowan and Reigart Lowry. The *Pawnee* arrived directly from Fort Sumter.

At about 1:00 a.m. on the morning of April 19, 1861, Reigart noticed a boat passing by with fifteen or twenty men aboard. He hailed them, and the boat came alongside the *Pawnee*.

"What are you doing out on the river at this time of night?" inquired Reigart.

"We are a select party to haul down the secession flag at Alexandria, Virginia," answered one of the men.

Seeing that some of the men wore uniforms, Reigart asked, "May I see your orders?"

The leader, a civilian lawyer named Fuller, blanched and said, "We do not have any orders."

Upon further investigation Reigart found that the men had no weapons and were absent without permission from their Massachusetts regiment. Commander Rowan had heard the commotion and came out to see what was going on. When Reigart told him what he had found, Rowan was furious. He ordered, "Place these men under charge of the Corporal of the Guard and throw them in the brig! We'll hand them over to their commanding officers in the morning."

Rowan left the scene, and Reigart proceeded to carry out his orders. Suddenly, with great alarm, the men remembered that they had left a seventy-five-dollar deposit as security for the safe return of their boat the following morning. This sum would be forfeited if the boat were not returned by that time. Finally, yielding to their pleas, Reigart applied to Commander Rowan for their release. Rowan directed that if there was a man of responsibility among the group, he should give his word that the men would return either to their camp or to Washington. Mr. Fuller, the New York lawyer, most eagerly volunteered his services for the position, and the men embarked a few minutes later.

Before the men left, however, Reigart had a few words to say to them. "There is a war going on. This is no game. You are violating military law in leaving your camp without orders. You have no right to undertake any such operation. When the government of the United States wants that flag hauled down, the government of the United States will issue the order and the flag will come down. And you, Mr. Fuller, have no right as a private citizen to thrust yourself forward and entice these men from their posts. The government has an Army and a Navy to carry out its wishes, and I see no reason to change this. Now be gone and I don't want to see you around here again."

Virginia seceded from the Union on May 23, and at that point, the government decided that the time had come to act. Alexandria had to be taken, and the Confederate flag had to come down.

15.
WE ARE PREPARED TO SEIZE THE PLACE, AND IT WOULD BE USELESS TO RESIST

---•◦•---

ALEXANDRIA WAS IMPORTANT, NOT ONLY BECAUSE IT BOR-dered Washington, but also because it was linked by rail to Richmond, Virginia. Colonel Elmer E. Ellsworth's "fire-eating" Zouaves were assigned the duty of taking the city. These Zouaves were energetic and enthusiastic firemen from New York City who wore colorful uniforms. Early on the morning of May 24, they were loaded onto two transports that soon steamed down the Potomac toward Alexandria.

The *Pawnee* had been lying off Alexandria for three days. Rowan spotted the steamers at about 4:30 a.m. He waited until they came into full view so as not to expose the secrecy of the mission, and then sent Reigart ashore to demand surrender of the town.

Onshore, Reigart conferred with Major George P. Terrett, Commander of the Virginia secession forces at Alexandria. In Commander Rowan's name, Reigart demanded the surrender of the city adding, "We are prepared to seize the place, and it would be useless to resist. I am influenced only by a desire to spare the shedding of blood of women and children."

The conference was held in the open street. Excited soldiers and civilians surrounded Reigart and Major Terrett. Major Terrett replied, "I will evacuate. I promise that I will use no hostilities if none are used on me."

This was agreed to, but when Terrett asked, "How much time do I have?" Reigart answered, "I do not know, but I do know that no time is to be lost."

"I will need until 8:00 a.m. to evacuate such women and children and property as I would require," asserted Major Terrett.

Reigart acquiesced saying, "Very well, I will go at once to the *Pawnee* should the troops land and you make no resistance. I have no doubt that no harm will be done to the town and its inhabitants, but should the *Pawnee* be obliged to open her batteries, no one knows better than yourself what would be the result."

Reigart hastened to the river and reached the wharf just in time to meet the colorful Zouaves who were then landing. He sought out Colonel Ellsworth and announced, "Sir, I am an officer of the *Pawnee*. I have been on shore with a flag of truce demanding the surrender of the town. The commanding officer is already evacuating; he promises to make no resistance. The town is full of women and children."

Colonel Ellsworth replied, "All right, sir. I will harm no one."

Reigart then informed Ellsworth, who landed his regiment with great rapidity, of the whereabouts of the telegraph office and other buildings. Reigart then returned to his ship to report his activities to Commander Rowan. Rowan directed Reigart to go back on shore, cooperate with the troops, and take part in what should occur. Reigart took a few men from the *Pawnee* along with him. Not finding Colonel Ellsworth at the head of his regiment, Reigart advanced to the upper part of the town. He marched his men through the town and hoisted the American flag on a street flagpole and on the staff of the Custom House.

Ellsworth's absence at the head of his regiment was explained later. He had seen the Confederate flag flying over the Marshall House Hotel in full view of Washington and the White House, so he rushed up to the roof and tore it down. On his way down the stairs, Ellsworth encountered the owner of the hotel, Mr. James T. Jackson, who blasted Ellsworth with a shotgun at close range. Ellsworth's aid, Corporal Francis E. Brownell, immediately fired back, and both Colonel Ellsworth and Mr. Jackson lay dead. Colonel Ellsworth was the first Union officer to be killed in the Civil War.

In the meantime, Reigart and his men met up with another contingent from the *Pawnee* under Lieutenant J. C. Chaplin. They joined forces and with a few extra Army troops, the men marched to the railroad station, led by Reigart. When they arrived at the station, Reigart instructed the men to seize the train. As the men boarded, however, the engine escaped. Reigart left a couple of Army troops on the remaining cars of the train, and he, Lieutenant Chaplin, and the other seamen returned to the *Pawnee*.

Later, when Secretary Welles learned that Rowan had sent Reigart ashore at Alexandria, he was furious. Welles read Rowan's report with pain and surprise. Rowan had had no orders to take Alexandria, and Welles expressed stern disapproval of Rowan's interference with the Army's operation. He concluded that while the interference in this instance was not serious, it might have caused the defeat of the object intended and could have been followed by serious disaster.

About a week later, the Navy had its first encounter with battle. The five boats of the Potomac flotilla engaged in heated gunfire with the Confederate batteries near Aquia Creek for two days. Damage was so heavy on both sides that neither side claimed victory. Flotilla Commander, James Harmon Ward, was proud of the conduct of his men in their first encounter with battle. Rowan's praise for his officers was also of the highest order. Their cool and gallant bearing had won his warmest admiration. Every man performed his duties promptly and intelligently, showing that his ship was in a high state of training. Rowan felt that he had been ably seconded by his divisional officers, Lieutenant J. C. Chaplin and Master Blue, and above all by his able executive officer, Lieutenant Reigart Lowry, whose fine bearing on the occasion was everything that he could have wished.

Now that the war was really under way, more stringent controls had to be put on the transportation of food and arms to the South. Commander Rowan and Reigart began watching suspicious looking activity around a fish house on the Maryland shore owned by a Mr. Carpenter. After about two weeks of observation, Commander Rowan sent Reigart ashore to inspect the fish house. When he arrived on shore, Reigart demanded the keys to the fish house. He went in with a few of his men. Boxes, barrels, and crates were piled everywhere. Reigart instructed his men to take an inventory of supplies. Included in the fish house were nearly 10,000 pounds of bacon, three barrels of whiskey, two barrels of sugar, and two bags of coffee.

Commander Rowan sent the list of the goods to the Navy Department and asked Secretary Welles for permission to seize the wares. Under the assumption that the goods were about to cross the Potomac to Virginia, Welles ordered them seized. Within a few weeks, Mr. Carpenter's character had been cleared and his goods had to be returned.

On the night of June 26, 1861, a tragedy occurred. The *Freeborn* had been engaging some batteries at Mathias Point. Commander James Harmon Ward, Reigart's old friend and teacher, was right out with his men. As he was lining up one of his big guns, preparing to fire at the battery, James Ward was shot and instantly killed. Ward was the first Union naval officer killed in the war. Ward's death hit Reigart hard. Reigart knew that men would be killed in the war, but Ward was the first man whom Reigart had known and liked well. Reigart and many of Ward's other former students mourned his death.

Few had been so close to Ward when he had taught, and few had been so close to Ward when he died. Soon after Reigart had heard of his friend's death, he was called into Commander Rowan's cabin. Rowan, the next senior man in the flotilla, had become the new flotilla commander.

His first official duty was to assign Reigart to command Ward's boat, the paddle wheeler *Freeborn*. Reigart was proud to take over his mentor's vessel. Not only had this been James Ward's boat, but it was also Reigart's first command.

As he was preparing to take his new command, Reigart came across a stray dog. He stopped to pet it and soon found that the dog would not leave him. It was a large black mongrel, and it followed Reigart wherever he went. He soon became as attached to the dog as it had become to him and eventually named the dog "Jack" after his friend James Ward. Jack went to the *Freeborn* with Reigart as the ship's mascot. Reigart and Jack would be constant companions for more than a dozen years.

Reigart immediately began to see a boat commander's responsibilities in a different light. He was now responsible for an entire boat and all the crew of that boat. He had wondered in his earlier days why commanders acted differently from the crew, and he was beginning to find out. What would have seemed acceptable conditions to him a day before now became deplorable conditions which could not be tolerated.

Only one day after accepting command of the *Freeborn*, Reigart submitted a report declaring that the vessel was far from serviceable. The crew was worn out from exposure, bad quarters, want of fresh provisions, and constant severe duty. The ship's account of stores, men, and ammunition seemed to be in utter confusion; ammunition and provisions were running low.

The *Freeborn* was steaming down the Potomac River one night shortly after Reigart took command. Reigart saw some suspicious looking lights on some vessels down the river. He ordered full steam and all men to quarters. When he got down to where he had seen the lights, Reigart found three ships hard aground on the shoals. The vessels were the government steamer *Mount Vernon*, the government steamer *Yankee*, and the schooner *J. W. Maitland* from Philadelphia with 280 tons of government coal on board. The *Mount Vernon* had freed herself and resumed down the river before Reigart arrived. He came within hailing distance and anchored. Since this was the same place that Virginia Rebels had burned a vessel under similar conditions, Reigart decided to remain by these boats until morning. At 3:30 a.m., the *Yankee* floated by. Reigart hailed her as she steamed within twenty yards of the *Freeborn*.

Someone on the *Yankee* shouted back, "Halloo!"

Reigart shouted, "This is the *Freeborn*. That schooner is loaded with government property. I want you to lie by me till I get her off, when I want you to convoy her to Mathias Point."

To Reigart's utter surprise, the *Yankee* took no further notice and steamed directly up the river. Reigart was angry. He found the *Yankee's* actions reprehensible and disrespectful. He wanted to give chase but did not feel that he could leave the *J. W. Maitland* defenseless.

When morning came, Reigart went over to the *Maitland* to confer with her captain. The two men decided that the best way to float the *Maitland* was to transfer some of her coal to the *Freeborn*. Reigart returned to get some of his men to help. Together, the crews of the two vessels transferred over twenty-five tons of coal to the *Freeborn*. At that point, a four-and-a-half-inch rope was attached to both boats, and the *Freeborn* towed the *Maitland* to safety. Returning from the incident, Reigart again stressed the need for repairs to his vessel.

A few days later, Reigart was sent with the *Freeborn* to protect the *George Weems* from seizure. There had been rumors that the Confederates would attempt to capture the *Weems*. A band of Confederates had captured the *St. Nicholas* a few weeks before.

Reigart found the *George Weems* and warned her captain of the danger. While he was on board the *Weems*, Reigart and his officers were insulted by several women on board who did not hesitate to sneer at the men and shout, "Three cheers for Jeff Davis." Upon return from this mission, Reigart again stressed the dire need for repairs to his vessel.

The beginnings of the Civil War had seen some carelessness and rough times. People had not yet taken the war seriously. As late as July 1861, women and children went with picnic lunches to watch battles. Men like those from the Massachusetts regiment had not yet grasped the seriousness of the situation. At the same time, everyone was over-zealous and most eager to do a good job. Rowan had sent Reigart ashore at Alexandria without orders. He was reprimanded but went on to serve well through the rest of the war.

Now, in 1880, while Reigart was before Rowan during his examination preparatory to his promotion, Vice Admiral Rowan was the second highest-ranking member of the United States Navy. Reigart and his old commander reminisced about the Civil War when they had last worked together. When he left, Reigart felt a great sense of satisfaction and pleasure, having seen his old friend and commander once again.

When Reigart returned to New York, he dropped in at the New York Club. His old friend Ben Butler was there.

16.
IF IT TAKES ALL NIGHT TO DO IT, THIS MUST BE DONE

———•◦•———

BEN WAS AT THE CLUB WHEN REIGART ARRIVED, AND REIGART joined him. "Well, hello, Reigart," greeted Ben when he saw his old friend. "You are looking good. You must he happy that the Jouett thing has been taken care of."

"I am," said Reigart smiling. "You didn't have anything to do with stopping it, did you?"

"You know that I can't tell you that," Ben responded.

Reigart could tell by the look on Ben's face that Ben had done something to stop it. "Well, I know that you did all that you could," Reigart said, deciding to let the matter drop. Reigart had just been reminiscing with his old commander, Stephen Rowan, and could not resist reminding Ben of some of the old times he and Ben had had together. They had first met during the Hatteras operation in 1861. Reigart had been instrumental in starting the plans for the Hatteras operation, though Ben got and took most of the credit for it.

The North Carolina coastline consisted of an offshore bar, extending south from the Virginia border for 240 miles. There were only three navigable inlets along this whole 240-mile stretch: Hatteras Inlet, Ocracoke Inlet, and Beaufort Inlet. Inside the bar lay the Pamlico and Albemarle Sounds, both sizable bodies of water. Countless miles of navigable rivers, streams, and canals flowed into these sounds. Among these was the Chesapeake and Albemarle Canal in which Reigart was a partner with his father-in-law. Reigart had only had an ownership interest in this canal for less than four years. It was now under Confederate control.

Reigart had studied the charts of the area very closely, ever since he had joined Milton Courtright in the venture. He knew that inland waterways gave the Confederates easy access from the ocean to Norfolk and Richmond. If President Lincoln's blockade were to be effective, the Hatteras Capes had to be controlled by the North. By only blockading the three main inlets, 240 miles of coastline and thousands of miles of inland waterways could be cut off from the outside.

Besides cutting off trade from the outside, Reigart knew that the vast inland water trade must be stopped, too. The shores of these inland waters abounded in rich productions such as cotton, grain, lumber, turpentine, and corn. There were excellent fisheries that were productive and extensively worked. Reigart knew that these were products the South would need to carry on their war effort.

Reigart put his thoughts together and sent them, along with charts and maps, to Secretary of the Navy Gideon Welles. As he sat in his cabin Reigart wrote, "I believe it to be my duty…to suggest that an effective blockade (of the North Carolina coast) is absolutely necessary to cut Norfolk and Richmond from communication with the sea, and to prevent rebel privateers from putting to sea from the waters of North Carolina, and to effectively blockade her ports." He knew that there was no part of the country that could so easily and so terribly feel the power of the United States.

Reigart believed this aim could be accomplished simply by station-
ing two vessels of the *Pawnee* class outside the bar, while several steam
canal boats could patrol the waters inside the bar. He felt that the steam
canal boats could carry enough arms and men to defend themselves, and
they could always fall back on the larger vessels outside the bar.

A few weeks after receiving Reigart's suggestions, Secretary Welles
sent them to Commodore Silas H. Stringham, senior officer of the
Atlantic Squadron. Commodore Stringham did not agree with Reigart in
all respects, but he did like many of the ideas put forth in Reigart's letter.
Commodore Stringham concluded that "the inlets may, for the time being,
be cleared, and while our ships are in sight, nothing will venture out, but I
am satisfied that permanent benefit can only result by a cooperating land
force to occupy the forts…at the mouths of the harbors."

The Navy Department decided to proceed with Reigart's operations
with one variation. The plan was to obstruct the North Carolina inlets
by sinking old whaling vessels in them loaded with stone. Reigart was
detached from the *Freeborn* and ordered to report to the department in
Washington to help formulate plans for the operation. Commander Henry
S. Stellwagen was selected for the important duty of sinking the vessels
in the North Carolina inlets. Secretary Welles sent Reigart to work with
Stellwagen and to organize a body of pilots for the operation.

Commander Stellwagen, commanding the chartered steamer
Adelaide, and Lieutenant Lowry, commanding the chartered steamer
George Peabody, went to Hampton Roads, Virginia in mid-August and
began preparing for the expedition. Nineteen whaling schooners were
loaded with blocks of granite, and all arrangements were completed within
a few days. Reigart and his commander were about to leave when they
received some disturbing news. The Confederates had armed the forts at
Cape Hatteras and placed some armed vessels there too.

A change of plans became necessary. Reigart soon knew the new
strategy. The North would capture the forts at Hatteras Inlet and then sink

the vessels as had been planned before. The Army would attack the forts by land from the north while the Navy attacked by sea from the south. The *Adelaide* and the *George Peabody* under Stellwagen and Lowry and the tug *Fanny* under Lieutenant Pierce Crosby would transport the Army's troops to their landing spot north of the forts.

The Army's troops would be commanded by Major General Benjamin Franklin Butler whom Reigart had not yet met. Commodore Stringham would command the Navy's forces. Upon consultation, Stringham and Butler decided that it would be worthwhile to keep Hatteras Inlet open as an access point to the inland waters for the North. This decision completed the final development in the plans for action on the North Carolina coast. The Hatteras forts would be captured, fortified, and occupied by the North, and a few steamers would be put on blockade duty at that point. The sinking of vessels would obstruct the remaining inlets.

The need for taking over control of the North Carolina coast was becoming critical. The area had a stormy character and a reputation for many shipwrecks. The Confederates had extinguished the light in the Hatteras lighthouse and removed buoys from the area, increasing the danger to Union ships along the coastline. Stringham was concerned about the seaworthiness of the *Adelaide* and the *George Peabody* in the stormy area. Welles was shocked and asked for reports on these vessels. Stringham remained concerned but Stellwagen claimed that they were as seaworthy as these kinds of boats usually are if they were used in a calm sea. He added that a calm sea was the only time that the expedition should be attempted.

Reigart was becoming anxious to see his idea come to fruition. He felt glad that he had recommended action on the North Carolina coast and was sure that the impact of a blockade there would be great.

The plans had been worked out and the preparations made. All that remained was to put them into action. General Butler's troops were made ready. Each man was provided with ten days rations and 140 pounds of ammunition. The troops boarded the three transports and left Fortress Monroe for Hatteras on the afternoon of August 26, 1861.

The entire squadron rounded the shoals of Hatteras early the next morning. That afternoon, Colonel William F. Martin of the Confederate States Army looked out from his fort and sighted the large fleet off Hatteras. He panicked. He knew that an attack was imminent, and he was not prepared. He did not have enough men to fight off both a land and a sea force; he sent a man to Portsmouth, North Carolina to get some aid. It would take over two days for this aid to arrive, and by then it would be too late.

The Northern forces made final preparations by the next night. Reigart was shocked when he received an order from General Butler. Butler told Reigart to see to it that enough rations were cooked for Colonel Max Weber's battalion. Butler ordered that they should have a good breakfast and a day's ration of beef besides. Ben concluded his note with "if it takes all night to do it, this must be done. The Captain of the *George Peabody* will be held responsible that it is done."

Reigart was shocked. He was tempted to ignore Butler's order altogether. His zeal for the public service only prevented him from totally disregarding it. He felt that the tone of the letter was not courteous nor its style official and he told Butler so in his response. Reigart was only a Lieutenant in the Navy, but he felt that Butler's letter lacked any consideration for him which he felt he was entitled to, "even from a Major General in the US Army."

Reigart did perform these duties, and Butler, who had the reputation of being somewhat of a beast, took a liking to this young Lieutenant who had stood up to him. Ben Butler would be even more impressed the next day when he saw Reigart in action.

17.
THE FIRST NAVAL VICTORY
OF THE WAR

———•◦●◦•———

TWO FORTS GUARDED HATTERAS INLET. FORT HATTERAS WAS located on the westernmost point of the beach and was octagonal in shape. Its walls were only five feet high but were twenty-five feet thick at the top, sloping down on the outside at about a forty-five-degree angle. It was built of sand and covered by turf. In all, it covered about two acres of ground. In July 1861, the Confederates had begun building a second fort, Fort Clark, a short way eastward and seaward of Fort Hatteras. It was similar in design but only about one-half the size.

The segment of the bar on which the forts were located extended north from Hatteras Inlet about forty miles and averaged about one mile in width. It was a barren strip of sand with a few scattered clumps of dwarf oak and a few little marshes covered with marsh grass.

Reigart would land the troops on his boat two miles above the forts on the seaward side of the bar. Reigart woke the men on his boat at 4:00 a.m. and gave them an early breakfast. He noticed that there was a heavy surf and wondered how it would affect the landings. Commodore Stringham gave the order to disembark the troops and the operation was under way.

The troops landed swiftly from the *George Peabody*, *Adelaide*, and *Fanny* and were covered and assisted by the *Pawnee*, *Monticello*, and *Harriet Lane*.

While the troops were landing, the *Wabash*, with the *Cumberland* in tow, and the *Minnesota* moved in toward the forts. The *Wabash* and *Cumberland* began firing on Fort Clark. Ten minutes later, the *Minnesota* passed inside the *Wabash* and *Cumberland* and opened fire. As the ships passed back and forth past the forts, they did not follow in each other's paths or follow the same path twice. This was the first time that this tactic had ever been used, and Commodore Stringham introduced it. The tactic proved to be effective. The firing from the forts was irregular, either passing over or falling short of the ships, even though the forts had many heavy guns. The *Susquehanna* joined the other ships in the use of the new tactic a short while later.

Once the troops had landed north of the forts, they began to move down toward them. They could hear the heavy firing as they approached. While the men moved down the beach, the larger ships that had been covering the landing joined their squadron and battled the forts from the sea. At 12:25 p.m., the flags were down in both forts. The rebels who were seen running toward Fort Hatteras and leaving the shore in boats were evacuating Fort Clark. When the flags went down, Commodore Stringham signaled to his boats to stop firing. When this happened, some of the troops marched down the beach and occupied the now empty Fort Clark. A sailor whose landing boat had been swamped while disembarking the troops raised an American flag at 2:00 p.m.

Since there was still no flag flying over Fort Hatteras by 4:00 p.m., Stringham ordered Commander John P. Gillis to feel his way into the inlet with the *Monticello* and to take possession of the fort. Gillis had only gone in a short way when he was fired upon from Fort Hatteras. The other Union vessels all opened fire at once. The *Monticello* was exposed and was struck several times. Finally, under cover of her sister ships, the *Monticello* was able to draw back without much serious damage. The Confederates later asserted that no flag had been flying over Hatteras on that day. Their flag had been blown to shreds by the wind, and no replacement had been received.

That evening, most of the ships backed off for the night. The three vessels that had covered the landing of the troops, rejoined the three chartered steamers to protect the troops. After dark, 250 reinforcements arrived for the Confederates. Commodore Samuel Barron and Major W. S. G. Andrews also arrived. Major Andrews held a brief consultation with Colonel Martin, and these Army officers decided to give Commodore Barron the total command of the defenses as they had complete confidence in his abilities.

The next morning, the weather was pleasant, and the sea was much calmer. The *Pawnee* and *Monticello* were left behind to cover the troops while the rest of the ships moved in to battle at Fort Hatteras. Commodore Stringham noticed that most of his shots here falling short and ordered a cease-fire. Longer fuses were put on the shells, and when firing resumed, the shots began falling in and around the fort with great effect. All Confederate fire fell short of the ships.

Reigart watched the entire battle from a distance with great interest. He knew that the North would be victorious and that it was only a matter of time. He wished that he could be in there fighting, but his boat was not heavily armed, and he still had some Army troops on board who had not landed the day before. Reigart was watching Fort Hatteras through his telescope when he noticed that a white flag had been raised. This sent a chill through his spine. He knew that the battle was over. He prepared to move the *George Peabody* in toward the shore as Stellwagen did the same with the *Adelaide*. They knew that the time had come to land the remaining troops, either in case of recommencement or cessation of the hostilities.

Reigart saw Ben Butler come in on the *Fanny* after the other troops had landed. He then watched Ben go on shore and thought what a pompous man Ben Butler was. Reigart had still not forgiven Ben Butler for the nasty order he had sent him. Once Butler reached the shore, he sought out the three rebel commanding officers, Barron, Andrews, and Martin, and brought them back to the *Monticello* for the surrendering formalities.

Ben Butler also sent a messenger to Henry Stellwagen and Reigart Lowry, requesting their presence on board the *Monticello*. Reigart was surprised but set right out for the *Monticello*. Reigart arrived just before Ben Butler came on board with the Confederate commanding officers.

When Butler had gotten settled, he asked, "Where's Lowry and Stellwagen? I want to see them." Reigart came first and wondered what this haughty man should want. "Are you Lowry?" Butler queried.

"Yes, sir," Reigart replied.

"That was quite a letter you sent me the other day," Ben began. "You really told me off. I watched you bring my men in. I was pleased with your care and conduct and have so informed Stringham. Stringham told me that you were in great part responsible for the initiation of this operation. You and Stellwagen performed so well, Stringham and I have decided to let Stellwagen and you officiate at the surrender ceremonies."

Reigart would later learn that this kind of behavior was typical of Ben. Ben would not apologize for his letter, but he would give out praises and commendations instead. Reigart felt so honored to be able to officiate at the surrender ceremonies that he forgot about Ben's letter. Reigart and Stellwagen took the surrender documents to the various parties who signed them. Reigart then presented the fully signed documents to Major General Butler and Commodore Stringham.

The two forts were surrendered unconditionally. Six hundred and seventy-eight prisoners were put on board the *Adelaide* and the *Minnesota* to be taken north. As a result of the operation, not only were nearly seven hundred men captured but also a thousand stand of arms, twenty-five pieces of artillery, a large quantity of ordnance stores and provisions, five boats, and two forts, all without the loss of life or one injury to the Union side. On the other hand, two dead and thirteen wounded Confederates were found, and it was presumed that many more dead and wounded had been removed on rebel steamers before the capitulation.

This battle was the first major victory for the North in the Civil War. It came as a pleasant relief to Northerners who had suffered early defeats at Fort Sumter and Manassas. Commander Stephen Rowan considered the capture of Hatteras "the most important event of the war." He noted that there was immediate widespread panic throughout all parts of North Carolina near water. The administration was also much encouraged by the victory. In Secretary Welles's congratulatory note to Commodore Stringham, Welles said, "It is, I trust, but the beginning of results that will soon eventuate in suppressing the insurrection and confirming more strongly than ever the integrity of the Union."

Hatteras was a personal victory for Reigart. Not only was he praised for recommending the operation, but also for his role in it. General Butler praised Reigart in his report to Major General John B. Wool: "[Lowry] brought in his vessel with safety, with the troops, who were pleased with his care and conduct." Stellwagen in his report to Secretary Welles also praised Reigart. Gideon Welles, himself wrote Reigart a letter of thanks, saying:

"I omitted making acknowledgements to you in the summer of 1861 for valuable information which you communicated in June of that year, relative to the navigation of the inner waters of North Carolina... The maps and reports relative to Albemarle Sound, the Hatteras Inlet, and the Chesapeake and Albemarle Canal, all at that time in possession of the rebels, were valuable...In command of the chartered steamer *Peabody* you accompanied the memorable expedition under Flag Officer Stringham, which resulted in the first naval victory of the war.

The changes and activity of operations of that period caused me to omit the thanks for suggestions and information then communicated, but which were duly appreciated, and for which it is my pleasure and duty now to make this acknowledgment."

During the days following the capture of the forts, the Union forces concentrated on restoring the facilities. Reigart was charged with the duty of placing buoys in the channel. He had with him a body of pilots who knew the area well, and together they charted and buoyed the channel to make it safe for federal vessels. The rest of the naval forces worked on the forts under Commander Rowan. Rowan became critical of the Army's troops, who did not appear to appreciate the necessity of repairing the fort or even know how to work with the artillery.

After he buoyed the channel, Reigart was sent back north with a captured Confederate ship and given a two-week leave. This segment of the operation was over. The main entrance to the vast system of the inland waterways of North Carolina was now in the hands of the Union. Richmond and Norfolk were cut off from the sea. The North was given a new ray of hope by this victory. The only remaining problem was the closing of the minor inlets at Ocracoke and Beaufort.

18.
WARRING AGAINST NATURE IN ONE OF HER MOST IRRESISTIBLE FORMS

———•◐•———

RIGHT AFTER THE CAPTURE OF THE HATTERAS FORTS, GIDEON Welles directed Stringham to begin sinking the stone laden vessels in some of the inlets. Welles wanted Oregon and Loggerhead Inlets blocked first. He wanted Ocracoke Inlet seized, but he did not want it obstructed for the time being as originally planned. Commander Stellwagen was placed in charge of the operation of sinking the ships in the channels. Stringham directed him to start with Oregon Inlet.

Soon, however, changes in command took place in the North Carolina area. First, the department relieved Stellwagen of his duties concerning Oregon Inlet. Then Stringham, Commander of the Atlantic Squadron, asked to be relieved of his command and placed in a more humble and less responsible position. Stringham had been the victim of a vicious press that had censured him severely. He was given a desk job in Washington, D. C.

Louis M. Goldsborough took command of the Atlantic Squadron. Welles, in his instructions to Goldsborough, emphasized the importance of a tight blockade. "There must be no commercial intercourse with the ports that are in insurrection," instructed Welles, "and our Navy must, by its power, energy, and activity, enforce the views of the President and the government on this subject." The obstruction of the inlets of North Carolina had become an obsession to Welles by this time, and he told Goldsborough to waste no more time or money and to get the job done. He even reversed his order regarding Ocracoke and ordered that it, too, be obstructed.

Commander Stellwagen was reassigned the duty of obstructing the inlets, he had worked so well with Reigart during the earlier Hatteras operations that Stellwagen asked for Reigart to help him in his new operation. Reigart was given command of the *Underwriter* and told to report to Stellwagen. Reigart was glad to know that his work was appreciated, and he set right out even though his doctor had recommended against it. Reigart had developed a severe case of skin discoloration which left purple blotches on his face.

Goldsborough was in a hurry to block the inlets so that he could carry out the wishes of the department. He told Stellwagen to start without Reigart. Stellwagen was ready to go, but bad weather and gale winds, which characterized the coast, kept him from venturing out. When the weather cleared, Stellwagen went out with two ships to the Hatteras Cape, each with two stone-laden schooners in tow. Stellwagen found the situation critical. The Union troops were in a poor defensive position. The *Fanny* had been captured inside the bar only two days before. The water was still rough in the area. Each ship lost one of its schooners during the rough passage. Between the rough seas and the poor security, Stellwagen returned without accomplishing his mission. He even expressed doubts about the worth of sinking the vessels as a blockade.

In the meantime, Reigart arrived and went to meet Stellwagen. He arrived during a gale storm and had an extremely rough voyage. On anchoring, the 850-pound anchor on Reigart's ship snapped off, leaving him with only his 400-pound anchor. After being there only one day, Reigart formed opinions like those that Stellwagen had expressed. Reigart observed that the Union was now in a critical defensive position rather than the offensive position in which it should have been. The rapid currents, he observed, made the situation more critical. The sand on the bar was constantly changing position. It had become considerably altered just in the month and a half since the battle. In the gale, then prevailing, Reigart visibly observed the sand being washed away from around the forts. The Army scarcely had a foothold, and Reigart thought that they would have to move to high ground when the next gale came along.

Reigart picked up some local pilots, and from them he learned that the situation inside the bar was bad. Though the ocean trade had been cut off, Reigart learned that the inland waters were crawling with Confederate vessels. Over twenty armed Confederate vessels operated out of friendly harbors and were able to offer or decline battle as they desired. Reigart learned from his pilot that the Confederates had all the pilots they needed to navigate the waters.

Reigart had originally been for taking quick control of the inland waterways. Now, he felt it was too late. The inland waters should have been taken right after the Hatteras forts were captured. Reigart was as disappointed as anyone when the waters were not taken but he saw little use now.

Stellwagen continued to express doubts about the viability of the stone fleet concept. The more he studied the project, the more skeptical he became. Stellwagen finally asked to be relieved of his duty. Flag Officer Louis Goldsborough granted Stellwagen permission to leave since his mission was "impossible" to carry out.

Goldsborough then turned around the very next day and assigned Lieutenant Commander Reed Werden to this "impossible" duty that Stellwagen had failed to carry out. Many of the men who had been hired to work with Stellwagen had left when he did. Many of the schooners were in bad or leaky condition or hard aground on the shoals or already sunk. Werden told Goldsborough how impractical the obstruction of the inlets was, and he also asked to be relieved from this duty. Goldsborough refused to relieve Werden until Werden distinctly informed him of the difficulties in blocking Ocracoke in particular.

Weather again delayed the project, and it was two weeks before Werden was able to send Reigart to Ocracoke to investigate these difficulties. In the meantime, Werden submitted the views of two pilots on this subject who both agreed that the project was entirely impractical. One of these men, Jacob Westervelt, cited an instance he had witnessed in 1857. A ship had sunk in one of these channels, and in only one week a new channel, as navigable as the original, had been cut out around the ship where there had been only three feet of water before.

The weather finally cleared, and Reigart went to Ocracoke. Two months earlier, while preparing the stone fleet, Reigart had thought the idea to be practical. He had reported that the vessels could be sunk in such a way as to effectively block the channels for months to come.

Now, as Reigart approached Ocracoke, he had been working off the Hatteras Capes for over two months. He had overseen a group of pilots and had buoyed the main channel. On this trip, he took his best pilot with him so that the pilot could advise him on the conditions and characteristics of the inlets.

After a thorough investigation, Reigart reported back that the obstruction plan was not practical. It was only on the inside of the bar that any obstruction could be accomplished, and even there could only be for a limited amount of time. Reigart told Werden that it only took but a brief observation of these channels and their currents to convince even the most skeptical that new channels would soon form around the sunken ships.

Captain Charles H. Davis, who performed a similar function further south less than a month later, also expressed his objections to his duty: "I am bound to put down vessels laden with stone, or the stone fleet as it is called. This is a disagreeable duty, and one of the last I should have selected. I always considered this mode of interrupting commerce as liable to great objections, and as of doubtful success."

In a short time, Lowry, Stellwagen, Werden, Jeffers, Westervelt, Davis, and several pilots began to look quite expert. "Nature in one of its most irresistible forms" went to work. Within a week, only a few of the vessels could be seen above water, and in less than two months, the ships had disappeared completely. Undercurrents formed new channels, and the granite-filled vessels found themselves engulfed in the sand and mud at the bottom or broken up and washed away.

19.
CRUELTY IN REFUSING ASSISTANCE TO THE COMMANDER OF THE PRONY

———•◦•———

DURING THE WEEKS FOLLOWING THE STONE FLEET DEBACLE, Reigart cruised around the southern part of the Hatteras Capes in the *Underwriter*. He had with him three other vessels that shared his blockading duties, the *Ceres*, the *O. M. Petit*, and the *Ellen*.

One afternoon, as Reigart approached Ocracoke, he spotted a vessel near the shore. Knowing this to be a dangerous area for boats to be in close to shore, he decided to investigate. Reigart, with a few of his men, went to pay the other ship a visit. As his boat approached, Reigart could see that the other ship was grounded. Reigart and his men boarded the ship and met its captain who had seen them coming.

The captain told Reigart, "We are the French Men of War, *Prony*. We have been making every effort to get off since daylight. If the bad weather comes in, I am afraid we will have to throw our guns and ammunition overboard and abandon the ship."

"We will see what we can do to help you," Reigart said hesitatingly. He could see that a wind was beginning to blow, and he knew this area only too well to expect the sea to remain calm for very long. "You never should have been this close to shore in this area," Reigart continued.

"We did not see any markers," the French captain replied.

Reigart began to fume. He was incensed at the viciousness of the Confederates. They endangered innocent ships when they put out the lights and removed the buoys along this treacherous coast. The water was beginning to get a little choppy, so Reigart told the French captain that he had to get back to his own vessel.

As he returned to the *Underwriter*, Reigart looked up at sky. Dark clouds were racing toward the area; he had seen this sky before and knew that he was in for a treacherous gale. Reigart sent orders to the *Ceres* and *O. M. Petit* directing them to return to Hatteras Inlet at once. If they could not get back in time, Reigart told them to take every precaution for the safety of their vessels and to get in at early daylight.

Reigart then sent a directive to the commander of the *Ellen* to stay with the *Underwriter*. Reigart was worried when he received word back from the *Ellen's* commander that the *Ellen* was damaged and could not keep the sea. It was too late to go into Hatteras or Ocracoke, so the commander of the *Ellen* took her in close to shore and anchored her there.

Reigart tried to keep the *Underwriter* within sight of the *Prony*, but it was too late to help her now. Reigart's only hope was that the gale would end shortly and that the *Prony* would not break apart before then. By 10:00 p.m., the weather had settled into a full-blown gale. The sea was raging and pounded unrelentingly against the ships. Reigart had to move the *Underwriter* out to sea for fear that it would go crashing into the shore. Reigart had not seen a storm like this since Vera Cruz and the China Seas.

The *Underwriter* was suffering terribly. Several times, her deck was filled with water. Some of this water seeped down to the boiler room, flooding her engines. At one point, Reigart ordered his men on deck to knock away the bulwark, the sides of the ship above the upper deck, in order to prevent the ship from foundering.

Reigart wanted to help the *Prony*, but when the gale continued through the next morning, he saw nothing that he could do. The sea was running so high that he did not dare approach within several miles of the *Prony*. By this time, Reigart's own vessel was in imminent danger, and his own safety and that of his crew had become a subject for serious consideration.

Reigart reluctantly left the scene and returned to Hatteras. He had wanted to help the Frenchman and offer all the assistance in his power. He knew the importance. If the Confederates rescued the ship, it might have serious bearing on political questions. Reigart blamed the whole incident on the Confederates. By extinguishing all the lights on the coast, the Confederates had made it the most dangerous in the world. When Reigart returned to Hatteras, he urged that help be sent to the *Prony* as soon as the storm cleared.

The *Prony* was lost in the storm. Reigart was shocked but not surprised when he learned that the French government had charged him with "cruelty in refusing assistance to the commander of the *Prony*, lately wrecked at Ocracoke Inlet." Commodore Joseph Smith launched an investigation. Every commander in the area verified that Reigart had done all that he possibly could under the circumstances. The French legation to the United States thanked the United States for investigating the incident. They apologized to Reigart and thanked him for his efforts. They were pleased to learn that the "casualties of navigation alone interfered with the kind purposes of the American commanders and prevented them from carrying succor to the *Prony*."

A few days after this incident, Reigart was given a short leave of absence. This phase of the Hatteras operation was over. More ships would be brought to North Carolina in 1862. By the end of 1863, the entire North Carolina coast, including the inland waters, except for the port of Wilmington was under Northern domination. By 1864, the North Atlantic squadron was the largest of the Union's four squadrons, and the Hatteras station was the largest in the squadron. In February 1865, the largest fleet ever assembled by the United States Navy up to that time, consisting of forty-eight vessels, attacked and captured Wilmington, thus completing control over the North Carolina waters.

Reigart would not see any of this later action. He would go to the other fronts. His work was done at Hatteras. He had met Ben Butter there for the first time but not the last. Had Ben not written that nasty letter to Reigart, they probably never would have become friends. Now, nineteen years later, Reigart stopped in to see Ben whenever they were in the same city. Reigart thanked Ben for whatever role Ben had played in stopping Jouett from jumping over the other sixteen captains' heads. As Reigart left, he commented, "Well, Ben, I'm glad this Jouett thing is over. I guess we've heard the last from him for a while."

"I hope so," said Ben. "I sincerely hope so."

Those last words troubled Reigart as he returned to the Coleman House. Reigart knew that Ben often could not tell him everything, but what could he mean by "I hope so"? It was not like Ben to say something like that unless there was something he knew. What could it be? What could he know? What could Jouett be up to now?

20.
WE HAVE LOWRY THE DARING

——•◦•——

WHEN REIGART GOT BACK TO THE COLEMAN HOUSE, HE found a letter he had been anxiously waiting. Even though Jouett had been stopped, temporarily at least, Reigart had decided to get his file in shape in case there would be any trouble with his own promotion. He had spoken out against two Presidents and two Secretaries of the Navy. They might try to pass him over even though he was now next in line.

Reigart had written to some of his old commanders for letters of recommendation. The one he had most wanted to hear from, Thomas T. Craven, had finally answered. Craven had been Reigart's favorite commander, and Reigart longed to see his old friend again as he read the letter.

Craven wrote: "Be sure, my dear friend, [the receipt of your letter] has caused me no little pleasure, and I have been thinking all day how much I would enjoy a grip of your hand." Reigart knew just how Craven felt. He, too, would like to see Craven again. Craven continued, commenting that the death of Reigart's Annapolis classmate, Edward Barrett, had brought Reigart up for promotion sooner than he could have expected. "I never supposed," wrote Craven, "that an officer with such a record as you must have at the Dept. would be required by the Board of Examiners to furnish testimonials, etc., but nevertheless I most cheerfully comply with your request and herewith enclose the paper." Reigart had to smile at this last sentence. Such a record as he must have at the department! In the last four or five years, he must have built up quite a file.

Craven had been following the Jouett case with considerable interest and was glad that Jouett had failed to consummate his outrage. Ben Butler's "I hope so" echoed in Reigart's mind as he read this part of the letter. Reigart was glad to hear from Craven. He had to pause and think about Tom Craven several times while he read the letter. When he got to one point, Reigart thought if he ever got a chance that he would go visit his friend. Craven wrote, "Should you ever in your wanderings be passing near this place and feel like making a man happy, you can always do so by dropping in and hanging up your hat as long as you please."

Reigart had first met Tom Craven during the Civil War. Reigart had been made executive officer of the *Brooklyn* of which Captain Thomas T. Craven was commander. After serving on the North Carolina coast, Reigart had been transferred to the *Brooklyn* in the Gulf Blockading Squadron. The first few months on this duty were spent blockading the mouth of the Mississippi River.

In Washington, the decision had been made to take control of the entire Mississippi River. Secretary of the Navy Gideon Welles selected sixty-year-old Captain David Glasgow Farragut to head this operation. Farragut was a veteran with forty-nine years service stretching back to the war of 1812.

Two forts guarded the entrance of the Mississippi River and the approach to New Orleans—Fort Jackson and Fort St. Philip. Farragut's mission was to capture these forts and move up the river. At the same time, the river fleet would move down from Cairo, Illinois, under command of Andrew H. Foote and later Charles N. Davis.

The *Brooklyn* with Reigart Lowry and Tom Craven on board would become part of Farragut's fleet. Farragut decided that the attack on Forts Jackson and St. Philip would be made on April 24, 1862. Seventeen ships and gunboats, under Flag Officer Farragut, and twenty-one mortar schooners, under Farragut's foster brother Commander David Dixon Porter, would participate. The fleet would proceed in two divisions, one to direct its attack on Fort Jackson and the other to direct its attack on Fort St. Philip. At the same time, five steamers belonging to the mortar fleet would try to silence Fort Jackson as the fleet passed.

On the morning of April 24, from 3:00 a.m. to 4:50 a.m., the *Brooklyn*, along with the rest of the fleet, engaged in battle with the two forts and some sixteen rebel gunboats. The fighting began at 3:10 a.m. when the *Brooklyn* opened fire with shells, grape, and canister of which some one hundred and five rounds were fired from the nine-inch guns on her broadside.

Reigart was all over the ship, encouraging his men and helping them whenever he could. The conduct of the men was of such excellence, he thought as he observed them, that any officer would have been proud of them. They met Reigart's highest expectations in drill and efficiency, and although the battle was fought in almost total darkness, Reigart believed that nothing could have exceeded the rapid and precise firing, the prompt readiness to repair damages, and the care for the dead and wounded. As Reigart made his rounds, he found one gun crew where eleven out of seventeen of the men had been killed or wounded, but the remaining six valiantly worked the gun until the end of the action. During the first day of the battle, the total number of casualties in the squadron was one hundred and forty-six wounded and thirty-seven killed.

The *Brooklyn* bore an important part of the fight and suffered severely. Her place in line was right behind Farragut's ship, the *Hartford*. Craven and Lowry soon lost sight of the *Hartford* in the darkness and blinding smoke and could only follow what they supposed was the line of the *Hartford's* fire. They suddenly found their vessel running over the hulks and rafts that bore up a chain that had been stretched across the river by the Confederates. Entangled in these, the *Brooklyn* got off her course, swinging athwart the river and her bow striking the shore. While in this position, the *Brooklyn* received severe fire from Fort St. Philip that cut her up severely.

Scarcely had the *Brooklyn* gotten loose and turned upstream when she was struck quite seriously by the *Manassas*, but the chain armor that had been hung along the side of the *Brooklyn* received most of the blow and saved the ship. A few moments later, the *Brooklyn* found herself under a raking fire from Fort Jackson. One shot from Fort Jackson struck a rail and plowed nearly all the way across the deck of the ship. Another struck the signal quartermaster, Barney Sands, and nearly cut his body in two. Reigart, who was all over the ship during the battle, came across Barney Sands and asked, "Who is that?"

One of the men answered, "Barney."

Reigart, in all the noise of the battle, thought that the man had said Bartlett, and as he roamed about the rest of the ship, Reigart spread the word that he had sent down all that was left of poor Bartlett. As he was in all parts of the ship, most of the men were quite surprised when Bartlett showed up!

As the *Brooklyn* got out from under Fort Jackson's guns, she came alongside a three-masted Confederate propeller ship that opened fire on her. The guns on the *Brooklyn's* port broadside were trained on the enemy vessel, and at only fifty yards, the whole force of the *Brooklyn's* broadside was hurled into the vessel simultaneously. There was a resounding crash that sounded like an echo from the guns; shells exploded in the enemy vessel's sides and on her deck. Flames burst out a moment later, and the shattered wreck drifted helplessly away.

By this time, the *Brooklyn* had come almost abreast of Fort St. Philip. Since the *Brooklyn* only had a few moments when all her guns bore on the fort, Craven and Lowry poured in all the fire they could. Before they had passed, they had completely silenced the fort. Reigart Lowry and Tom Craven felt a great sense of accomplishment when they saw in the flashes of the exploding shells the enemy running like sheep for more comfortable quarters.

Reigart was proud of his men on this first day of battle. As he sat in his cabin that night, he wrote his report to Craven: "As your executive officer, it becomes my duty as it is my pride to call attention to the excellent bearing of every officer and man on board this ship. The advancing and victorious squadron in succession ran down, sank, blew up, and fired by shells, eleven of the enemy's sixteen gunboats…I, without hesitation, assert that the attack of our squadron upon two strong and garrisoned forts, coming within grape and canister range, and to a great extent silencing their fire, and destroying nearly all the enemy's fleet, is not to my knowledge surpassed, if equaled, on the record of any Navy in the world."

On the second day of battle, the *Brooklyn* fought at close range next to the *Sciota* but was forced to stop firing when the *Sciota* rushed in between the *Brooklyn* and the shore batteries. Again, all the men worked quickly and efficiently, and the only loss of life was one Dennis Leary who fell overboard by his own carelessness.

During the two days of battle, the *Brooklyn* suffered severely. Both mainstays, several shrouds, lanyards, jib stays, and much of the running gear, as well as many other important parts of the ship, were cut by the sixteen shells which struck the *Brooklyn*.

At the conclusion of the battle, Captain Graven prepared his report for Farragut. Like Reigart, Torn Craven was pleased with the heroic way all his men had performed. He seemed surprised at their perfect coolness and self-possession as they were under fire from the forts for half an hour before he had given the order to "open fire." Craven was especially pleased with Reigart's performance. He wrote, "I have to congratulate myself on being so ably assisted by my executive officer, Lt. R. B. Lowry. He was everywhere, inspiring both officers and crew with his own zeal and gallantry…"

Farragut moved his fleet up past the forts toward New Orleans while Commander David B. Porter remained behind with the mortar fleet. The forts surrendered to Porter a couple of days later. The battle of New Orleans had been a tremendous success for the Northern Navy, and the seamen were rightfully proud of their performance. Songs and poetry instantly appeared, and the men who had participated in the battle quickly learned them. A song was written about the *Brooklyn's* role in the battle, and it was often sung on board the vessel during evening jam sessions. Part of it went as follows:

> *On board the good ship Brooklyn, we are sailing in the van,*
>
> *We can do the work before us if any sailor can.*
>
> *We will drive the rebel forces from their stronghold to the sea,*
>
> *And we'll live and die together in the Navy of the free.*
>
> *Chorus:*
>
> *The Navy of the free brave boys, the Navy of the free*
>
> *Hurrah, hurrah for the Brooklyn crew wherever they may be.*
>
> *The Brooklyn has the bravest crew of any in the fleet,*
>
> *And when in battle fighting, they can do their work so neat.*
>
> *Then our gallant Captain Craven calls, all ready will we be,*
>
> *To follow him forever in the Navy of the free.*
>
> *Chorus:*
>
> *We have Lowry the Daring, we have Bartlett the Cool.*
>
> *Where could we learn the art of war within a better school?*
>
> *Add Selmer to the list of names, and with me you'll all agree.*
>
> *That we have the bravest officers in the Navy of the free.*
>
> *Chorus:*

A poem, "The Ballad of New Orleans" also described the battle. A part of it described the *Brooklyn's* exploits:

> *And into our vacant station*
>
> *Had glided a bulky form;*
>
> *Was Craven's stout Brooklyn, demanding*

Her share of the furious storm.

We could hear the shot of St. Philip

Ring on her armor of chain,

And the crash of her answering broadside,

Taking and giving again.

We could hear the low growl of Craven,

And Lowry's voice clear and calm,

While they swept off the rebel ramparts

As clear as your open palm.

As a result of the action at Forts Jackson and St. Philip, two vacancies occurred in the squadron, one on the *Colorado* and the other on the *Wissahickon*. As for the *Colorado*, the most senior officer without a command, Commander John De Camp, declined on the grounds that it was not his proper command, but he did not hesitate to grab the opening on the *Wissahickon*. He, therefore, deprived Reigart of a legitimate vacancy to which his position as senior Lieutenant in the squadron entitled him. Moreover, John I. Davis, Reigart's junior, took command of the *Colorado*. Reigart wrote Secretary Welles, saying that he wished to be "placed in command of a vessel, as I think my rank and services entitle me to." He received no reply.

The North had opened the southern portion of the Mississippi River. The New Orleans operation had been a tremendous success due to good planning and gallant fighting by the professional Union Navy. Now came the time for the Navy to move up the river and deep into enemy territory.

21.

WE ARE NOT ON A COTTON OR NIGGER OR CHICKEN-STEALING EXPEDITION

———•◯•———

THE UNION NAVY'S FIRST REAL CONTACT WITH SOUTHERN people—black and white, rebel and faithful—came right after the attack on Forts Jackson and St. Philip. Now the Navy was attempting to obtain control of the Mississippi River and was, as a result, penetrating the interior of the South. Reigart was about to find many contrasts in the behavior of different groups of Southerners.

Governor Thomas O. Moore, the Confederate governor of Louisiana ordered that all cotton, sugar, and molasses be destroyed when he learned that the US Navy was coming up the river. He wanted all measures taken to ensure that these goods would not fall into Union hands. One afternoon, Captain Craven sent Reigart ashore at Belle View Plantation in Louisiana for the purpose of communicating with the residents and obtaining provisions. This was Reigart's first real contact with Southerners since the war began.

Upon arriving at the plantation, Reigart was met by a large crowd of Negroes of all ages who seemed happy and content. Upon making inquiry, he learned that this and the five neighboring plantations belonged to a

Mr. Ackland. Reigart sent for this man, and in a short time Mr. Ackland arrived on horseback, greeting Reigart cordially and expressing pleasure at seeing him. Mr. Ackland was laboring under intense excitement. He had just received an imperative order from a captain of an irregular band of militia to burn his cotton within five days. If he did not comply, he ran the risk of having it burned for him, with the additional threat that he would be hanged.

Reigart explained his mission, saying, "I am here only to procure fresh meat and vegetables for which I will pay a fair price. I am not here to steal your cotton."

Ackland looked relieved but replied, "I am sorry, but I have no provisions. I have over one thousand Negroes to feed and clothe, and I have been unable to give them any kind of meat for three weeks. My Negroes have the liberty to raise their own poultry and vegetables, and you are free to buy from them."

As the two men talked, Mr. Ackland proceeded to give Reigart a history of his persecutions by and sacrifices for the Confederate government. "Men of substance," he stated, "are constantly pressed by the government for money, provisions, teams, wagons, and Negroes. I have been asked time after time to burn my cotton, but I have steadily refused to do so."

Ackland raised between five and six thousand bales of cotton each year. He still had the previous year's entire crop, and since he depended on the sale of this cotton to clothe and feed his Negroes, he believed that every principle of right and law forbade him from burning it. He was perhaps the wealthiest man in all of Louisiana, but he believed that the revolt of the South was wrong. Ackland had not taken an active part in the rebellion but had been on the plantation the whole year, separated from his family who was residing in Nashville. Ackland concluded his description of his affairs by saying with a little bitterness, "It seems as if those who had nothing to lose are intent on lowering to their own positions all those who have."

"Would you desire armed protection?" Reigart inquired of Mr. Ackland.

"No. I don't think so," answered Ackland. "I am afraid that it would subject me to the fury of the mob after the force was withdrawn. Don't worry. I will protect my property against the Davis emissaries with my life."

Reigart returned to his ship. That night, as he sat in his cabin, Reigart thought about his visit with Mr. Ackland. He thought that it was incredible that men born under a free government, with the rights of speech and suffrage, should in so short a time be brought under the iron heel of remorseless and cruel tyranny. Reigart reflected that Ackland's vast estates and great wealth were no protection to him in a region where all government had ended, and only unbridled passions of men ruled the hour. Reigart was more convinced than ever that the United States government should extend its protecting arms over its offending yet deluded and helpless children, to save them from utter ruin and degradation.

Reigart soon learned that the suffering of this planter was not an isolated case and that the opening of the Mississippi River would be welcomed by many of the residents of the area. Many small militia groups and guerilla bands were forming, and the sooner the Mississippi River was opened, the safer these plantation owners would be. Reigart knew that all those who had anything to lose by the privation of property would hail the security that the United States government could offer with secret joy.

Now that the Navy was past New Orleans, it was able to penetrate further into Confederate territory. As the vessels steamed up the river in early May, Reigart noticed large crowds on the shore. In front of the large sugar plantations, he saw the white occupants collected in groups and gazing askance at the Union vessels, while the ladies often turned their backs. Then as the vessels passed groups of Negroes, particularly if they were hidden from their masters' views by intervening houses or trees, who showed great joy in seeing the Union Navy by jumping, bowing, and waving to it.

One day, Reigart witnessed only one true demonstration in favor of the Union, and that was on the part of a brave lady. She was standing on the levee in front of her mansion, alone, under the shade of a large oak tree. Her servants were grouped together about fifty yards up the river. Above and below were two large parties of ladies and gentlemen who looked scornfully on both her and the Navy. As the vessels neared, the woman ran up to her servants and unrolled a large Union flag. She handed it to her servants and made them spread it out and wave it over their heads, while she waved her kerchief and wiped the tears from her eyes.

Reigart and his captain were moved by this demonstration. That night, Captain Craven wrote to his wife and told her about the woman: "The flag was our own; the flag of our beloved but sore stricken Union. God bless that brave woman! I felt at the time as if I could jump to the shore and kiss her as if she had been one of my nearest and dearest kin." It was becoming noticeable to the Navy that many Southerners did not support the Confederacy.

The next evening, the *Brooklyn* anchored about eight miles below Baton Rouge, in front of a plantation owned and occupied by a French Creole and his family. As was his custom at any stopping place, Captain Craven sent Reigart ashore to deliver a speech. Reigart made his way to the plush residence of the Frenchman, who, with his wife and grown daughters appeared to be terribly frightened. After learning that Reigart was not on a "nigger stealing" expedition, and that all his property was safe, the Frenchman calmed down. As his reserve wore off, the Frenchman became cheerful and friendly. The planter told Reigart how an emissary had just visited him from Governor Moore, who had ordered him to destroy his sugar and molasses. If the Frenchman did not immediately comply with this demand, a party of men would soon follow and not only destroy his property but also hang him. The Frenchman had been under a lot of strain, not knowing whether his own friends would destroy his sugar and molasses and then hang him.

Reigart returned to the *Brooklyn*. The next morning, he sent some men ashore with the planter's hearty permission to buy poultry, eggs, and vegetables from his Negroes. While these men were on shore, a bouquet arrived on the *Brooklyn* for "the Captain" from his unknown, unseen, fair friends, the young ladies.

Only two days later, when the *Brooklyn* passed the mouth of the Red River, Reigart saw a gentleman on shore rush to a pile of cotton on the bank of the river and set it on fire. This seemed to be a general signal, for in a few minutes, smoke was rising from other heaps of cotton as far as Reigart could see. As the *Brooklyn* sailed on, Reigart saw a lot of cotton in the river which could not have been burned because of a danger of setting fire to buildings. Governor Moore's order to burn cotton was having quite an effect with many plantation owners.

As the *Brooklyn* headed back toward New Orleans the next morning, Reigart saw another heap of cotton going up in flames. When he went on his usual visit to shore, Reigart asked the overseer of this cotton, "What are you burning your cotton for?"

The man answered, "My owner ordered it, I suppose, to save it from falling into your hands."

"We are not on a cotton or nigger or chicken-stealing expedition," Reigart explained.

"Well, there are 1,500 bales gone," the overseer replied. "If it had been mine, I wouldn't have burned it."

Reigart later found out about the effect of guerrilla bands on small towns. Before this, he had spoken to plantation owners on the topic. In mid-June, Reigart was sent ashore at Bayou Sara, accompanied by about one hundred men, for the purpose of destroying the telegraphic apparatus and cutting the wires. Reigart informed the authorities that the *Brooklyn* was on the river to enforce the laws of the country. He warned them that if there were any demonstrations made against the *Brooklyn* by thieves or guerrillas as it passed by, the town would be held responsible. The mayor told Reigart that a band of guerrillas had been through only three days before. The mayor added that the townspeople feared these men more than they did visits from the Union Navy. Before leaving the town, Reigart, with the flag of the Union at the head of his party, marched his men through some of the principal streets of the city to the tunes of "Yankee Doodle" and "Dixie."

Reigart had seen two kinds of people—those who were intimidated by the bands of guerrillas and those who were not. Most townspeople and small farmers and plantation owners did not have the will or the resources to resist Governor Moore. The large plantation owners, however, had too much to lose. These latter men, the largest slaveholders in the South were against the war. Their own side was destroying the slavery system and ruining them financially.

Reigart would see one more type of Southerner during the coming months—the Southern mayor.

22.
MISSISSIPPIANS DON'T KNOW, AND REFUSE TO LEARN, HOW TO SURRENDER

———•◎•———

FOLLOWING THE FIRST DAY OF FIGHTING BETWEEN THE Union Navy and Forts Jackson and St. Philip, Farragut had taken the Hartford and a few other vessels up the river to New Orleans. He sent Captain Theodorus Bailey, second in command of the federal fleet, ashore to demand surrender of the city of New Orleans and to hoist the United States flag over the customhouse, the post office, and the mint. Bailey sent for General Mansfield Lovell, in charge of Confederate forces in New Orleans, and stated his demands. Lovell refused to surrender the city, his forces, or any portion of them. Instead, he offered to evacuate his troops and leave the city officials to do as they deemed proper.

General Lovell evacuated, leaving the city defenseless. Farragut then restated his demands to the mayor of New Orleans, John T. Monroe. Mayor Monroe saw no need to surrender since the federal Navy could take the city at any time. He flatly refused to raise the American flag on any public building. Farragut became so offended by the exchange of correspondence with Mayor Monroe that he terminated it. When Major General Benjamin

Butler arrived in New Orleans, Farragut turned over the charge of the city to him, and Farragut resumed his naval duties.

The capture of New Orleans was a great step towards gaining control of the Mississippi River, but the long stretch of the river between New Orleans and Vicksburg, Mississippi was still controlled by the Confederates. Early in May, the fleet began to move up the river.

On May 8, Commander James S. Palmer, commanding the *Iroquois*, contacted the mayor of Baton Rouge, B. F. Bryan. Palmer offered Bryan the same terms that had been offered to New Orleans. The terms were an unconditional surrender, and the flag of the United States had to be hoisted over the arsenal. The mayor refused to surrender and said that he could not raise the flag over the arsenal as he had no control over it: "The city of Baton Rouge will not be surrendered voluntarily to any power on earth. We have no military forces here and are entirely without any means of defense; its possession by you must be without the consent and against the wish of the peaceable inhabitants."

At half past one the next afternoon, Reigart went ashore and personally hoisted the stars and stripes above the Baton Rouge arsenal.

Commander Palmer advanced the squadron up the Mississippi River, and on May 12, he demanded from the mayor of Natchez, Mississippi, John Hunter, the same terms of surrender which had been offered at New Orleans and Baton Rouge. Mayor Hunter replied: "Coming as a conqueror, you need not the interposition of the city authorities to possess this place. An unfortified city, an entirely defenseless people, have no alternative but to yield to an irresistible force, or uselessly to imperil innocent blood. Formalities are absurd in the face of such reality. So far as the city authorities can prevent, there will be no opposition to your possession of the city; they cannot, however, guarantee that your flag shall wave unmolested in the sight of an excited people, but such authority as they do possess will be exercised for the preservation of good order in the city..."

As Farragut moved his vessels up the river, Foote and Davis moved their fleet down. While Farragut captured New Orleans, Baton Rouge, and Natchez, the river fleet had won victories at Island No. 10, Fort Pillow, and Memphis. Now in the middle of 1862, these two fleets approached each other at Vicksburg, the only point on the Mississippi River remaining in Confederate control. Vicksburg was strategically important for a couple of reasons. It was situated on the Mississippi River at a point where it made a sharp U-shaped turn, and the city was situated on a hill that rose two hundred feet above the river.

S. Phillips Lee, commanding the *Oneida*, led an advanced naval division to Vicksburg to demand its surrender. He delivered a surrender demand to the military authorities from Farragut and Butler. James C. Antry, Military Governor and Colonel commanding the post replied, "I have to state that Mississippians don't know, and refuse to learn, how to surrender to an enemy. If Commodore Farragut and Brigadier General Butler can teach them, let them come and try."

The stage was set. The Union had to fight for Vicksburg.

23.
EVERY MAN KNOWS THAT IT IS HIS DUTY TO FOLLOW HIS LEADER

———•◐•———

FARRAGUT HAD RECEIVED ORDERS DIRECTLY FROM PRESIDENT Lincoln, as early as January 20, 1862, to open the Mississippi River. Much of this had been accomplished, but problems had developed which made Farragut begin to doubt his ability to complete this order. His boats needed repair; he had no reliable pilots to navigate the Mid-Mississippi; he was short of coal; the water level of the river was beginning to fall; his vessels were running aground; and he was outnumbered by twenty to one. With these problems, added to the curve in the river and the height of the batteries at Vicksburg, Farragut expressed his concerns to the Navy Department, but to no avail.

One possible solution was to dig a canal across the narrow neck of land formed by the hairpin curve. The land here was only three-quarters of a mile across, and it was felt that by building a canal across it that the course of the river could be changed, bypassing Vicksburg and completing Northern control over the river. The order to proceed with the canal came from Secretary Welles on June 25. General Benjamin Butler sent about 5,000 troops to Farragut under General Thomas Williams. Williams, with his small force and some Negroes, began digging. The line for the canal, however, was not well located, for it was perpendicular to the direction of the current. This, combined with the fact that the water level of the river was dropping, led to the ultimate failure of the project.

In the meantime, plans went ahead for a naval offensive against Vicksburg. Farragut ordered his fleet to get under way at 3:00 a.m. on the morning of June 28. At about 4:00 a.m., the Confederates opened fire on the advanced vessels of the squadron. When the *Brooklyn* arrived below the lower batteries, Reigart noticed that Porter's mortar fleet, which seemed to be without any form of order, had passed between the *Brooklyn* and the riverbank. The *Brooklyn* had to stop its engines, and its progress became delayed. When Porter's mortar boats got out of the way, Reigart discovered that the only gun that would reach the hill batteries was his eighty-pounder rifle. Therefore, he ordered vigorous fire from this gun.

At sunrise, when the smoke cleared, Reigart could not see the rest of the ships, except for the *Kennebec* and the *Katahdin*. Reigart consulted with Captain Craven who told him to resume fighting with the hill batteries. The firing from the *Brooklyn* still had little effect, and later that day, Reigart would point out in his report the futility of using wooden vessels against hill batteries at 1,000 to 1,500 yards from the water at an elevation of 200 to 300 feet. He used the example that the fleet had not been able to permanently silence the batteries, even after long battle.

The southern forces had found that the best defense during this naval engagement was to flee from the batteries and return when the firing from the ships died down. Farragut became convinced that Vicksburg could not be taken without a land force of 12,000 to 15,000 men attacking from the other side. He told Welles how tremendous the gunfire had been and how little effect it had had. In his report to Welles, Farragut also noted: "The *Brooklyn*, *Kennebec*, and *Katahdin* did not get past the batteries. I do not know why."

During this operation, the ships were supposed to follow the *Hartford* up past the batteries. When the *Brooklyn*, *Kennebec*, and *Katahdin* did not, Farragut demanded an explanation. Captain Craven answered that Farragut had said in his general order that "Should the action be continued by the enemy, the ships and the *Iroquois* and *Oneida* will stop their engines and drop down the river again." Craven also described a conversation between Farragut and himself during which he had asked Farragut whether he should leave any battery unsilenced. Craven alleged that Farragut replied, "No, sir, not on any account."

Farragut answered Craven with a letter of censure. He regretted to say that he had read with great surprise Craven's explanation of the causes that led to his not coming up the river. Farragut had no recollection of ever saying to Craven that he was not to leave an unsilenced battery, nor did he remember saying that Craven was to drop down again. Farragut forgave the commanders of the *Kennebec* and the *Katahdin* as they had just arrived and had been assigned to the rear, "and every man knows that it is his duty to follow his leader." Farragut continued, "But, sir, when you presume to shelter yourself under the idea that I left you or any other officer the right to stop at pleasure and change my general order, you assume the right to annul my orders, or act according to your own will." Farragut felt it strange that no other officer took Craven's view of the general order. The order had read when the ships reach the bend in the river, should the enemy continue the action, the ships should drop down. Farragut asked, "How did I explain this part of my order to you all? Did you ever reach the bend in the river? I can answer for you, that you were never within a mile and a half of it."

Captain Craven asked to be relieved of duty and sent north the next day. He felt that he had been slighted and treated unfairly by Farragut several times during the past few months. He cited specific instances. On April 24, at New Orleans, Farragut assigned one of Craven's juniors to the command of one of the four columns, yet Craven had no such command. On May 2, Farragut gave Craven an order to proceed to Vicksburg to take possession of that place and to destroy the railroads and telegraphs. On

May 7, Craven was replaced in this duty by a junior officer and ordered down to Baton Rouge. On June 25, Farragut assigned a junior officer to a position Craven felt should have been his. Now, this letter of censure added to Craven's feeling that he had lost or never had the favor of his commanding officer.

Farragut claimed not to have consciously inflicted injustice upon Craven. In most cases, Farragut stated that it had been the ship and not the man whom he had chosen. Farragut relieved Captain Craven and transferred command of the *Brooklyn* to Commander Henry H. Bell, the junior commander who had superseded Craven in all the above instances!

Reigart followed Craven's situation closely. He liked Captain Craven and was his friend. Moreover, Reigart, too, had felt slighted under Farragut's command. Reigart reopened the whole affair the day after Craven was relieved when he requested to be relieved from his post on the *Brooklyn* and to be placed in command of a vessel. He felt that it would be extremely repugnant to him to serve under any officer, other than Craven, in a position lower than several of his juniors then served. He, too, felt an injustice. Reigart reasserted the complaint he had made in New Orleans. In his letter to Flag Officer Farragut, Reigart concluded, "I have served faithfully, and I can see no prospect ahead by which I can gain any name or fame for myself in this squadron. After the important operations of the squadron are finished, I shall consider it far from an honor to succeed the command of a gunboat, after some invalid Commander has satisfied his own ends and proceeded to reap the laurels after all the fighting is over."

Reigart's letter disturbed Farragut, and he instructed Commander Bell to clear up the whole matter. Farragut had always felt a desire to do something for Reigart, and he had placed Reigart in command of the *Montgomery* earlier in the year. But now, Farragut urged Bell to make Reigart sensible of his error and induce him to withdraw his letter. "If he will not, suspend him from duty, and allow him to take passage home...A first officer with so insubordinate a spirit can be of no use to you. No one can more deeply regret than I the whole affair, but the discipline of the service must be maintained."

Henry Bell went to Reigart and told him how seriously Farragut wanted the letter to be withdrawn. Bell convinced Reigart that he should withdraw the letter and Reigart did. Farragut contacted Reigart at this point. He told Reigart that he was pleased by his frank and manly tone, but he thought that the whole affair had been taken in the wrong spirit. Farragut added that there had been no deliberate intention to do harm to anyone in the matters mentioned by Reigart, and he hoped that this idea would be obliterated from Reigart's mind.

Had Reigart not withdrawn his letter, Farragut would have relieved him of duty. Reigart did withdraw it, though, and only six days later, he was detached from the *Brooklyn* and given the command he had demanded. Perhaps writing the letter in the first place had paid off. When Reigart left, Commander Bell made the following entry in his diary: "Lieutenant Lowry, the indefatigable First Lieutenant of this ship, left her to take command of the gunboat *Sciota*."

Farragut had now reached Vicksburg, but on his first pass he had failed to capture it. Now, most of his fleet was above the city, but three of his vessels remained below. He had had to relieve one of his senior officers from duty and nearly lost another fine officer in the process. But now, with these troubles behind him, his major problems lay ahead. He had to find a way to complete control of the Mississippi River as had been ordered by the president. He faced far superior forces at Vicksburg, and he knew that he had a major dilemma facing him.

24.
THE RAM MUST BE DESTROYED

———•○•———

DAVID FARRAGUT KNEW THAT HE NEEDED HELP TO CAPTURE Vicksburg. After he had passed by the city and confirmed his beliefs about its strength, he contacted Flag Officer Charles Davis, commanding the Union river fleet to the north, and General Henry Halleck, commanding the Union Army forces in the area. Davis's boats were already approaching Vicksburg, and he was willing to provide any assistance he could. General Halleck's troops, however, were in a scattered and weakened condition, and he could not provide Farragut with any troops. He expressed a desire to help, but he felt that it would be several weeks before he could send any men.

The unsuccessful attempt at a canal, lack of military success in eastern Mississippi, and a realization that a military victory was not imminent at Vicksburg finally brought Secretary Welles over to Farragut's viewpoint. On July 14, Welles wrote to Farragut that perhaps greater objects could be accomplished in the Gulf. Mobile, Alabama, was a target that Washington felt should be attacked and taken. Therefore, Welles ordered Farragut to move his fleet back south of Vicksburg with as little injury and loss of life as possible.

Farragut was preparing to return down the river when an event occurred which caused him deep mortification. Some of the gunboats of

Davis's flotilla had been sent up the Yazoo River to obtain information concerning the ironclad ram, *Arkansas*, which was being built there. The vessel was called a ram because its bow was low in the water and pointed. The vessel was used to ram enemy ships, puncturing their sides below the water line and sinking them.

Reigart had just taken command of the *Sciota* a few days before. He was getting his boat ready to go back down past Vicksburg when he heard heavy gunfire coming from the direction of the Yazoo River. The cause of this gunfire soon manifested itself when Reigart saw the gunboat *Tyler* appear, closely followed by the *Arkansas*. The *Arkansas* seemed, from her movements, to entirely trust her invulnerability for a safe run to the cover of the Vicksburg batteries. The *Tyler* made a running fight until within the federal fleet's lines.

The federal boats began firing as the *Arkansas* passed right through their lines. Reigart ordered his men to fire the eleven-inch gun at the enemy vessel. It fired; the shell struck the *Arkansas* fairly, but the shell glanced off her iron side almost perpendicularly into the air and exploded. Reigart then ordered his men to keep up small arms fire so that the Confederates could not man the port side of the *Arkansas* until she passed. Reigart's officers and men had been ready, but since the *Arkansas* only took about five minutes to pass, they did not have enough time to disable her.

That evening, Flag Officer Farragut issued a general order to his men directing them to pass down below the city of Vicksburg. While he did not plan to attack the city itself, he made it clear that no one would do wrong by tackling with the *Arkansas*: "The ram must be destroyed."

Reigart was fifth in line on the *Sciota*. Nearing the point opposite the city, he came under heavy fire from hill and water batteries and from sharpshooters in the woods. Bullets flew thickly over the *Sciota*. Sick and wounded who were not able to work the *Sciota's* large guns fired rifles and concentrated on the riflemen in the woods. When the *Sciota* got out of range and damage was surveyed, Reigart found it surprisingly light. Only two men were seriously wounded on the *Sciota*. The fleet had passed Vicksburg with a loss of fifteen lives and thirty wounded, but the ram was not destroyed!

For Reigart, one event made the day a happy one. The young officer, who only a week earlier faced dismissal from the fleet, received a promotion to Lieutenant Commander by order of President Abraham Lincoln. Lieutenant Commander was a brand-new rank and Reigart was among the first to receive it. It had become an official rank on the day he became commissioned. The same law had also created the ranks of Rear Admiral, Commodore, and Ensign (replacing Passed Midshipman).

Since the passing of Vicksburg had been at night, attack on the *Arkansas* had been difficult. Only one shot struck it fairly, but this one did a great deal of damage. Repairs were begun immediately, but the North did not learn how bad the damage was for a few days, or they would have gone in and finished the *Arkansas* off.

It had already been decided that Vicksburg would not be captured, but the *Arkansas* was another matter. While it was a threat, its military potential was limited. But the fact that a whole fleet had been unable to destroy it—twice—had made the *Arkansas* a tremendous psychological threat. Farragut and Davis knew that the *Arkansas* had to be destroyed, even before they received a letter from Secretary Welles expressing the absolute necessity of capture or destruction of the vessel. The Navy Department had been mortified and deeply embarrassed by the affair.

The river was now rapidly falling, and Farragut was anxious to return down the river to deeper water. It was with great relief that he received the order to go downstream on July 20. On July 27, Farragut's fleet started down the river, while Davis's returned up the river, leaving Vicksburg entirely free.

Confederates were causing disturbances around Baton Rouge during the early part of August, so Farragut ordered several of his vessels to that area, including Reigart's *Sciota*. There was a minor skirmish there on August

6, and General Thomas Williams was killed when a Minié ball pierced his heart. Reigart stayed at Baton Rouge to watch for more trouble, but one of his fellow officers took the *Essex* up the river to investigate reports that the *Arkansas* was only about five miles away.

The *Arkansas* had been having engine trouble. At about 9:00 p.m., the *Essex*, under Commander William D. Porter, came around a point and opened fire on the *Arkansas*. At this time, the *Arkansas's* engineers reported her ready, and she started for the *Essex* with the intention of ramming her. Suddenly, one of the *Arkansas's* engines stopped. When the *Essex* continued to advance, the captain of the *Arkansas* realized that his vessel did not have a chance, so he ordered his men to abandon ship and to set the fire to the *Arkansas*. Even after the Confederates reached shore, Bill Porter continued to fire upon the disabled vessel furiously, until his firing, combined with the fire within the *Arkansas*, blew up all that remained of the vessel.

"It is one of the happiest moments of my life that I am enabled to inform the Department of the destruction of the ram *Arkansas*," wrote Farragut the next day, "not because I held the ironclad in such terror, but because the community did."

The Navy had eliminated this menace, and this part of the mission was successful. Vicksburg remained in Confederate hands, but the rest of the river was now in Northern hands. Commerce was interrupted, if not stopped, for the whole length of the river, so the fact that this one city remained in Confederate hands had little military advantage for them. Its main advantage, as with the *Arkansas*, was psychological and had more meaning in the press than to the military. The Confederates had issued a challenge to Butler and Farragut to come and try to teach them how to surrender. Confederates at Vicksburg would not learn how to surrender for nearly a year.

This period of war on the Mississippi River had been eventful and exciting for Reigart. He had seen a lot of fighting and had performed with distinction. But with all this, one of his best memories was working with

Thomas T. Craven. Tom Craven was not only a great captain, but he was a genuinely nice man. Reigart had been shocked when Farragut censured Craven, but Reigart's spunk in the aftermath of the Craven affair had gotten him a command that was long overdue. Reigart would remember Tom Craven for the rest of his life and always look up to him. It was for these reasons that Reigart had asked Tom Craven to write him a letter of recommendation. As Reigart finished Craven's letter, he put it down and reflected about his old friend.

Reigart was in a good mood, and he decided to drop by the New York Club for what he hoped would be a quiet uneventful evening.

25.
THERE WAS NO USE OF RUNNING WHEN YOU COMMENCED TO SHOOT

———•◦•———

REIGART DECIDED TO READ A NEWSPAPER IN THE PRIVACY and quietude of the New York Club reading room before adjourning to the lounge for a few sociable drinks with his friends. As he read his paper, Reigart noticed a familiar figure approach. It was his old friend, Captain Francis A. Roe. Captain Roe had been number five on the original captain's list. Now he was number three.

"Well, well," greeted a jovial Reigart, "What gives me the pleasure of meeting you here tonight, my good Captain Roe?"

"I've got some news," whispered Roe. "Can I talk to you in private?"

"Of course," assured Reigart. "Let's go into the lounge."

On the way to the lounge, Reigart told Roe that he had received a letter from Tom Craven. Roe was interested in hearing about Tom as he, too, had known him during the Mississippi operations, though not nearly as well as Reigart.

The two captains went over to their usual corner table and ordered a round of drinks. "What kind of news do you have?" inquired Reigart.

"The worst," Roe began. "Jouett has gone back to Congress. This time, he's taking the more indirect route of a Vote of Thanks."

Reigart was taken aback. He had known Jouett was up to something from the offhanded remarks Ben Butler had made. "Damn. I thought we'd stopped that bastard," Reigart cursed under his breath.

"Me, too," echoed Roe. "It's going to be awfully hard to get the men organized again. The fight has gone out of them."

"Exactly what does a Vote of Thanks do for Jouett?" Reigart asked.

"All he needs is approval of the Secretary of the Navy for a promotion," Roe replied.

"That's what I thought," Reigart sighed as he sank back into his chair. Reigart was worried. A confirmation was a lot easier to fight than a Vote of Thanks. A confirmation gave a man a promotion right then and there. A Vote of Thanks only gave a man praise. If any promotion came out of it, Congress could place the blame on the Secretary of the Navy. Jouett had the support of the Republican administration. If there were a Vote of Thanks, his promotion would be automatic. Secretary Robeson had been corrupt. The new Secretary of the Navy was merely stupid. A story Reigart and all the high-ranking officers knew was that Thompson had expressed surprise upon finding on his first visit to a naval vessel that ships were hollow. Reigart knew that Thompson was only a puppet, and that the captains had to worry about the coming events.

Reigart told Roe that they would have to organize the captains again. Roe agreed; the two men sat at the table and began to make plans. Reigart had last worked with Francis Roe during the Civil War. After the *Arkansas* had been destroyed, the Navy settled down to patrolling the river, convoying troops, and fighting Confederate troops along the shores. Reigart had been in the same division as Francis Roe, and they saw each other often.

Even though Reigart and Francis were on different ships, they often encountered similar problems and separately reported them to the appropriate authorities. While the two men worked in Louisiana, they saw a great number of French flags. This flag, in certain positions, resembled the Confederate flag so strongly that Reigart prepared his guns to fire at it at one point. He only refrained from firing a moment too soon when he discovered his mistake. Francis Roe, commanding the *Katahdin*, experienced similar problems. The only difference in his case was that he had fired at a French flag, thinking it was a rebel pennant.

These two men behaved similarly a few weeks later under a completely different set of circumstances. Both their vessels were part of a convoy of Army troops. When the convoy arrived at Donaldsonville, Louisiana, they landed a party of Army troops and began receiving sugar and other merchandise on board. It was later reported, by both Reigart and Francis, that a company of these troops had pillaged a large mansion and carried off wine, liquor, silver plates, and clothing belonging to ladies. Reigart and Francis had also seen these men get drunk on the wine and liquor.

Reigart was basically an honest person. He believed in law and order. He saw the reason for being in the South was to protect the laws of the United States. Pillaging and robbing the Southerners seemed to be against everything he had been fighting for. What was more, Reigart feared that the Navy would be considered accomplices since they were present and witnessed the pillaging. Reigart, disturbed by all of this, wrote to Commodore Henry Morris, the senior officer in the fleet, for explicit and written instructions relative to his duties as a convoy.

Morris told Reigart to consider it his first duty to cooperate with the Army, affording them all the aid and protection in his power in carrying on operations against the enemy. Reigart should patrol the river and disperse any enemy he came across. He should give convoy protection to merchant steamers and Army transports up and down the river when it did not interfere with his other duties.

Concerning the question of the soldiers on board Army transports pillaging on shore while engaged in their duties, Reigart was not on any account to withdraw his vessels and leave them unprotected and liable to

capture by the enemy. But Morris wanted Reigart to report all pillage, spec-
ifying the troops, the locality, the names of the owners of the houses so
pillaged, and any other pertinent details so that Morris could give General
Butler enough information to investigate and punish the responsible parties. Morris did not think that the mere presence of the gunboats would
implicate them in the lawless acts, but even if it did, the duty of protecting
the transports was paramount.

Reporting the pillaging to Butler was a touchy matter. Butler, himself, had been accused of pillaging in New Orleans. Some people said that
he had taken silver spoons from some of the wealthier households in that
city. Whether or not this fact was true, the rumors and the publicity that
they had received made General Butler extremely sensitive about the subject. Morris asked Reigart and Francis to confine themselves to a plain nar-
ration of the facts in their reports without using any "harsh" terms such as
brutal, outrageous, wanton, and malicious. Morris explained that it embarrassed him to report the pillaging to Butler, and this kind of language com-
plicated matters.

Roe had also written complaints about the pillaging directly to
General Butler. Reigart had known better. Ben Butler answered Roe: "The
acts of the troops pillaging (if true) are without palliation or excuse, certainly no more to be justified than this improper, bombastic, and ridiculous rodomontade (sic) of a sub-lieutenant of the Navy."

Reigart was on a regular patrol some time later. He was about ten
miles above Donaldsonville. The fog was so thick that he could not see
the other three ships in his division. Reigart was on the deck watching the
shore carefully because of the dense fog. Suddenly, the fog cleared, and
Reigart saw a large herd of cattle. Reigart hailed the cattle driver, shouting,
"Hello, there. This is the commander of the *Sciota*. Where are you going?"

Instead of replying, the men made efforts to escape. Reigart told his
men to fire over their heads, and if the men did not stop, to shoot them
down. In the meantime, he took a few of his men who were standing

nearby and personally led a landing party. The cattle drivers stopped, and Reigart and his men seized them and took them to the *Sciota*. The cattle drivers consisted of six men. The owner, a man named Clifton, produced a pass from Confederate General Richard Taylor. Upon interrogation, one of the other men said, "Well, there was no use of running when you commenced to shoot."

At this point, the other boats in the division had shown up. Lieutenant Commander George M. Ransom, Reigart's divisional commander, came on board the *Sciota*. Ransom questioned the men and learned that they were going to New Orleans. The naval division had no facilities for holding all six men, but they could not let them go. Therefore, Ransom, in consultation with his other commanders, decided to execute four of the men. The other two men were taken into custody.

The cattle were intended for Confederate camps. They were captured on Confederate soil with a pass from a Confederate commanding officer in their possession. Reigart knew that the capture of the cattle had been lawful and just. He also knew that he had only made the capture because the fog had helped him surprise the drivers who knew the *Sciota* patrolled the river.

Lieutenant Commander Ransom sent Francis Roe down to New Orleans to procure transports for the cattle. Roe returned with five transports provided by General Butler. Thirteen hundred head of wild but very heavy cattle were loaded onto the transports. About two hundred head had to be left on shore because they were too wild and unmanageable.

The transports began down river under convoy of the *Sciota*, *Kineo*, *Katahdin*, and *Itaska*. About two miles below Donaldsonville, the *Sciota* met up with seven pieces of artillery and nearly nine hundred infantrymen. The battery had been so skillfully concealed that Reigart had not seen it until he was right abreast of it. Fire against the boat was heavy, but the *Sciota* was moving so fast that it was out of range before firing more than three rounds. Reigart ordered the convoy to seek safety in flight. He then rounded and went back to engage with the enemy. Reigart had nearly silenced all the fire from the enemy when the *Kineo* came in and helped him to drive the remaining enemy to flight.

Reigart's executive officer, Lieutenant Charles H. Swazy, was mortally wounded during the battle; he was struck in the hip by a 12-pounder rifle shot. Reigart eulogized Swazy: "This officer was characterized by all the elements which make up the hero—brave, inbred with patriotic ardor and professional ambition, chivalric as a gentleman, gentle, and with a heart full of Christian principles. His last words were: 'Tell my mother that I tried to be a good man.'"

The convoy and the transports continued to New Orleans after the skirmish at Donaldsonville. Ransom put Reigart in charge of the convoy during this latter part of the trip. Reigart Lowry and Francis Roe continued to serve the southern Mississippi River during the rest of 1862. At Port Hudson, as at Vicksburg, the Mississippi River took a sharp turn. The east bank was quite high, and the west bank was very low. For these reasons, plus strong currents and shallow water, utmost skill was required to navigate through the waters. Reigart reconnoitered the batteries at Port Hudson and reported that the place was strongly fortified and by nature, the most formidable object on the river. The rebel fortifications appeared to be in such a position that the Union Navy, having passed or silenced one of the lower batteries, other concealed batteries would open, throwing a crossfire from batteries yet to be approached or silenced. This reconnaissance would prove invaluable a month later when the Union would make a successful attack on Port Hudson.

Toward the end of his assignment on the Mississippi, Reigart received a present that he would long cherish. A group of his friends in Philadelphia sent him a beautiful dress sword as a testament of their appreciation for the eminent services Reigart had performed during the Civil War. Reigart could not thank these men enough. He felt that the sword was so complementary to him and felt that the men had given it to him more out of friendship than because of his military record.

Reigart knew of nothing that was so much worth striving for, after his country's thanks, as the approval of those who knew him and watched him grow up since boyhood. The receipt of the sword from so many of his boyhood friends filled his heart with joy and helped him forget the dangers and hardships he had gone through.

Reigart laid aside his old battle sword, the gift of a good and noble mother, to wear and use the new sword. He asked the same blessing from it that he had received with the other and prayed to God to give him the continued resolution, courage, and fidelity to wield it with the same untarnished honor for his country and himself.

Reigart had been kept busy during the second half of 1862, convoying, patrolling, transporting, and blockading on the lower Mississippi River. During the period, he dealt with Francis Roe more than any other individual. Little did he realize that they would be brought together again eighteen years later.

As they sat in the New York Club lounge, Francis Roe asked Reigart, "I have heard that your version of Jim Jouett's heroism is not quite the same as his. Would you tell me your version so that I can relay it?"

"Of course," assured Reigart.

26.
THEY WOULD BUNGLE
THEIR WAY RIGHT
INTO HEROISM

------- • ◉ • -------

WHILE THE RESOURCES OF THE UNION NAVY HAD BEEN BUS-
ily setting up blockades on the east and west of the Confederacy, the
South—the Gulf of Mexico—had been neglected. Farragut and others had
entertained thoughts of setting up a blockade at Mobile, Alabama, but
delays set this project back time after time. In the meantime, Farragut did
take positive action in the western Gulf. He sent four vessels to Galveston,
Texas, in October 1862. Jim Jouett commanded the *Santee*, which was one
of the ships in this new division.

Reigart ordered another round of drinks for Francis Roe and himself as he began to tell of Jim Jouett's exploits. "You know," started Reigart
with a twinkle in his eye, "Jim Jouett and I tell this story the same way. I
just emphasize different parts." Reigart had heard the story many times as
he had come to Galveston only a short time after this one incident in Jim
Jouett's career on which Jouett made his claim to fame. He had heard the
story from Jim Jouett as well as other members of Jim's crew.

Jim Jouett decided one night to try to take the Confederate steamer,
General Rusk. He took two rowboats each filled with men and each armed

with a small howitzer. He took these boats past the forts and into the entrance of the harbor. Everything went fine until then, but now one disaster after another occurred, caused by the bungling of Jouett and his men. The result would be that they would bungle their way right into heroism.

First, Jouett's boat crashed upon the rocks. The second boat then crashed into Jouett's boat, smashing several of its oars. The racket alerted the Confederates. Jouett realized that he would never get to the *General Rusk* in time to capture her, so he directed his men to go for the *Royal Yacht* which was closer.

Jouett ordered the men in the second rowboat to board the *Royal Yacht* while he went around to the other side. One man had boarded from Jouett's boat when Jouett fired his howitzer. The recoil of the gun pushed the launch away, and the rapid tide carried the boat further away. Jouett's other boat had not gotten close enough to board and had also drifted downstream. The men in the second launch spotted Jouett's boat, mistook it for the enemy, and opened fire with her muskets, killing Jouett's pilot. The second launch then turned tail and fled, to be seen no more that night.

By this time, several other naval officers who were in the lounge at the New York Club had heard Reigart telling the Jim Jouett story. Most of these men knew both Reigart and Jim and were familiar with the story. Somehow, Reigart's version of the story, even though he used the same facts, always turned out to be more interesting and amusing than Jim Jouett's version. Jouett always made himself the great hero, and most of the men were bored with Jouett's vanity. As Reigart continued to tell the story, all these old sea captains and commanders were doubled over with laughter at Jouett's blundering.

Jouett next took his boat alongside the *Royal Yacht* and led his men on board. There was a lively fight on the deck and several men were killed and wounded on both sides. By this time, the Confederate batteries on shore began firing and the Confederates on board the ship sought safety below. One of the last men turned before going below and rammed a boarding pike through the muscle in Jim Jouett's arm and through his right side, piercing his lung and pinning him against the mast. The Confederate and Jouett then struggled. Jim Jouett tore himself free from the mast and the boarding pike broke, leaving a piece about a foot long protruding from his body. The Confederate ducked below. Jouett wrenched the pike from his body, and as the blood began to gush out of his body, he stuffed a piece of his shirt into the wound.

As Jouett struggled to his feet, he found that he was alone on the ship. His last man was just going over the side into the launch, presuming Jouett to be dead. Jouett leaped over the side of the *Royal Yacht* into his launch which was leaving, and pointing a gun at his own men, led them back aboard the *Royal Yacht*.

Reigart had the men convulsing by this time with his antics as he held his side and pretended to point a gun at the men. He staggered around the lounge, imitating a wounded Jouett. The men loved it. "What happened next?" one of them shouted, urging Reigart to continue.

Reigart resumed. He knew that Jouett exaggerated this part of the story, but he told it that way, too, because it made a better story. Jouett led his men back onto the vessel to the forward hatch. Jouett looked down the hatch and demanded that the Confederates surrender. When they refused, Jouett led his men down the hatch to another hand-to-hand fight. Reigart's imitation of Jouett, fighting with his one good hand, set the men to laughing again.

The Confederates finally agreed to surrender, but when Jouett looked around him, all his men were gone again. Reigart looked at his listeners, and pretending they were the Confederates and he as Jouett, said, "Wait here a minute, gentleman. A near mortally wounded man like me could easily handle all of you, but I'm going on deck to see where all my men are off to." Reigart went running across the lounge, holding his right side, and moaning and groaning all the way. When he got to the bar, he pretended it was the rail of the *Royal Yacht*. He pretended to look off into the horizon for the launch and upon spotting it, he shouted "Come back, you cowards. I, the great Jim Jouett, though about to drop dead from a terrible wound, have captured this ship single-handedly. Are you men going back to the *Santee* to tell them you deserted me after the ship was captured?"

Jouett's men finally came back, and Jouett once again called down the hatch and ordered the Confederates to come up. When they refused, Jouett threatened to drop a shell with a lit fuse down the hatch. The men came up. They were put in the launch and safely secured. Jouett then set fire to the *Royal Yacht*. Reigart, pretending to be Jim Jouett, attempted to light a match without success. It was rather difficult since he was only using his left hand. In fact, Jouett did light a fire on the *Royal Yacht*, and in fact, it was a poor one. As soon as Jouett and his men left, Confederates boarded the *Royal Yacht* and easily extinguished the fire. Jouett and his men returned to the *Santee*, but their launch was almost destroyed as they passed through the breaking waves. Jouett was taken aboard and received immediate attention from the surgeon, having had gaping wounds in his body for over three hours.

Reigart concluded his story by collapsing in his chair to the applause of all the men in the lounge. "Reigart," an admiring Francis Roe said, "I wish you could tell that story to Congress the way you told it here. Jim Jouett would be laughed right out of there."

"Yes," Reigart sighed, "but I suppose we would never get away with it."

27.
A STRANGE SAIL HAD BEEN SIGHTED TO THE SOUTHEAST

————•◉•————

REIGART HAD GONE TO GALVESTON SHORTLY AFTER THE Jouett incident. Before Reigart arrived, the area had at first been controlled by the Union. In December 1862, Major General John B. Magruder, Confederate States Army, secretly surveyed the Union position and formulated a plan for recapture. Early on New Year's morning, 1863, Magruder attacked; violent fighting on land and sea ensued. A few hours later, when the battle had ended and the smoke had cleared, the Confederates had gained control of Galveston and had captured the *Harriet Lane*, the Union's largest and most powerful ship in that port. Union Army troops under General Isaac S. Burrell surrendered.

Three of the Union vessels escaped. Magruder claimed that they had escaped under a flag of truce. Magruder was doubly bitter because he had felt that original Union control had come under another false use of a flag of truce. The Union officers disagreed with Magruder. They admitted that flags of truce had been raised. While the flags were raised, the situation was supposed to remain status quo, but the Confederates were accused (by the Union leaders) for improving their position. They continued shooting for ten to fifteen minutes, made prisoners of men on shore, moved their artillery into a better position, and towed the *Harriet Lane* to the wharf. This, combined with the complete unacceptability of the surrender terms, led to the decision for the Union to lower the flags and retreat.

The defeat at Galveston sent shock waves through the Navy. Farragut and Welles were stunned. Farragut immediately sent eager Commodore Henry H. Bell, commanding the *Brooklyn*, to Galveston to reestablish the blockade. Bell took with him three other vessels, including Reigart's *Sciota*.

The day after the new division's arrival, Magruder sent a boat out to Commodore Bell under a flag of truce. Bell sent a cutter out to meet it and to bring it to him. Bell received on board Major Eustis of General Magruder's staff and Captain McGreal, both of Confederate States Army. Bell offered these gentlemen wine, cigars, and newspapers while he sent for Lieutenant Commanders Reigart Lowry and Chester Hatfield. Upon arrival of these latter two officers, the meeting began. The Confederate officers brought a letter from General Magruder to Commodore Bell, protesting the Union violations of the flag of truce on January 1. Magruder claimed that all but one Union vessel left its assigned area before the time agreed in the truce. He asked Bell if the white flag was to be recognized and respected as a flag of truce.

Reigart and Hatfield, swapped stories with Confederate officers while Bell drafted a reply. The atmosphere was congenial, though each side tried to out-brag the other. Bell finally came back with his reply that said that he had never violated the flag of truce and had no intention to if the other side respected and observed it.

The next day, these men who had talked so freely and been so friendly fought each other. Bell moved his fleet in and attacked. During the shelling, Reigart concentrated his vessel's fire on the *Harriet Lane*, a ship he had served with earlier in the war. Twice during his barrage of fire, the Confederates had to move the *Harriet Lane* because he was coming too close.

The next afternoon, Bell called all his commanders together for a conference. The topic of the meeting was what to do next. Should they attack? Should they only blockade? Bell only had one reliable pilot, a small force, and treacherous waters. While all his commanders were ready and willing to attack Galveston again, a few had reservations. Reigart spoke for most of the men when he said, "My biggest fear is that we might ground a few ships. If this happens, the North will suffer a grievous loss. It might be better to only blockade and not to risk another defeat until we have more strength." Bell reluctantly gave up the idea of recapturing the city, though he would maintain his blockade.

As this conference began, it had been interrupted when a strange sail had been sighted to the southeast. Bell sent the newly arrived *Hatteras* out to investigate, and the meeting continued. The stranger lured the *Hatteras* about twenty miles from the other vessels. In the meantime, the meeting had ended, and all the commanders returned to their vessels. At about 7:30 p.m., Reigart looked off toward the *Hatteras* and saw distant flashes and heard heavy incessant firing.

Reigart headed the *Sciota* to the southeast and was soon followed by the *Brooklyn* and *Cayuga*. After he had gone out about twenty-three miles, Reigart tried to calculate the distance from the firing by the clashes and booms. The firing was so incessant, however, that this proved to be impossible. Reigart's best guess was that the fighting was about fifteen to twenty miles further away. By 10:00 p.m., the firing had stopped and Reigart had lost sight of the *Brooklyn* and *Cayuga*. Reigart took his ship to the west and discovering nothing, he returned north to the Galveston blockade.

The next morning, Reigart set out again to see what he could find. A few hours later, he came across a white five-oared boat, manned by five men and steered by Acting Master Partridge. Reigart ordered his men to help these other men aboard. Partridge told Reigart that they belonged to the *Hatteras*. They had an amazing story to tell.

28.
WE ARE THE CONFEDERATE STEAMER ALABAMA

———— • ◎ • ————

THE *HATTERAS* HAD CHASED THE STRANGE SHIP THAT HAD been acting suspiciously. At dusk, they lost sight of her, but suddenly, after 7:00 p.m., they had come upon her. Lieutenant Commander Homer C. Blake, an Annapolis classmate of Reigart's and a dear friend, commanded the *Hatteras*. When the *Hatteras* had come alongside the strange ship, Homer Blake hailed the stranger, shouting, "What steamer is that?"

A voice from the other ship answered, "Her Britannic Majesty's steamer, *Spitfire!*"

Homer Blake announced, "Thank you. I will send a boat on board of you." A boat was lowered and manned with sailors under Acting Master Partridge.

As the launch left the *Hatteras*, the strange craft again replied, "We are the Confederate steamer, *Alabama*."

At that moment, from about fifty yards, the *Alabama* opened fire on the *Hatteras*. Both vessels steamed ahead, side by side, hotly engaged with each other. During the next thirteen minutes, fifty shots were fired from the *Hatteras* and a greater number from the *Alabama*. The Confederates tried boarding the *Hatteras* but without success. They tried a second boarding, and this time they were successful. Cheers rose from the *Alabama*, and in a few minutes all was silent. The crew of the *Hatteras* was taken to the *Alabama*, and the *Hatteras* was sunk. The crew of the *Alabama* had forgotten about the men in the rowboat and left them.

Reigart was concerned about his friend, Homer Blake, but he would later learn that Homer and the others had been taken to Jamaica where they were released. After talking to the men in the small boat, Reigart went out to look for the *Brooklyn*. When he found her, Reigart saw that Commodore Bell had come across the sunken hulk of the *Hatteras*.

While stationed at Galveston, the *Sciota* ran low on oil, and her crew ran low on money. Reigart registered a complaint with Rear Admiral Farragut. Concerning these problems, Farragut answered that oil should have been taken on before Reigart's departure from New Orleans. As for money, Farragut said that the *Sciota* crew would "have to do as others are doing," and that there was more reason in their case since they could not spend it where they were.

Reigart wrote back to Farragut to strengthen his stand and to once again complain about the supply of oil and money. Reigart explained to Farragut that he had left New Orleans in quite a hurry and that he had made every effort to get oil before he left. As for money, Reigart was sorry to say that he could "not do as others are doing for the reason that all the others had money to pay for their grog and rations." His crew had not had a cent paid to them for five months. They had had several opportunities to purchase supplies and spend money, and many of the men had families who relied on part of this money. Farragut finally came through with some oil and money, but it would be some time before the men would receive all the back pay that was due to them.

Later in January 1863, another Confederate boat came out under a flag of truce. Again, it was a messenger from General Magruder. The general sent a verbal message that he would parole the crew of the *Harriet Lane* if Commodore Bell would provide them with transportation north.

Reigart was present during the entire meeting. The Confederate officers brought with them a package of letters written by the crew of the *Harriet Lane* and some rebel officers to relatives in the North. Reigart read the letters and then arranged for their delivery. The Confederates left with assurances from Bell that passage would be provided for the crew of the *Harriet Lane*.

Reigart spent the next several months patrolling and blockading the entire coast of Texas. Galveston gave the Union several serious setbacks during the early months of 1863. First, the city had fallen to Magruder, and then the *Hatteras* had been sunk by the notorious *Alabama*. The Union came back, and although it did not reoccupy the city of Galveston, it did successfully resume the blockade of the Western Gulf region. The issue of the flags of truce used by Magruder, while at no time a proven charge against the North, became overshadowed by the arrival of the *Alabama*. The *Alabama* falsely flew the British flag, and this issue would rage unsettled for a decade.

On May 1, Reigart was sent back north after having served actively in the war for over two years. On his trip home, Reigart prepared a plan for manning seacoast defenses with naval officers and seamen who were not being employed at sea. Reigart pointed out how successfully this had been used by the Confederates, but Gideon Welles told Reigart that these fortresses came under the control of the Army. Therefore, that force would do any manning of these works.

29.
CAN YOU NOT SEND LOWRY DOWN HERE?

━━•◉•━━

WHEN REIGART LEFT THE NEW YORK CLUB, HE WAS UPSET. HE had defeated Jouett once, but Reigart did not know whether he could muster enough support to defeat Jouett again. There were now only fourteen captains senior to Jouett, after the promotions of Stephen Quackenbush and Earl English. Reigart knew he could enlist the help of Stephen and Earl, but their support would not be as enthusiastic as it had been prior to their own promotions. Jouett was no longer jumping over their heads and was no longer a direct threat to them.

Reigart knew he could count on Francis Roe whom he had just left. Reigart also knew that his support would be strongest from the men at the top of the list. These men were due for promotion the soonest and would feel the impact of Jouett's promotion the most. These men were up for promotions during the next several months. If Jouett jumped over their heads, their promotions might be pushed back a few months. A position these men had dreamed of all their lives, commodore in the United States Navy, was in sight without Jouett. With Jouett, it became still a dream and a hope. Reigart was affected the most directly; he was now at the top of the list. There was a spot now open, and it was rightfully his. If the President or Secretary of the Navy delayed Reigart's promotion, a Jouett victory in

Congress might give Jim Jouett Reigart's own position! Reigart fumed when he thought of this possibility. He had been actively fighting corruption for a decade. If, now, Jouett might take his spot, this would be too much for Reigart.

As Reigart walked home, he decided that he would enlist the support of only the first five of the captains. As these men were most threatened, they would be most willing to help. These men had been active before, and Reigart knew he could count on their help. This way, he could avoid the tremendous chore of trying to bring all fourteen men together again, unless it became necessary.

Reigart had only three men to contact. He was now number one and Francis Roe was number three. John Upshur was number two; Reigart's boyhood friend, Sam Franklin, was number four; and Bill Whiting was number five. Reigart decided to contact John, Sam, and Bill the next day to enlist their support.

The following morning, Reigart arose early to go out and find his friends. He soon learned that John Upshur and Bill Whiting were in New York and sent word to them to come to the New York Club. Sam Franklin was in Philadelphia, so Reigart wired him, asking Sam to come to New York at his earliest convenience. Francis Roe was in New York and Reigart let him know about the coming meeting at the New York Club. After sending these messages, Reigart went straight to the New York Club to wait for the other men.

He went into the lounge and secured the usual corner table for the meeting. Francis was the first to show up. Reigart told Francis about his idea to enlist the support of the top five captains to carry the burden of this latest fight with Jouett. Francis concurred. When John Upshur and Bill Whiting arrived, Reigart and Francis told them about Jim Jouett's latest maneuver. "If Jouett gets this Vote of Thanks from Congress," Reigart cautioned his friends, "it will directly affect every one of us. Everything we fought and stood for before still stands. Our careers are at stake now.

Others will follow if Jouett is successful. Then the whole Navy will be at stake. I suggest that you all contact the men you know in Congress and try to learn all you can about Jouett's progress. We'll meet back here in two weeks, and once a month after that until we defeat him for good."

John Upshur spoke up, raising his glass of bourbon. "I propose a toast to the success of our mission and to the defeat of Jouett's dastardly plans."

"Aye, aye," all the men chimed in.

The four men finished their drinks. Reigart told them that he would bring Sam Franklin up to date about the meeting, and the four men parted.

When Reigart returned to the Coleman house, he found a telegram waiting for him. He opened it. He had been promoted to commodore! Reigart could not believe his eyes. This was the moment he had been waiting for all his life—Commodore Reigart Bolivar Lowry. It hardly seemed real. Reigart did not feel any different than he did when he had been a captain only a moment before, but he did know that he felt good. He wished that he could share this good news with his family, but that was impossible since Bess had divorced him several months before.

Reigart knew that his friends had all left the New York Club when he had and that there was no sense in going back there. His friends? What would they think? He knew that they would be happy for him, but they would wonder about his desire to continue against Jouett. Reigart knew that his hatred for Jouett would not subside. Reigart had been fighting men like Jouett for several years and was not about to be stopped now. He would continue to work with the captains if they needed him.

Reigart was lonely. He had no one with whom to celebrate his good fortune. His former family was in Erie, and his friends had left the club for the night. Reigart decided to round up his fellow boarders at the Coleman House and throw a party none of them would ever forget. The boarders were glad to celebrate with Reigart, and his party lasted far into the night.

Reigart soon learned that he did still have a great number of friends. Word of his promotion spread quickly, and Reigart began to receive letters and telegrams from all over. One that thrilled Reigart was from his old friend Ben Butler. Ben and Reigart had become good friends over the years. They were complete opposites in many ways, alike in others. Few would have thought that these two men could have become friends, but they had.

Their first contact had not been a pleasant one. Ben had ordered Reigart to cook breakfast for Army troops. Reigart had not liked Ben's tone or style and let him know about it. Ben had liked Reigart's spunk. Ben might have tried to destroy Reigart had he wished, but the two men hit it off. When Ben saw Reigart in action, he admired Reigart even more. Reigart had landed Ben's troops quickly and efficiently and performed excellently before the general.

Had Hatteras been their only contact, their friendship may have become only a memory, but these men met again during 1862 on the lower Mississippi River. Reigart had played an active role in New Orleans, and Ben had heard of his exploits. Ben led the Army into New Orleans and occupied that city. Ben and Reigart would have much contact during 1862 as Reigart convoyed, transported, and provided Ben's troops with any other support he could offer.

It was during this period when Ben acquired a reputation which made Ben's and Reigart's friendship even stranger. Ben became known as "Beast Butler" and "Spoons Butler." While occupying New Orleans, Ben issued an order stating that any woman who insulted or showed contempt for his soldiers would be "regarded and held liable to be treated as a woman of the town plying her avocation." Confederate President, Jefferson Davis, declared Ben "an enemy of mankind." Women volunteered to spin the cord to hang Butler, and their daughters asked to be allowed to adjust it around his neck. Ben, as a Congressman, would later lead the prosecution at the Impeachment trial of Andrew Johnson.

Ben, hated by so many, had made a friend in Reigart during 1861 and 1862. After Reigart returned north in 1863, he performed several assignments in Philadelphia and Washington. In Washington, Reigart served on a board reviewing naval regulations. Reigart's year in the North was briefly interrupted in the spring of 1864. On May 1, Ben Butler sent a telegram to Captain Gustavus V. Fox, Assistant Secretary of the Navy: "Can you not send Lowry down here? Let him report to me since the Navy gunboats are going to aid the Army."

Butler was preparing for an expedition against Richmond. The plan was for Grant to come down from the North and for Butler to go up from the South, along the James River. The two men would join forces and capture Richmond.

Reigart gladly joined Ben to head up the transport fleet for Ben's Army. During his time there, Reigart helped Ben's forces fight back the Confederate troops at Drewry's Bluff. In the end, though, Butler's drive was not quite as successful as had been hoped. He stopped at Bermuda Hundred, just a few miles below Richmond. Though Richmond was not taken during this drive, this was an important part of the entire Richmond mission. Reigart had played his part, and he returned home.

Reigart was pleased to hear congratulations from his friend, Ben, now that Reigart had become a commodore. He began to answer all his friends who had written or wired him since his promotion.

He also began to prepare for the next meeting of the captains at the New York Club.

30.
CATECHISM OF SEAMANSHIP AND GUNNERY

———•○•———

WHEN REIGART ARRIVED AT THE NEW YORK CLUB FOR THE next meeting, he found two of the captains already there. John Upshur and Bill Whiting had come early to congratulate their good friend on his promotion. John and Bill greeted Reigart with warm handshakes and embraces. One of their men had made it. It was particularly significant that Reigart got his promotion. Of all the captains, Reigart had been the most outspoken critic of the corrupt Republican administrations. If the President and Secretary of the Navy could not prevent or delay Reigart's promotion, perhaps the seniority system would survive.

"Well, how does it feel, Commodore?" John Upshur inquired, proud of Reigart but a little bit jealous.

"It feels great," beamed Reigart. "It has taken forty years to get this promotion, and I plan to enjoy it." Reigart had not gotten used to being called Commodore, and he still felt a little uncomfortable when John used the new title.

The men moved back into the lounge and settled down at their usual table. These three men—Reigart Lowry, John Upshur, and Bill Whiting—all had a great deal in common. As well as being close to each other in seniority, these men had been great naval educators. All of them had joined the Navy in a training program and had graduated from Annapolis. Reigart had later taught on several receiving ships, including the *North Carolina* where he had started. John Upshur had taught at the Naval Academy. Reigart's greatest contribution to naval education came during the last year of the Civil War, and both John Upshur and Bill Whiting played a role.

The Navy had played a critical part in the Civil War, but it had done so by tremendous expansion. The blockade extended 3,549 miles from Virginia to Texas. Nearly 200 harbors, river mouths, and inlets had to be guarded. The Navy patrolled 3,615 miles of the Mississippi River and its tributaries and about 2,000 miles of other rivers, sounds, bayous, and inlets along the Atlantic and Gulf coasts.

To work the blockade, the Union increased its number of ships from 90 to 670. To man the ships, the number of seamen went from 7,500 to 51,500, and the ranks of naval officers increased from 1,300 to 6,700.

This rapid expansion of officers and men proved to be a real problem for those who wanted to maintain a professional Navy. While Reigart had been in Washington serving on the Naval Board on Regulations, Secretary of the Navy Gideon Welles had noticed him. Welles asked Reigart to develop a new system in naval education. The purpose of this new apprentice system would be to recruit young men who were desirous of becoming naval officers but who lacked the education required for the positions. The education not only encompassed the maritime knowledge required for a midshipman, but also reading, writing, and arithmetic.

Reigart was given charge of the first group of apprentices on board the *Sabine*. He much preferred his new setup to that which he had encountered on the *North Carolina*. There was not only far more class time on the *Sabine* but also actual cruises enabled the seamen to put their book learning into practice. As the program progressed, Reigart used his more advanced students to aid him in the classroom. This apprentice system worked so well that it was continued for several years after the Civil War and prepared many young men for the Naval Academy.

The base from which the *Sabine* operated was New London, Connecticut. The first recruits assembled there during the summer of 1864. Three hundred bright-eyed sailors, representing all the states of the Union, became pioneers in this new program. Reigart called them all on deck on the first day of class. He introduced himself and his executive officer, Bob Mauly. After discussing the school and its rules with his students, Reigart began the first class.

Because of his good training background, Reigart wrote his own textbook for his students. He called it *Catechism of Seamanship and Gunnery*. Reigart started his first class by asking, "What is a ship?"

The boys all looked at each other, and a few tried to answer the question. It sounded like a simple question, but when none of the recruits had been able to answer it, Reigart told the boys, "A ship is a vessel which has three masts and carries square sails on all three of them." He continued by explaining the differences between a ship, a barque, a schooner, a sloop, a brigantine, a barkentine, and a topsail schooner.

In later classes, Reigart would teach the boys about the various parts of vessels: the hold, fore, aft, port, starboard, and various decks. As the classes progressed, the terms became more specialized and more difficult. The apprentices learned about knots, ropes, blocks, tackle, sails, masts, and yards. As he taught them about specific parts of the vessels, Reigart took his students to the part of the ship and showed them what he was talking about.

Everyone soon settled into the daily routine. The men and boys were awakened each morning by a piping. During the day, they swarmed upon the rigging, worked, and played. Some learned weaponry, practicing with swords and rifles, fencing, drilling, and target firing, while others attended the various classes.

After dinner, the boys wrote letters, read in the library, or attended jam sessions where they swapped stories and sang sea chanties. Reigart was always welcomed at these gatherings since he could tell a story as well as any man. He was a hero to these boys. He had had an exciting career, and many of his exploits during the then present Civil War had been written up in newspapers all over the Union.

While primarily stationed at New London, the *Sabine* made frequent cruises along the Atlantic coast from Maine to the Capes of Delaware. These cruises enabled the boys to put their training to practical use. During one of these cruises, while the *Sabine* was in Portland, a calamity took place. Several houses caught fire and completely burned down. The people of Portland had been kind to the crew of the *Sabine*, so Reigart and his students donated $308 to help the poor people who had been made homeless.

The *Sabine* spent part of the first year of the apprentice program in the Union blockade off Virginia. Looking for blockade runners gave Reigart's students training which could not be had any other way.

In all, Reigart headed up the apprentice system for nearly four years. During this period, he was promoted to the rank of Commander. By the end of his term, Reigart had made the new apprentice system workable and successful. When he left, Reigart transferred his boys to John Upshur on the *Saratoga* who would take over the school. John Upshur and Bill Whiting would run this school on the *Saratoga* for the next three years.

As Reigart, John, and Bill celebrated Reigart's promotion, they talked about the apprentice system. They were all proud of their contributions to this program.

31.
DRUNKENNESS, BRAWLING, AND GENERAL MISCONDUCT WERE OTHER COMMON PROBLEMS

—•◦•—

AFTER REIGART TRANSFERRED THE SCHOOL TO JOHN UPSHUR, he took command of the USS *Severn*. This command would be a big let-down for Reigart. The next year would probably be the most boring year of Reigart's active duty. The *Severn* was in poor condition, and its crew was insufficient to handle her. The war was over. The Navy's duties became routine again. Reigart became bogged down with administrative details in his daily work.

Paperwork and interpretation of naval regulations took a great deal of Reigart's time. Once there was a disagreement concerning who got which room on the *Severn*. The matter went all the way up to the Navy Department. The solution seemed simple. The ordnance and navigation officer being the same person would occupy but one room, thus leaving a vacant room. In the forward wardroom, the two engineers would occupy the room on the port side, while the two ensigns would occupy the room on the starboard side. This was the ridiculous kind of minuscule detail that kept Reigart and the Navy Department busy.

Details concerning the crew took most of Reigart's time. The *Severn* never had a full crew. The *Severn* had four boilers and thirty furnaces. Reigart only had enough men to man one boiler and nine furnaces. Reigart often asked the department how he should distribute his work.

The crew was temporary in nature, mostly young seamen who needed discipline and training. At one point, Reigart transferred his entire crew to another vessel and received a new crew himself. Some of the boys coming to the *Severn* were apprentices from the US Training Ship *Saratoga*, under John Upshur who had taken over Reigart's training program.

Deserters were a problem. Morale was low, and many boys wanted to leave. In September 1869, Reigart advertised Mate Albert C. Smith as a deserter from the *Severn* and offered a reward of fifty dollars for his apprehension. Another time, when anchored at Hampton Roads, Virginia, Reigart sent his executive officer ashore for coal. Several men were granted permission to go ashore with the executive officer. When the men landed ashore, the executive officer directed them all to meet at a certain time, and they would return together. But when the launch returned to the ship, Mate Myers and Paymaster's Clerk Coleman were not aboard. When these men had not returned by the following morning, Reigart decided he could not waste any more time and so he left with his ship for Key West, Florida. Mate Myers caught up the next day, but Paymaster's Clerk Coleman never returned.

Reigart also encountered insubordination on board the *Severn*. He reported Lieutenant E. L. Amory for general inattention, neglect of duty, and disrespect. There were a variety of reasons. One took place when Reigart asked Amory to take charge of the usual ceremonies when Admiral Charles Poor was about to leave the ship. A half hour later, when Reigart came onto the gangway with the admiral, Reigart found only half the normal complement of boys there, and three of the four boys were not in the proper uniform. Then Reigart asked Lieutenant Amory why the gangway was not properly attended, Amory replied that he had passed the order and could do no more. Amory often bothered Reigart about small details. Reigart felt that Amory's manner was improper, defiant, and tended to create insubordination on the vessel. Reigart reported Amory to the Navy Department for general inattention and want in zeal in the execution of his duty and relieved Amory from duty.

Drunkenness, brawling, and general misconduct were other common problems. One night, Mate W. S. Baldwin came on board the *Severn* in a state of intoxication, created a disturbance, behaving in a violent and scandalous manner. Reigart was forced to report Baldwin to the Secretary of the Navy for conduct unbecoming an officer. In another case, Reigart reported Patrick Connolly for violently assaulting and beating his superior officer, William Wills, machinist, breaking Wills's arm and disabling him for several weeks. In still another instance, Reigart reported Mate G. M. Bowers for ungentleman-like and ruffian conduct. Bowers had assaulted Admiral's Clerk, James J. Farrell, striking him several times, drawing blood, and had to be removed by force.

Because Admiral Poor used the *Severn* as his flagship, there was a band on board, and even this, at times, caused problems. Reigart found that one of the musicians, Antonio Poreti, had steadily refused to play any instrument since he had been on board the *Severn*, alleging that he could not play and did not understand a note of music. As Poreti was Italian and did not speak a word of English, Reigart considered him useless and recommended that Poreti be discharged without pay as a fraudulent enlistment. Reigart also informed the department that Poreti had been enlisted on the *Vermont* where he supposed that Poreti's qualifications as a musician had been examined.

Fortunately, all was not bad. Every once in a while, Reigart had the opportunity to praise those in his command. When new young officers completed six months of duty, it was Reigart's responsibility to send an appraisal to the Navy Department. In May 1870, he submitted such an appraisal for J. C. Chevalier: "It gives me great pleasure to testify to the ability and zeal of Mr. Chevalier in the performance of his duty (sail maker), and speak in high terms of his officer-like deportment and correct moral conduct while under my command, and I recommend him to the Navy Department as in every way worthy to receive his warrant as a sail-maker in the US Navy."

Reigart's men were well trained, and in time of crisis, they reacted with speed and effectiveness. One afternoon, while the *Severn* laid at anchor in Key West, the US Iron Clad *Terror* that was entering the Harbor, collided with her, causing considerable damage. During the emergency of a few minutes, Ensign Leutze and Mate Sylvester Poole displayed cool energy and promptness. Several officers and men had been forward of the gun deck when the collision seemed inevitable. They all left except for Leutze and Poole, who with the Ship's Cook released twenty fathoms of chain down alongside the ship at the very moment of collision. Reigart believed this action saved his ship from being sunk.

During this period, there were a few attempts at innovation. Even though there had been steam vessels as early as 1809, the Navy had been slow in implementing steam into its ships. The introduction of ironclad and iron-sided vessels during the Civil War had forced the increased use of steam. Sail power was no longer sufficient to move the heavier ships.

The *Severn* was a steam vessel, and Reigart was charged with testing this steam power with various types of screw propellers. He also tested the speeds the *Severn* could make under different heads of steam. In one of his reports, Reigart reported that he was confident that under fifty-five or sixty revolutions, the *Severn* was one of the fastest ships in the world. He praised the two-bladed screws over the four-bladed ones. It propelled the ship at least as fast and retarded it less. At one point, the *Severn* reached fifteen knots. On these voyages, as on all voyages, Reigart was on the bridge day and night. At the end of a trip, he would be exhausted, and it would take him a couple of days to recuperate.

The fact that the *Severn* carried Admiral Poor's flag meant that Poor was on Reigart's ship. Having one man as commander of a ship with a higher-ranking officer on board always led to conflict. For Reigart, it was no exception. On March 13, 1870, Poor directed Reigart not to leave the *Severn* without his permission and to always report his return. Reigart felt humiliated and annoyed that he had to ask permission every time he wished to go over the side.

Reigart decided to appeal to the Secretary of the Navy to decide whether the commander of a flagship, alone of all other commanders in a fleet, had to report every time he left the ship or returned. Reigart was angered by the fact that Admiral Poor required that either the commander or the executive officer be always on board. Reigart knew that this was in violation of naval regulations. Reigart considered Poor's orders oppressive and unusual. To avoid the humiliation of having to ask permission before going over the side, Reigart decided not to leave the ship until the Secretary of the Navy settled the question. Reigart wrote his request to the Secretary of the Navy on April 14. He wrote again on June 8, informing the Secretary that the letter remained unanswered. On July 19, his original letter still being unanswered and Reigart still being on the ship, he wrote one more plea for a reply.

In the meantime, Reigart had asked to be relieved of his command of the *Severn*. Among the trivial clerical work, Admiral Poor's oppressiveness, and the political situation, Reigart had many reasons for this request. Reigart was finally detached on August 29, 1870. He had commanded the vessel for one year and three days. He had not left the ship for the last four and a half months.

Reigart was now free to play a more active role in politics. He had always had deep political feelings. He was a Northern Democrat in a land of Republicans. His Commander-in-Chief and his Secretary of the Navy were both Republicans. Reigart disagreed with their political views, but even more, he disagreed with their corrupt behavior. Reigart knew he could speak more freely about them if he were not on active duty.

32.
A FIRST-CLASS PILOT, A RELIABLE, ENERGETIC AND TRUSTWORTHY MAN, AND AN EARNEST, THOROUGH, HARD-WORKING REPUBLICAN

FRANCIS ROE AND SAM FRANKLIN SOON JOINED JOHN UPSHUR, Bill Whiting, and Reigart in the lounge. This was the first meeting in which all five men had participated. Reigart had brought Sam up to date about the last meeting. Francis and Sam congratulated Reigart on his recent promotion to commodore. Once the social amenities were over, Reigart called the men to order.

"Gentlemen, let's get started. I must admit that when I suggested that there be a committee of five senior captains, I never thought that it would turn into four captains so soon."

"Reigart," John Upshur interceded, "May I ask you a question?"

"Of course," Reigart said, faintly smiling and knowing full well what John was about to ask.

"Now that you have been made Commodore," John began, "you no longer have a direct stake in Jouett's promotion."

"That is where you are wrong, sir," Reigart admonished. "You, I, and all the country have a stake in Jouett's promotion. This may seem like a small matter to many, but it represents the worst instinct of man—greed. Greed leads to more greed. Men like Grant and Robeson are the ultimate result."

"Well," John continued, "We were hoping you still felt that way. Will you continue to lead us in our fight against Jouett?"

"I have been fighting corruption for ten years," Reigart stated. "I'm not about to stop now. I'm in this Jouett thing until the finish. If you would like to choose a new leader, feel free. I'll still work with you."

John Upshur looked around the table at the other men. Each one of them nodded affirmatively. John turned to Reigart saying, "Well, I guess it's settled. You were our leader when only number three on the list. You are still welcome to be our leader even as a commodore."

Reigart was pleased that he retained these men's confidence. He continued the meeting. The men had all talked to contacts in government. Jouett was still trying to get his Vote of Thanks. The best that the men could figure showed that Jouett was still short of the required number of votes. Congress knew that the captains were organized, and this was having its effect. The men knew that if they disbanded, Jouett would become a shoe-in. They also knew that they had to remain in constant touch with as many members of Congress as possible to keep the Congressmen aware of the opposition to Jouett.

The meeting adjourned, and the men went their separate ways. Reigart still had been given no command. The Navy had nothing to offer, even to a high-ranking officer like himself. Therefore, Reigart decided to spend some of his free time in Washington meeting with politicians. During the past decade, Reigart had played an active role in politics, and he had many friends whom he had helped place in office.

Reigart had always had an interest in politics. After he left the *Severn*, Reigart had become an outspoken critic of the Republican Party right up to the President himself. Being a colorful, high-ranking naval officer, Reigart was a popular stumper and could often be found as the main speaker at public meetings. Reigart became especially critical of the scandals and corruption that pervaded the Grant administration.

Reigart had been promoted to Captain during this period. After eighteen months of politicking and lack of duty, Reigart had been reassigned to teaching duty. He went to Boston to take command of the US Receiving Ship *Ohio*. Reigart was restless, though. The *Ohio*, being a Receiving Ship, just received and trained new recruits. This command would be worse than the *Severn*. Not only would he be plagued by administrative details but the *Ohio* never even left the harbor.

Reigart and Bess had been living in New London since 1865 when Reigart commanded the *Sabine* there. The term of the commandant of the Navy Yard at New London would expire in a few months, and Reigart decided to try to obtain it. Reigart had been trying to get this appointment since he had left the *Severn* in 1870, but the Navy had been slow to react. Since Reigart felt that politics was impairing his chances for the command, he wrote to his old friend, Ben Butler, who was then in Congress from Massachusetts. Ben agreed to investigate the matter for Reigart. Reigart told Ben that he felt confident that the people in New London would prefer him over the other applicants. When the present commandant, John Upshur, was detached, it finally looked as if Reigart would get the post.

The Secretary of the Navy issued Reigart orders to report to New London. But two weeks before Reigart's term began, the orders were revoked. This was the beginning of a harassment that would never end during Reigart's life. The Secretary told Reigart that the orders had been revoked because the people of New London had asked for it. This really hurt a man who only a year before had thought that the people in New London would prefer him at that station. It had not been all the people who had wanted Reigart out of New London. It had been a few Republican people whom Reigart had alienated during his political activities of the past couple of years. They had requested from Robeson that a good Republican be placed in command of the New London station, and Robeson, of course, was happy to comply. This was Robeson's first move against Reigart. It would not be his last.

Secretary Robeson soon found a way to get Reigart out of his hair for a couple of years. Robeson transferred Reigart to the Treasury Department for duty as a Lighthouse Inspector in the Fourth Lighthouse District. A high-ranking naval officer and a high-ranking Army engineer in each district ran the Lighthouse districts, under the auspices of the Treasury Department. Eventually, the Coast Guard would assume these duties.

The Fourth Lighthouse District extended from New Jersey to Virginia. Under jurisdiction of the district were thirty-two lighthouses, four light ships, two fog signals, 131 buoys in place, and 196 spare buoys. Reigart worked out of his old hometown, Philadelphia. Reigart was the disbursing officer for the district. He did not like this duty, and as soon as he began in his new job, Reigart began to long for the sea again. His heart was on a ship far out at sea and not at a desk as a disbursing officer. Reigart asked to be assigned to the first available vessel and detached from lighthouse duty.

Reigart was appealing to deaf ears, though. Secretary Robeson was in no hurry to get Reigart back under his jurisdiction. It took two years for Reigart to get out of the lighthouse position, and when he did, he found himself back in another political controversy. Reigart had dabbled in Philadelphia politics while he had been on duty there. This had kept both local people and the naval secretary aware of Reigart's political leanings.

When Reigart knew that he would be leaving, he had made a recommendation for his replacement. Soon after, Secretary Robeson received a letter from a freshman Congressman named Loftland. Loftland had learned about Reigart's recommendation and had assumed that Reigart had submitted the name of a Democrat. Loftland strongly recommended to Robeson that George H. Maull replace Reigart because he was a first-class pilot, a reliable, energetic, and trustworthy man, and an earnest, thorough, hardworking Republican.

Loftland played the role of the loyal servant perfectly. He told Robeson how his state, Delaware, was just emerging from Democratic rule. Delaware had cast its vote for Grant in the last election. Loftland could not stress the importance of this appointment enough. He told Robeson that Reigart was trying to have a Democrat put in his place, and that Reigart was willing to go outside the district to fill the position rather than have a Republican fill it.

Reigart was astonished when he learned of Loftland's letter. Examinations had been given, and Reigart's candidate had obtained the best score. Reigart knew that under no circumstances could he let his political beliefs influence his official conduct. To the best of his knowledge, his candidate was a radical Republican! When Robeson asked Reigart to defend himself, Reigart told Robeson that Loftland's letter was a result of Loftland's ignorance and his lack of association with officers and gentlemen. Reigart told Robeson that he had no explanation to make because there was nothing to explain.

Reigart's candidate did not have a chance. The Navy had succumbed to politics. As an outspoken Democrat, Reigart was becoming very aware of this fact. It was because of this that Reigart's next command would come as quite a surprise. It would not only be the highlight of the decade of the 1870s for Reigart, but also the beginning of the end.

33.

THE MOB SEVERED THE HEADS FROM THE STILL WARM BODIES, PLACED THEM ON PIKES, AND MARCHED WITH THEM THROUGH THE CITY

—•◎•—

NOW BECAUSE OF THE JOUETT AFFAIR, REIGART MET WITH Congressmen he had gotten to know since the early 1870s, when he had become active in politics. He surprised even himself when he realized that during the past ten years he had worked with or campaigned for nearly all the Democrats in Congress. His reception in Washington was warm as long as he steered clear of the Republicans. While President Hayes was a Republican, the Democrats controlled Congress, and this was the one thing that was preventing Jim Jouett from getting his Vote of Thanks. The administration was putting pressure on the Congressmen, though, and many of Reigart's friends were quick to tell him not to let up.

While he was in Washington, Reigart took the opportunity to contact some of the captains senior to Jouett who were on duty there. One afternoon, Reigart came across Stephen Bleecker Luce. Stephen Luce, like Reigart, John Upshur, Bill Whiting, and many of the other captains, was a great naval educator. Stephen had taught for several years at Annapolis, and while there, had written a book called *Seamanship* that became a basic text for midshipmen. Stephen Luce also played a key role in helping Reigart develop the Apprentice system during and after the Civil War.

Before the Jouett case, Reigart had last seen his friend Stephen at Key West in early 1874. Stephen commanded the *Minnesota*. He, Reigart, and nearly all the US Navy had gathered at Key West because of the *Virginius* Affair. The *Virginius* Affair had brought the country and the Navy to life.

Stories of the *Virginius* Affair had made headlines in the newspapers every day for months. The *Virginius* was a ship that had been caught smuggling arms and ammunition into Cuba. The events that followed were beyond belief.

The *Virginius* had been built as a blockade-runner during the Civil War, and so, it seemed appropriate that this ship would continue in this kind of duty after the war. The boat had been sold after the war to John F. Patterson for $9,800. Patterson registered the *Virginius* at the Custom House in New York. Although the vessel never again returned to the United States, her papers had been kept up to date at American consulates in Caribbean ports.

From the beginning, Patterson chartered the *Virginius* to the Cuban Junta, an organization opposed to Spanish rule of the island of Cuba. The Cuban Junta ran arms, men, and ammunition to various parts of the island of Cuba in what were called "filibuster" expeditions. The *Virginius* became a notorious "filibuster" ship, and Spain often complained to the United States about her activities.

In July 1873, Captain Joseph Fry went to New York to find a job as commander of an ocean steamer. There, he met General Quesada, a leader of the Cuban Junta. Quesada offered Captain Fry command of the *Virginius* at one hundred fifty dollars per month. An old Confederate blockade-runner, Fry knew the dangers of his new command, but he desperately needed the money and the job.

On October 23, 1973, the *Virginius* set out from Kingston, Jamaica, for Cuba, loaded with war supplies. Bad leaks caused the *Virginius* to pull into Port-au-Prince for repairs. There, her presence was noticed by Spanish authorities who alerted the commander of the Spanish man-of-war *Toronado* that the *Virginius* was on her way to Cuba.

On the night of October 31, the men on the *Toronado* caught sight of the *Virginius* about ten miles off the coast of Cuba and gave pursuit. A seven-hour chase ensued. To lighten her load, the crew of the *Virginius* threw arms, ammunition, and even horses overboard. This was all to no avail, though. The *Virginius* again began to leak badly from the strain of the chase. This caused her to slow down and to come within firing range of the *Toronado*. After being fired at four times, the *Virginius* rounded to and surrendered within about six miles of Jamaica.

Spanish officers boarded the *Virginius* and demanded that someone "take down that damned rag and hoist the Spanish flag." The American colors were lowered, and the Spanish flag was raised in their place, where-upon the Spaniards kicked and trampled upon the American flag. Captain Fry handed over his American papers and pointed out that the ship flew American colors and had an American crew. In reply, the Spanish officer said, "I do not care what flag the ship carried; it is a pirate ship, and you are all my prisoners."

The *Virginius*, with her one hundred and fifty-five crewmembers and passengers, was taken to Santiago-de-Cuba where it arrived at 5:00 p.m., November 1, 1874.

The next day, a court martial was held on the *Toronado* trying the entire crew of the *Virginius* as pirates. The results were sent to the Captain General, and all the men except four Cuban leaders—Ryan, Del Sol, Verona, and Cespedes—were put in the local jail. At dawn on November 4, the four Cuban leaders were led down to the "slaughterhouse." The prisoners were forced to kneel and then were shot in the back. Ryan was not instantly killed, so a Spanish officer stepped forward and thrust his sword through

Ryan's heart. A bloodthirsty mob then came down upon the corpses. The mob severed the heads from the still warm bodies, placed them on pikes, and marched with them through the city. General Don Juan N. Burriel, Governor and military leader of Cuba, justified the deaths of these men by the fact that they were traitors to their country and insurgent chiefs.

The passengers were then tried summarily, without counsel, without notification to the American consulate, and without interrogation. On November 7, Captain Fry and thirty-six others were also led to the "slaughterhouse." The victims faced the wall with their backs to the firing party who were only ten feet away. Captain Fry was the only one to drop on the first volley, despite the proximity of the firing squad. Then a horrible scene ensued. The Spanish butchers advanced to where the wounded men lay in agony. Then placing their guns in some instances into the mouths of their victims, the Spaniards pulled the triggers, shattering the heads into fragments. Twelve more men were executed in a similar manner the next day.

In all, fifty-three of the passengers and crew of the *Virginius* were executed. Twenty-seven of the men were Americans or Englishmen. The summary trials and hasty executions would bring great reactions from the United States who would claim that the executions were in direct violation of Article 7 of the 1795 treaty between the United States and Spain, which guaranteed civil trials for Americans.

But reaction from the United States would come slowly at first. News was blacked out. The American consul had attempted to protest, but General Burriel placed sentinels completely around the consulate until after the executions. Immediately following the first executions, all foreign vessels were prohibited from leaving Cuban ports to prevent the news from circulating. The Spaniards then seized control of the telegraph lines and forbade their use to anyone. Even the American vice-consul was not permitted to contact authorities in Washington. In addition, the telegraph lines between Havana and Santiago conveniently broke down. Burriel claimed that insurgents had cut them. The government in Madrid, at the insistence of the United States, had sent a telegram ordering a halt to the executions on November 6, but Burriel claimed that he did not receive it until November 12.

These actions shocked the world, but to the Spanish rulers, death was the natural way to deal with the enemy. In Spain itself, Carlists were being executed at this same time for even less reason. The Spanish felt that the killing of a few men was small matter, and that the main question involved in this case was the legality of the seizure of the *Virginius*. Burriel could not be bothered with American protest of the executions and finally answered them saying that he had been busy and moreover, "the past two days were holidays."

When news of the first executions reached Kingston, the British Commodore in that port was notified. He sent the British ship-of-war *Niobe* to Cuba under command of Sir Lambton Lorraine. Lorraine left in such haste that several of his crew who were on shore had to be left behind. When he arrived in Santiago, Lorraine met with Burriel. Lorraine asked, "What is the meaning of the shooting now going on?"

To which Burriel replied, "We are only shooting some prisoners."

Lorraine was not satisfied. He asked, "Are there any English subjects among them?"

Burriel quickly replied incorrectly, "No, only Americans."

Lorraine stood strong. He told Burriel, "If you shoot another prisoner, whether English or American, until I can investigate the facts, I will bombard the town."

Burriel tried to hold his ground. He told Lorraine, "I am not in the habit of allowing myself to be overawed."

Lorraine returned to his ship, swung it about, and pointed his big guns at the heart of Santiago and said no more. Burriel must have been "overawed" because no more executions took place after this incident. Various American cities and organizations later honored Lorraine for his actions that exhibited the Anglo-American friendship that has prevailed throughout most American and British diplomacy.

A few days later, Commander William B. Cushing of the United States Navy arrived. He, too, demanded an audience with Burriel. When Burriel refused, Cushing threatened to bombard the governor's palace. Burriel had a sudden change in heart and agreed to see Cushing. At the meeting, when Burriel reached out to shake Cushing's hand, Cushing withdrew his hand. Throughout the interview, Cushing stared Burriel down and played a tough role. He advised Burriel not to shoot any more of the *Virginius* passengers without first removing the women and children from Santiago. Burriel agreed that there would be no more shootings.

Cushing was intensely patriotic and ambitious. He had gone to Santiago without waiting for orders when he first heard of the *Virginius* incident. While there, he acted on his own since contact with Washington was difficult if not impossible. Knowing Cushing's character and fearing that he might start a war, Secretary Robeson wired Commander Daniel L. Braine in New York: "For God's sake, hurry on to Santiago-de-Cuba. We are afraid that Cushing will do something."

Meanwhile, back in Washington, news of the *Virginius* Affair began to trickle into Secretary of State Hamilton Fish's office. Fish's first reaction was that this was merely another incident in a long line of troublesome instances with Spanish rule in Cuba. These had become rather common since 1868 when insurrectionists in Cuba had begun to try to rid themselves of Spanish rule. When news of the first four deaths arrived, Fish began to realize the gravity of the situation. The capture on the high seas of a vessel bearing the American flag presented a serious question that would need investigation. The summary proceedings resulting in the punishment by death with such rapid haste would attract attention as inhuman and in violation of the civilization of the age. Fish knew that if an American had been wrongfully executed, that the United States would require most ample reparation. Later, on the day that Fish learned of the first four deaths, word came in about forty-nine more executions. Fish now knew that he had a major incident on his hands and he put in a vehement protest to the government of Spain.

As the news trickled in, the newspapers began to pick it up. The reaction would result in a high point in military and diplomatic history of the 1870s.

34.
MASS INDIGNATION MEETINGS AROSE IN EVERY MAJOR CITY, TOWN, AND HAMLET

———•◦•———

WHEN REIGART PICKED UP THE NEWSPAPER ONE NOVEMBER morning, he was shocked. As he read of the events of the *Virginius*, Reigart realized that there was a possibility of war and that the Navy would have to be mobilized. After he had left the lighthouse duty, Reigart had been given command of the *Canandaigua*. Now that some action was possible, Reigart began to prepare his men and his vessel for any possibility.

As if the news from Cuba was not bad enough, rumors and false information began to appear everywhere. When Reigart picked up his newspaper on November 14, he saw a report that fifty-seven more passengers of the *Virginius* had been killed. This number appeared in the newspaper headlines for days and was also reported to Secretary Fish by Daniel Sickles, the United States consul in Madrid. This report proved to be erroneous; Fish was notified of the error on November 18, but most newspapers did not carry the retraction until November 21. Rumors were also generated concerning Sickle's health and welfare. Spanish demonstrations outside the United States embassy were reported way out of proportion, and on November 21, a headline in the New York Herald read: "Rumored Assassination of Sickles." This, too, of course, proved to be false.

False or not, all this news had done its damage. Reigart and all who had read these articles were enraged. The retractions did not lessen the rage. Once the newspapers had picked up the story of the *Virginius*, massive reactions appeared all over the United States. Mass "indignation" meetings arose in every major city, town, and hamlet. On November 20 and 21 alone, these meetings were held in New York, Brooklyn, Newark, Hoboken, New Orleans, Salt Lake City, Baltimore, San Francisco, Augusta, Columbus, Georgia, and Philadelphia.

The *Canandaigua* was stationed in Philadelphia. Philadelphia was Reigart's boyhood town, and he still had many friends and relatives there. He had lived in Philadelphia many of the years of his life and had served there for the past two years as a lighthouse inspector. During those two years, Reigart had become active in local politics.

Because he was so well known in Philadelphia, Reigart was invited to be one of the principal speakers at the Philadelphia mass meeting. Reigart told his audience how outraged he was that something like this could happen to his fellow man. Reigart and his crew were ready, as naval officers and men, to serve their country and participate in whatever military events that might occur. Throughout the meeting, there were cries for war. None wanted the Spanish butchers to get away with these mass murders.

The Cuban Junta also held meetings in New York and other major cities. General Quesada started to prepare another expedition and by November 9, already had 5,000 sympathizers enrolled. The Cuban anti-slavery committee took a petition with 600,000 signatures on it to President Grant on November 15. The clamor was great, and the cry for war was loud.

Throughout the addresses at the mass meeting in New York, the cries of "War! War!" were heard. General John A. Foster, who did not attend sent his regards and volunteered to get up his old regiment, fill it within five days, and lead it himself. At the mass meeting in St. Louis, speakers urged President Grant to suspend the neutrality laws for two or three months so that the American people could "inflict summary vengeance upon the bloodthirsty Spaniards and wrest the island of Cuba from their grasp." Many people felt that war was inevitable.

Even the preachers got into the act during their Sunday sermons. Henry Ward Beecher made an eloquent appeal for recognition of the Cuban insurgents, and his fiery denunciation of Spaniard cruelty brought down the house. When he said that the Cuban patriots "deserve liberty and the help of every honest man on the globe to achieve it," the congregation broke into applause, and the ladies waved their handkerchiefs.

The biggest proponent for war was the New York Herald. The view of the Herald was that the crime Spain had committed was so great that the only choice the United States had was to declare war. At the height of the mass meetings, November 21, the Herald said that the American Army should be in Cuba in ten days. If the Army needed more troops, the Herald felt that Grant could ask for 100,000 volunteers and that the country would back him up. A few days later, the war feeling in the country was subsiding, but not at the Herald. Finally, on November 25, the New York Times felt compelled to condemn the New York Herald for its stands on war: "The public has been treated to a great deal of rubbish in some New York newspapers concerning the duty of government in relation to the Spanish difficulty...Secretary Fish is as patriotic an American as any of the wild Irishmen who propound their views of international difficulties through the columns of the New York Herald...The government disdains to adopt the buccaneering swagger so dear to the New York Herald and journals of its class." The Herald continued, though, saying that it preferred a war that would lead to peace rather than a peace that would lead to war.

The war feeling had the ear of President Grant, but so did Hamilton Fish. Fish was worried about the crowd that surrounded Grant and in a letter to a friend said, "What a nasty crew to have about one! Drunken, stupid, lying, venal, brainless. Oh! That 'Somebody' were rid of such surroundings." Grant would talk of war with Spain with friends at the White House, and they would plan ways to wipe out Spain and to free Cuba. But when it came to actual decisions, Grant relied heavily upon Fish's thoughts.

The resounding war cries throughout November 1875 mingled with the din of working in the naval yards that had not seen such activity in years. Throughout the Navy, ships prepared for action. Reigart, too, got his men and his ship into shape. He had been watching the Navy decline ever since the end of the Civil War, and he saw the *Virginius* Affair as an opportunity for a rebirth of a great Navy. Every available vessel was ordered to prepare for sea. Secretary Robeson directed the entire Navy to rendezvous at Key West, Florida, at once. In all, the *Virginius* incident caused about $65,000,000 in direct expenses on the Navy for which no real return was received. The war scare caused naval appropriations to reach a high point in 1874 for all of the 1870s. The number of seamen increased from 3,500 in 1875 to 10,000 in 1879.

There were two objectives that could be reached through war. One was acquisition of Cuba by the United States. The London press took a favorable view to Cuban annexation, and certain Latin American nations were thrilled at the prospect. A few American politicians also preferred annexation, but they preferred that it take place without war. Then, of course, the New York Herald in its one plea for "peace" asked for "not only a piece, but the whole beautiful island of Cuba." The other objective was independence for Cuba from Spain which had been the goal of the insurgents and the original purpose of the Virginius expedition.

Feelings ran high among the Spaniards in Spain and Cuba. When news of the capture was made known in Santiago, the city was illuminated, and men marched in the streets. A few weeks later, a grand bull fight was given in honor of the crew of the *Toronado*. The Spanish press approved of the entire affair and offered its hearty "Hurrah!" In Spain, Sickles reported that the situation had become so grave that he feared that the United States legation might have to be closed. Mobs threatened violence, and there was a general clamor for blood in Madrid.

Reigart closely followed the events as they unfolded on the Virginius Affair. Reigart was perhaps more interested than most in these happenings. As a member of the United States Navy, it was likely that he would be called to serve in one way or another. If there was war, all senior members of the Navy would become involved; if the matter were to be settled peaceably, it was likely that the Navy would be involved in the diplomacy as it had many times before. There was a feeling of excitement in the air as Reigart prepared his ship for war. As soon as he was ready, he would join the other ships at the rendezvous.

35.
IMMEDIATE SURRENDER
OF THE VESSEL
AND SURVIVORS.

———••○••———

WHILE REIGART PREPARED HIS SHIP, THE GOVERNMENTS OF
Spain and the United States began negotiations. The issues involved were
deeply imbedded in international law. At first, Hamilton Fish named as
points of offense "the capture on the high seas in time of peace of a regularly documented United States vessel, under the United States flag, and
the conveyance of the vessel with those aboard to a port within Spanish
jurisdiction, the execution of a large number of the passengers, officers,
and crew, and the retention of the remainder and of the vessel." On the
other hand, Spanish authorities maintained that the *Virginius* was a pirate
vessel carrying the American flag illegally, that she was a notorious "filibuster" ship carrying contraband of war and operated by insurgent chiefs, and
that Spain had acted in self-defense.

Reigart, as most Americans, saw two separate important questions—
the capture of the vessel and the execution of fifty-three men. As to the
capture, the *Virginius* had kept its American papers up to date, and thus he
believed that she had the right to fly the American flag and to be protected
by it. Fish denied the right of capture of an American vessel in time of

peace even if it did carry contraband of war. According to a Senate resolution of 1858, any interference with a vessel carrying the American flag was "in derogation of the sovereignty of the United States." Since the *Virginius* carried the American flag, most Americans claimed that Spain had no right to interfere with her.

There was little question that Spain did not have the right to seize a legally documented American vessel, but there was some doubt as to the legality of the *Virginius's* American papers. Spain claimed that if the *Virginius* were not legally documented, then she would assume the identity of her owner that Spain claimed to be the Cuban Junta. Therefore, Spain claimed to have only captured one of her own vessels. The United States denied, however, Spain's right to decide whether the *Virginius* was legally documented or not; this was a municipal matter within the jurisdiction of the United States. This argument was dulled, though, by the fact that during the *Alabama* controversy, the United States had condemned the fraudulent use of neutral flags and papers.

Some Americans agreed that Spain had the right to capture even an American vessel if it were found in Spanish waters aiding the insurrection. Sickles felt that no question would have arisen if the vessel had been captured in Spanish waters, and a fair trial had been accorded to American citizens with respect to the treaty of 1795. However, the entire chase and capture of the vessel took place in international waters. The United States recognized Spain's right to self-defense but not past her own territorial waters. Britain also denied the right of Spain to chase a vessel outside of her own waters in time of peace. In fact, in a similar case, Spain had been forced to return a British ship, the *Deerbound*, which had been aiding the Carlist insurrection of Spain.

It was not the capture of the vessel that most aroused the emotions in the United States; it was the inhuman slaughter that took place in Santiago-de-Cuba. Even after hearing of only the first four deaths, Fish commented that "the executions…of these persons was forced on with indecent and barbarous haste, and in defiance of all humanity and regard to the usages of the civilized world." Under the treaty of 1795, the lives of Americans were sacred until a trial had been carried out in the presence of an American consul. Burriel's haste and inhuman actions, which he termed "strict fulfillment of the law" were against the laws of nations and fully justified ample reparations, even disregarding the legality of the capture.

Spain saw different issues. She justified both the capture and the executions on the basis that the *Virginius* was a pirate ship. A Spanish municipal law of 1869 had announced that anyone supplying aid to the insurrection would be considered enemies, treated as pirates, and would be immediately shot. When the *Toronado* had captured the *Virginius*, the Spanish officer in charge proclaimed that the *Virginius* was a pirate ship. The United States considered the Spanish definition of pirate erroneous, inexact, and absurd. Spain could not make men pirates by merely labeling them so. The definition of pirate accepted in international law was one who was not protected by any nation and enemy to all. In addition, piratical acts had to be committed at sea.

Spain partially justified her seizure of the *Virginius* on the fact that it was carrying contraband of war. There was no doubt in anyone's mind about the nature of the cargo, and many Americans felt that if the *Virginius* had committed a crime, it had been blockade-running or smuggling. Even Captain Fry's biographer admitted to this. In international law, enemy's goods in a neutral vessel, the vessel itself, and the men on board are subject to seizure. But technically, Spain had not recognized the belligerency of the insurrectionists, and so technically the *Virginius* could not have been carrying contraband of war. Had a war been recognized, a whole new set of rules would have applied, including the seizure of an American vessel on the high seas.

Perhaps Spain's most tenable justification for the seizure of the *Virginius* was a claim of self-defense. The *Virginius* was a notorious "filibuster" ship and was threatening Spanish security on the island of Cuba.

The *Virginius* was making a hostile expedition that threatened the peace of Cuba, and using this reasoning, Spain could and did claim self-defense. These were the issues that led to negotiations between the United States and Spain.

The United States' demands were restoration of the *Virginius*, release of the surviving prisoners, a salute to the American flag, punishment of Burriel and other Spanish officials, and indemnity for the families of those executed. Secretary Fish ordered Minister Sickles to begin negotiations with Madrid at once. On November 14, Fish wired his demands to Sickles and told him that if Spain had not met all of them within twelve days that Sickles was to close his legation and to leave Madrid. The Spanish minister, Mr. Carvajal, thought that Sickles had acted on his own and rejected Sickles's demands. Sickles assured Carvajal that his demands had come directly from Washington and were those of the government of the United States.

When, on November 26, these demands had not been met to the satisfaction of the United States, Sickles asked for his passport and prepared to leave Madrid. At 2:30 p.m., he received a note from Carvajal with important concessions. Spain pledged that "if it should be proved that the *Virginius* rightfully carried the American flag and that her papers were in regular form, her seizure would be declared illegal, the American flag would be saluted in the manner desired, and the *Virginius* with her surviving crew and passengers returned." Spain also promised to punish any Spanish officers at Santiago who had failed in their duty and offered that reparation questions be settled by arbitration. Sickles decided to stay and resume negotiations.

This offer, however, was too little, too late. When Fish had not received word of a settlement by his deadline time, he began his own negotiations in Washington with Spanish Minister Polo. When he heard of Sickles's progress, Fish told him to continue negotiations. Meanwhile, in Washington, Fish objected to the fact that Spain held the vessel and the surviving crew while Spain investigated the legality of the ship's American papers. Fish informed Polo of his feelings, and only two days after he had begun negotiations in Washington, Fish concluded an agreement with Polo, which was essentially the same as the one Sickles had negotiated. The primary difference was the immediate surrender of the vessel and the survivors, while only the flag salute would be deleted if it were proved before December 25 that the *Virginius* carried American papers illegally.

Fish had been glad to have the opportunity to negotiate directly. He did not fully trust Sickles and was concerned about his hot temper. When Fish concluded nearly the same treaty that Sickles had negotiated, Sickles felt he had been dishonored by his government and resigned.

Release of the ship and the men went right according to schedule. The *Virginius* was surrendered on December 16 in the harbor of Bahia Honda. Three days later, the *Virginius* went to sea in tow of the USS *Ossipee*. On the way north, the *Virginius* sank in eight fathoms of water off Cape Fear, North Carolina.

Cries came from both sides that the United States had sunk the *Virginius* for diplomatic reasons. The Spanish press, commenting bitterly on the accident, claimed that the United States sank the vessel in order to prevent investigation of its status because a ship must be in port before any action of libel can take place. The Spanish press felt that prize money was due to the crew of the *Toronado* and that the United States was trying to avoid payment of it. In the United States, the convenience of the sinking was also noticed. If the vessel remained afloat, it would be a source of embarrassment and annoyance to Secretary Fish and to the United States government.

Whether the sinking was convenient or not, it had been well known that the vessel's condition was critical. She had had to stop twice on her way to Cuba in October in order to repair her leaky condition, and one of the reasons she had been captured was this poor state of repair. When she was handed over to the Americans on December 16, water was found in all her compartments that had to be pumped out. Her leaky condition had been noted throughout her voyage from Cuba to the United States, and rough weather proved to be too much for her. A naval court of inquiry attested to her poor condition and placed the blame for her sinking on no one.

The one hundred and two surviving passengers were released to the USS *Juniata* under Commander Braine on December 18. The exchange took place during the night in order to prevent any disturbances at the request of General Burriel. The prisoner conditions had been rather poor, and the men were covered with filth, vermin, and rags. They were given fresh clothing and returned to New York.

Thus, the first two parts of the treaty had been concluded by December 12. Hamilton Fish felt pride in having both the men and the vessel back because he thought that it admitted guilt on the part of the Spaniards.

Reigart did not know it, but he would play a key role in the implementation of the next part of the treaty.

36.
SYMPATHY IS A PASSION OF THE SOUL WHICH CANNOT BE IMPOSED

<hr>

PERHAPS THE MOST INVOLVED PROBLEM OF THE ENTIRE *Virginius* Affair was the question of the vessel's right to fly the United States flag. The first reaction of the American people was that their flag had been dishonored and that action should be taken to restore that honor. Was our flag a dishrag or an emblem of power? This was the question that was asked by many aroused Americans. They demanded action. Any nation that permitted its flag and its citizens to be insulted in one instance would soon be insulted all over the world.

When members of one nation insult the flag of another, it is customary for an apology to be made by a flag salute. Arrangements were made in the protocol of November 29 for a flag salute to be given on December 25, unless before that date Spain could prove to the satisfaction of the United States government that the *Virginius* had been flying the American flag illegally.

While hundreds of naval orders and movements were published weekly in various newspapers, Captain Reigart B. Lowry, commanding the *Canandaigua*, slipped out quietly for Cuba under confidential orders from

Secretary Robeson on December 10. Reigart was to receive the salute to the American flag and return a salute to the Spanish flag hoisted above his vessel unless he heard otherwise before December 25. This was a distasteful duty for Reigart. He would much rather have gone to war with Spain and punish her for the inhuman actions of Burriel. Secretary Robeson realized that some of his men felt this way, so he instructed Reigart and his crew to observe the utmost courtesy while they remained in Cuba.

Reigart arrived in Santiago on December 19. The next morning, Reigart, the highest-ranking naval officer to be sent to Cuba during the crisis, notified General Burriel of his presence. It turned Reigart's stomach to have to deal with this beast, but it was his duty.

Burriel informed Reigart that he would deliver a salute of twenty-one guns to the American flag at Moro Castle at noon on Christmas day. Reigart was disturbed by Burriel's choice of Moro Castle since it was three-and-one half miles from his anchorage and out of sight from his vessel. International saluting had customarily been made at Battery Blanco in the upper bay of Santiago-de-Cuba. Reigart had received and returned a salute from there a year before. Reigart informed Burriel that it would be inconvenient and impossible for him to leave his anchorage on the 25th and trusted that it would be convenient and agreeable for both nations to exchange salutes in the harbor of Santiago-de-Cuba.

Burriel replied that Battery Blanco had been in poor condition since her guns had been fired a month previously. Burriel told Reigart that he feared for the safety of the battery and failure of the salute if this battery were used. Burriel felt that a salute in Moro Castle, out of sight from Santiago-de-Cuba, would arouse fewer emotions among his own people. Having to give a salute at all was embarrassing to him, and if he could deliver it unseen by his fellow compatriots, it would be more politically expedient for him. Burriel felt so strongly about this that he told Reigart that if the salute could not be given at Moro Castle, that he would have to cancel it altogether. Another crisis loomed.

In the meantime, Spain had been gathering evidence concerning the validity of the *Virginius's* papers. Spain argued that they did not want to apologize for an offense that they had not committed. They claimed that no insult had been made to the American flag by the capture of the *Virginius* because it was not entitled to carry the American flag. On the surface, though, most Americans saw no reason to doubt this validity. The ostensible owner of the vessel was an American citizen, John F. Patterson, who had registered the vessel in New York in 1870. Since that time, the vessel's papers had been kept in excellent order, and an American citizen had always commanded it.

Spain challenged the fact that Patterson was the rightful owner of the *Virginius* and felt that he had obtained the papers fraudulently. Voluminous testimony was delivered before a United States District Attorney and submitted on December 11 to Secretary of State Fish. Fish sent the evidence to Attorney General George Williams and asked him to deliver an opinion on the *Virginius's* right to carry the United States flag. Williams found from the evidence that the *Virginius* was owned and operated by General Quesada and the Cuban Junta. Therefore, since no vessel in which a foreigner is directly or indirectly interested is entitled to a US registry, the *Virginius* carried the American flag "without right and improperly."

Williams's decision satisfied Fish who at once informed Polo that the salute to the American flag would be "spontaneously dispensed with" by the United States. Polo acknowledged this decision and stated formally that "there was no offense to the American flag, and that no intention to insult it could or ever did exist." Fish then had Robeson inform Reigart of the decision. Reigart informed Burriel on December 22.

This decision had come at an opportune time since Reigart had been unable to agree with Burriel on the location of the salute, and these two men were considering dispensing with it anyway. The strained feelings between Reigart and Burriel, however, were not relieved by the cancellation of the salute. Reigart stayed in Santiago and reported to Burriel that he had information that property and lives of American citizens were in jeopardy. The American consulate had been threatened, and some of Reigart's officers walking on the public plaza had been treated with impertinence and offensive remarks made at or to them with hisses. Reigart was determined to restore peace and friendly relations between the respective peoples. He wanted to stop any public outbreak of violence before it started because he knew that public outbreaks are always sudden and for a time uncontrollable, and only suppressed after the storm has passed and committed its havoc.

Burriel was incensed. He protested vehemently and energetically saying that if there had ever been any insult to the Americans or any prosecution against them, it had been done according to the law. The tone of Burriel's letters became very defensive. He continually emphasized the "hospitality" and "honor" of the citizens of Santiago. Burriel admitted that the relations between Cubans and Americans were strained, but he pointed out that the presence of the United States Navy was not helping the situation. Burriel told Reigart that his government could not control the inner emotions of his subjects: "Sympathy is a passion of the soul, that cannot be imposed, born of the heart, over which there is no human power…" Burriel claimed that his people were kind and gentle by nature and were never lacking in their hospitality to foreigners. Burriel also commented that some people, both in Cuba and in the United States, wanted war, "for they mistakenly believe that then another flag will fly over this island." The behavior of these men, Burriel told Reigart, should be discounted. The strongly defensive nature of Burriel's letters showed that he felt a need to justify his own actions and those of his countrymen. Reigart decided to stay in Santiago for a few more weeks.

While Reigart stayed in Santiago, Fish tried to implement the remaining sections of the protocol of November 29. The protocol allowed for "reciprocal reparations." If the nations could not agree on the amounts, then the amounts would become subject to arbitration. On December 30, Polo presented Spain's demands to the United States. He showed that

the Spanish government had protested repeatedly concerning the operations of the *Virginius* on the Cuban coast. He compared the *Virginius* to
the *Alabama* because of which the United States had recently secured an
indemnity from Great Britain. Since Spain would not admit to a state of
war in Cuba, Hamilton Fish could find no reason that the United States
should pay an indemnity to her.

Great Britain, which had lost nineteen men during the *Virginius* executions, put in her claims for indemnity. In late August 1874, a settlement
was reached of £500 for each white man (£5,000), and (£300) for each black
man (£2,700), for a total of £7,700. This was embarrassing to the United
States who had been unable to procure a settlement by that time. Therefore,
Hamilton Fish began to negotiate with more vigor to obtain a settlement at
least as favorable as that of Great Britain, though he refused to make a distinction between the races on the amount paid. Finally, in February 1875,
the new minister to Spain, Caleb Cushing, accepted an offer of $80,000
unconditional indemnities. This amount was accepted, closing this part of
the protocol.

In the only remaining part of the protocol, Spain had agreed to punish anyone who had offended Spanish laws or obligations. The United States
repeatedly demanded the punishment of Burriel who "by his own deeds
of wanton wrong, rendered himself amenable to the penal laws of Spain."
Spain continually promised to punish Burriel, and finally "punished" him
by promoting him to the rank of Marshall of Spain for his eminent services.
The officers of the *Toronado* all received generous promotions, and a small
amount of prize money was distributed among them for their actions.

The *Virginius* crisis had ended, and it would be forgotten in future
generations. It had occupied newspaper headlines for months, and many
Americans were dissatisfied with its outcome. Reigart felt that America
had been insulted and that her honor had been stained. He, like many
Americans, would not have been satisfied unless America had gone to war
with Spain. Perhaps he was twenty-five years ahead of his time. Certainly,

some people must have recalled the *Virginius* incident when the *Maine* was sunk, but even then, the *Virginius* had been generally forgotten. Fish had won a peace, but only delayed war.

Reigart finally left Santiago after being there for several weeks. He joined the rendezvous at Key West. A large part of the Navy remained at Key West or in the Caribbean for the next several months in case another incident might occur. This had been the time when Reigart had last seen his friend Stephen Bleecker Luce. The two men talked about the *Virginius* Affair.

It had been the one high point for the Navy during the 1870s. Reigart concluded his visit to Washington and returned to New York. When he returned to the Coleman House, he picked up the pack of mail that had accumulated in his absence. As he opened one of the pieces, Reigart became livid.

37.
THOSE WHO BOTHER ME MOST WILL BE PAID LAST

———•◦•———

IT WAS A BILL FOR COAL REIGART HAD PURCHASED IN 1873. The bill said that Reigart owed $35.00 for coal plus seven years of interest at 6% per annum, or $16.33, totaling $51.33. There was a reason that this bill remained unpaid, even more of a reason than the fact that Reigart had a history of unpaid bills going back to 1845.

On June 18, 1865, Reigart had received a bill from John Earle, Jr., a merchant tailor, for some clothes he had bought in 1845. The principal amount was $122.00. Nineteen years interest added $161.04 for a grand total of $283.04. Reigart paid most of his bills, but anyone who was particularly bothersome about collecting his bills was likely to be paid late or not paid at all. This trait of Reigart's was later inherited by one of his sons. The son seldom paid his bills, and generally threw them away before even opening them. This policy was abruptly halted when it was discovered that one of the envelopes he had thrown away contained money and not a bill.

On April 12, 1875, Reigart received a letter from Charles Whelp, a New York attorney. Mr. Whelp presented a claim against Reigart in favor of C. F. North of Paris, France. The claim was for goods furnished to Mrs.

Lowry, and the statement was enclosed. Mr. Whelp wished to be advised whether he could expect a settlement. Reigart wrote back nine days later, expressing his inability to decide at once what he would do regarding the claim, but that in a few days he would be able to advise further. Reigart never did advise further.

On July 8, 1873, Reigart's lawyer received another claim, this one from a Philadelphia lawyer. This one also asked Reigart to make an offer. If none could be made, a suit was threatened. Reigart's lawyer responded, saying that Reigart felt hurt that the clients did not acquiesce, in as much as he had dealt with them for many years and paid them many hundreds of dollars. Reigart felt that this incident showed a lack of confidence in his honor. He could not be induced to renew even that, to say nothing of a more definite proposition. He added that it would be a waste of time and trouble to push the suit, as he had nothing whereupon a levy could be made, and the clients had no one to blame but themselves by not getting the money before this time.

It was not unusual for Reigart to have overdue bills, but when he opened this one bill for coal, he threw a fit. This bill from the Chappell Coal Dealers had caused him a lot of trouble, and he had vowed never to pay it.

Six years before, on November 14, 1874, while Reigart was in New Orleans following the *Virginius* incident and the naval rendezvous, George M. Robeson, Secretary of the Navy, received a letter from the Chappell Coal Dealers concerning Reigart's account. The Chappell Coal Dealers pointed out that Reigart's account was overdue. They told Robeson that they had repeatedly requested payment of the bill, but in most cases had received no reply. In one of the few times that Reigart had responded, he told them "those who bother me most will be paid last." Even though the amount of money was small, the Chappell Coal Dealers thought that there was a principle involved and, therefore, submitted the case to the department.

Robeson contacted Reigart and asked him to explain the situation. Reigart did not think that the Chappell bill was any of Robeson's business.

He told Robeson that he had no explanation to make for any private or civil offense. Any creditors with whom Reigart may have had business transactions, Reigart told Robeson, were referred to his lawyers. The courts of civil law were open to Messrs. Chappell if they wanted to go that far to get the money.

Robeson disagreed that the bill was none of his business. He differed wholly with Reigart's assumption that the department had no authority to take notice of a creditor's complaint. Robeson stated that he did not know whether the indebtedness existed. Even if it did, Robeson admitted that it could exist without affecting the character of the debtor as an officer or a gentleman. But Reigart had been given a chance to explain himself and had not. Robeson, therefore, relieved Reigart from duty as commander of the *Canandaigua* and placed him on furlough.

To furlough an officer of the United States Navy as a punishment had never been inflicted before. A furlough put an officer on waiting orders with one half the pay for his allowance and grade. Reigart's sea pay was $4,500 per annum; his waiting orders pay was $2,800 per annum, thus, reducing his furlough pay to only $1,400 or less than one-third of his normal sea pay. This was a rather severe punishment for Reigart's failure to pay a $35.00 bill.

Robeson had told Reigart that the furlough was because of the bill. Reigart knew that the bill was not the reason; Robeson knew that the bill was not the reason; everyone knew that the bill was not the reason. The New York Times covered Reigart's furlough on the front page. The article never even mentioned the bill. It did mention Reigart's political views and some articles in a publication called the *Canandaigua Journal*, a magazine published on Reigart's ship. Because of these factors, the Times indicated that Reigart had "incurred the displeasure of the Secretary of the Navy, and in consequence has been 'furloughed.'" An understatement. The article also mentioned that Reigart's furlough came right after the *Canandaigua Journal* had been publicized in a New Orleans newspaper.

Reigart acknowledged Robeson's letter that reprimanded him, relieved him from command of the *Canandaigua*, and placed him on furlough. Reigart condemned Robeson's action and promised him that he would appeal the decision. Reigart returned home. He began his appeal procedure immediately. There was no law permitting the naval secretary to place an officer on furlough. An act of March 3, 1835, said, "No officer shall be placed on furlough except at his own request." An act of June 1, 1860, reconfirmed this. Reigart was quietly removed from furlough on March 3, 1875, but he was not given any duty.

The Chappell bill had given Robeson the means to punish Reigart. Robeson had hated Reigart's political activities, and he had been looking for an excuse to throw the book at Reigart. The Chappell bill had allowed Robeson to put into effect a vendetta against Reigart. It would cost Reigart nearly $9,000 in salary over the next five years; it would lead to Reigart's divorce; it would ruin Reigart's life. He never again would hold a command.

It was not surprising, therefore, when Reigart became enraged at receiving the Chappell bill again in 1880. Even though Reigart knew that the Chappell bill had not been responsible for his problems, he had never forgiven the Chappell Coal Dealers for their role in the affair. Reigart knew, though, that the real reason for his problem had been Robeson's corruption and Reigart's public statements on the subject.

38.
THE MOUNTAIN HAS LABORED AND BROUGHT FORTH A MOUSE

———•◯•———

SOME PEOPLE MIGHT HAVE THOUGHT THAT REIGART WAS paranoid. The Grant administration was probably the most corrupt of any in American history. Grant was probably the only member of the administration who was not corrupt. He was just inept and naive. Corruption was all around him, though. His advisors, his Vice President, his private secretary, members of his treasury department, his Secretary of War, and his Secretary of the Navy were all known to be corrupt.

Secretary of the Navy George Robeson perhaps best personified a man who combined financial greed with partisan politics. During Robeson's term, he and his friends became richer by millions of dollars. During his eight-year term, Robeson's private bank account increased from $20,000 to $325,000. The worst part of all the money Robeson and his friends siphoned off was that it was done at the expense of the US Navy. During his term, Robeson reduced the Navy from a first-rate Navy to a twelfth-rate one. A typical way Robeson used his office was to sink a lot of money into ships and then sell them as scrap for little money. This was done a number of times. To cite a few: The *Shackamaxon* cost $1,300,000 and was sold for scrap for $18,500; the *Waxsaw* cost $600,000 and was sold for scrap for $3,000; the *Piscataqua* cost $1,000,000 and was sold for scrap for $5,000; the *Chickasaw* cost $390,000 and sold for $8,000. The list goes on. Even Ben Butler benefited from these deals. He purchased the prize-racing yacht, *America*, for only $5,000. Brand-new boats that cost over $1,500,000 required as much as $865,000 in repair bills in their first years.

Secretary Robeson was brought before the House of Representatives four times for investigations into his affairs: 1872, 1876, 1878, and 1878-9. The evidence and testimony taken at these sessions consumed 5,675 pages. Besides the robbery in sales and repairs of naval vessels, sinecures flourished under Robeson. One good example of this was the fact that he had twelve agents in Florida who were supposed to be guarding the growing timber of the Navy. These agents lived from fifty to one hundred miles from the timber which most of them had never seen. One of the agents, Henry Clews, testified:

Question: Are you a timber agent in Florida?

Answer: Yes, Sir.

Question: How far do you live from the timber you are expected to guard?

Answer: I do not know anything about the public domains and did not try to find out.

Question: Did you ever see or visit the timber?

Answer: No, Sir.

Question: Did you perform any service under that appointment?

Answer: No, Sir. Nothing but draw my pay.

Question: What was your salary?

Answer: Forty-one dollars a month.

Question: What is the politics of these agents?

Answer: They are Republicans.

It was this kind of corruption which had prompted Reigart to write his articles in the *Canandaigua Journal*. The *Canandaigua Journal* was a clever and sprightly little sheet published on board Reigart's ship. Reigart got along well with the men on the *Canandaigua*. A few of them had writing talent, and Reigart encouraged them to use it. The result was the *Canandaigua Journal*.

The "Journal" included many kinds of articles as long as they might be of interest to the men on the ship. Many of the articles were about the events that took place on the ship. An annual inspection by an Admiral would be a prime topic. The articles were lively and interesting, and when, in October 1874, the *Canandaigua* was in New Orleans, the *Daily Picayune* published some of them.

Occasionally, Reigart wrote articles for the paper. On a later trip to New Orleans, in December of the same year, the *Daily Picayune*, which had so enjoyed the *Canandaigua Journal* before, published some more articles from it. Reigart wrote one of these articles, and it concerned the President and his Cabinet. Reigart's furlough had come only sixteen days later.

The President and his Cabinet had just issued their annual reports to the nation, and Reigart wrote a scathing satire on them. His criticisms were valid, but these men were his bosses. Reigart knew the chance he was taking, but he felt that the American public should know the truth.

Reigart began his article by telling his readers that he would not republish the reports. He said that his lack of space and desire for good taste precluded any direct quotations from the reports. Reigart then went on to criticize the President and the Cabinet members one by one. Grant's message, he wrote, was the same old weary platitudes. Reigart was bored from reading the same report for six years straight. He hinted that perhaps Grant had reused last year's report.

Reigart's comments on the Secretary of Treasury were two-sided. When Reigart mentioned that the treasury secretary shifted money from one pocket to another, he not only referred to his bad habit of deficit financing but also his corrupt activities.

The Secretary of War asked for more funds and officers in his annual report. Reigart could not understand why. Exaggerating a little bit, Reigart pointed out that the Army already had seven officers to each man. It could not possibly need any more.

As for Robeson, Reigart had saved some comments. A man named Reynolds had taken over the Navy Department and was managing the office while Robeson tended to politics. Since Reynolds had been running Robeson's office, Reigart speculated that perhaps Robeson had spent the last several months working on his annual report. If that was the case, Reigart concluded, "The mountain has labored and brought forth a mouse." It was clear that Reigart had not been impressed by Robeson's report. Robeson had tried to convey the impression that the Navy was growing larger and stronger. Reigart knew better.

39.
IF THIS BE TREASON, MAKE THE MOST OF IT

———•◦◯◦•———

THOUGH REIGART'S FURLOUGH HAD BEEN LIFTED ON MARCH 8, 1875, he saw no more active duty in that year. He spent a good part of the year bickering with relatives over his brother's estate. The money in the estate did not cover what had been left in the will. Reigart was executor and caught in the middle. By the end of the year, he was getting desperate to get some active duty. He requested duty at New York, Philadelphia, or Washington.

Robeson's answer to Reigart was an assignment as executive officer at the New London station. Reigart could not understand this. When last ordered to duty at New London, his orders had been revoked at the request of certain citizens to whom he was personally and politically obnoxious. Reigart had positive proof that this antagonism on the part of the same persons still existed, and he knew that this would render his stay in New London uncertain. This position would be disagreeable to him both socially and professionally. Because of the uncertainties, he could not move his family to New London, so it would be a great additional expense for him to be separated from them while on shore. The present executive officer had applied to Reigart not to replace him. Because of all this, Reigart told Robeson that he was anxious for active duty but not at New London.

The Navy Department replied that the orders to New London would be revoked and orders to another point, probably Pensacola, Florida, would be issued. Sea duty might also be considered when there was a vacancy, though this kind of position was rare. Reigart asked to be assigned to the *Centennial*. The department declined ordering Reigart to the *Centennial* but informed him that as soon as Captain George E. Belknap's health permitted his removal from Pensacola, that Reigart would be ordered there. Reigart was happy. He thought he had finally gotten himself a command and placed himself in correspondence with Captain Belknap. Reigart made all preparations to go to Pensacola when he learned that Belknap was about ready to leave.

About a week before his departure, Reigart asked the department when his final orders would come. He was not prepared for the dirty trick Robeson was about to play on him. Robeson told Reigart that under a new organization, a commodore would take the Pensacola yard. The station was offered to Commodore John Cooper but he had declined. On hearing this and learning that no other captains or commodores were applying for the station, Reigart reapplied. This time Reigart was informed that a commander would command the station. The Pensacola station was hopeless. Reigart applied for duty at New Island, California, that his old friend, Tom Craven, commanded. His application was put on file. Reigart's disfavor in the department was becoming evident to all, but Reigart kept trying.

Meanwhile, while Reigart waited for an assignment, Robeson continued to harass him. At one point, Robeson called Reigart's attention to a bill from Roger Gordon. Reigart's steward had already paid the bill. The furlough had not been enough. Robeson had refused to give Reigart a command, and now he complained about a paid bill.

Robeson's harassment encouraged Reigart to become more active in politics. Reigart's political activities were continually reported to Robeson who became more steadfast in his refusal to give Reigart a command. Reigart took an active part in the politics of the day, playing the role of an outspoken politician. He denounced the President and members of the Cabinet, calling them thieves and scoundrels. During the presidential campaign of 1876, Reigart proclaimed, "If the Democratic Party cannot carry the election in 1876, they will carry it by the sword in 1880," and "If the Democratic Party does not carry the election in 1876, they will carry it by force of arms in 1880, and if this be treason, make the most of it."

The citizens of Erie, Pennsylvania, where Reigart did most of his campaigning, either loved him or hated him. Those who hated him reported his words to Secretary Robeson. Robeson was disturbed. A military officer threatening to seize the reins of government by force of arms was high treason. Reigart would not admit to the exact words of these speeches, but he told Robeson that since he was not on active duty, he felt that it was perfectly correct for him to express himself regarding the future of his country.

There was no question that Reigart was a vocal proponent of Democratic principles, and he did belittle the Republican leaders in the government. He only said what a lot of people were thinking. Reigart just forgot, every once in a while, that he wore the uniform of the United States Navy. He liked to use colorful, figurative language and sometimes got carried away with himself. When he used terms such as "force of arms," they were not meant in the literal sense. Reigart was a patriot who had given his life to the Navy, and though he had political differences with his leaders, he would gladly lay his life on the line for his country and its leaders.

In the meantime, Reigart continued to seek duty. In December 1876, Reigart was again assigned to New London. He again asked Robeson to revoke these orders as the duty seemed very hostile to him. Reigart referred Robeson to all the letters on file with a statement of his case. Robeson knew about Reigart's feelings. He had purposely offered this assignment because he knew that Reigart would refuse it. Furthermore, this way he could not be accused of not offering Reigart any positions.

It also gave Robeson the opportunity to accuse Reigart of declining duty. Reigart answered Robeson's charges. He had never declined duty except for the New London assignments for which he had cause. Reigart had evidence that the department had concurred with him about the New London assignments. Reigart had made repeated attempts to obtain duty. His record of active naval life, sea service, and duty in the merchant marine could not have been accomplished had he avoided duty.

Lack of active duty had punished Reigart financially. It had injured his professional reputation and crippled his ability to care for his family. Reigart had to congratulate himself for not accepting duty at New London. Robeson had played a double-edged dirty trick. He had been confident that Reigart would ask to be relieved of the New London duty, but if he took it, Robeson would not have minded. Robeson knew that the New London base was going to be closed two months later. A move to New London only to have it closed would have completely bankrupted Reigart. In his defense against declining duty, Reigart concluded, "In the performance of any duty, at any time, or place, I yield to no other officer in fidelity, zeal, patriotism, and ability."

Reigart continued to apply for duty. When a vacancy occurred at the Washington Navy Yard, Reigart applied for it. In late 1877, Reigart received orders to report to the US Training Ship *Constitution*, "Old Ironsides" in Philadelphia. The Navy had reinstated the apprentice system that Reigart had developed a decade before. It had been dropped in the early 1870s, and now it was being started up again, this time with four training ships. Reigart's duty on the *Constitution* would be like that on the *Sabine*. The day after he took over the command of the *Constitution*, Reigart applied to be relieved. The pay was not adequate, and it was the same kind of duty Reigart had performed as a Lieutenant Commander. After only thirteen days, Reigart was detached from the *Constitution*.

Reigart never got a real command after the articles published in the *Canandaigua Journal*. The only offers he got were commands Robeson knew he would refuse because they were far beneath the dignity of a captain or were personally repugnant to Reigart. This lack of duty eventually caused the end of his marriage and his move to St. Catharines. Receipt of the Chappell bill brought back all these bad memories for Reigart. He went to the New York Club to have a few drinks to help forget.

40.
IT HAD GIVEN HIM A PURPOSE IN LIFE

———•●◉●•———

REIGART SPENT THE NEXT SEVERAL MONTHS WORKING ON the Jouett case. He attended the monthly meetings at the New York Club. He met privately with many of the captains. In between, he went to Washington to keep his lines of communications open with Congress. Since he had had no command in nearly five years, fighting Jouett gave Reigart something to make him forget all his problems. He looked forward to the meetings with his friends. It gave him something to do and made him feel useful.

The November meeting took place during the third week of that month. Sam Franklin had just returned from Washington and had some news for the men. As soon as Sam arrived, the men adjourned to their table in the lounge.

"What's up, Sam?" Reigart began.

"Jouett has given up his campaign for a Vote of Thanks," beamed Sam.

There was a commotion around the table. The men had been waiting for this for months. When the surprise was over, Reigart asked, "Tell us more, Sam. How did it happen?"

"He just could not get enough support. The presidential election sealed it. Even though a Republican President and Congress were elected, there were too many new faces. Jouett had to sell too many people before he could get a majority. Besides, President Hayes and Secretary Thompson were his biggest supporters. They will he gone in a few months when the new administration takes over."

The men toasted their success, and other naval officers in the club, who had been following their activities, soon joined in the celebration. The party lasted most of the night.

When Reigart returned to the Coleman House, he felt like something was missing. It had been a great achievement to defeat Jouett. But now that it was over, there was a big hole in Reigart's life. Since he had been without a command, he had lived for another day of struggle against Jouett. It had given him a purpose in life.

Without the Jouett case, Reigart did not have much. His marriage was over. He could not get a command, even though he was a commodore. The Republicans had been reelected, and the new President, John Garfield, had been linked with scandal in the Credit Mobilier affair. It appeared, except for Jouett, that there was no end to his problems.

Reigart had been too busy to notice the pain from his medical problems—rheumatism, gout, and diabetes. Now he began to feel the pains again. Between the pains and his depression, Reigart began to drink again.

On Saturday night, he decided to go to the New York Club to see if he could find some company. On his way out of the house, he stubbed his left foot against a chair. After cursing the chair out, Reigart went on his way. His foot hurt, but he continued. When he got to the club, Reigart met up with Commodore Alexander Rhind. They had been drinking and socializing for a while when Reigart felt ill. His foot still hurt, and he began to feel weak. Chills ran through his body.

Commodore Rhind became concerned. He took Reigart to a druggist where Reigart got a prescription. Then Commodore Rhind escorted

Reigart back to his apartment at the Coleman House. Rhind came back to the Coleman House Monday morning to check on Reigart's condition.

Reigart had become weaker and was in extremely poor condition. Rhind decided to take Reigart to the Brooklyn Naval Hospital, and Reigart was in no shape to argue.

The Brooklyn Naval Hospital was a splendid building surrounded by heavy foliage and full-grown trees. The hospital could comfortably hold about one hundred patients. Reigart was admitted to the hospital in a helpless condition. He had a gouty diathesis and was also a diabetic. Hence the inflammation in the left instep and ankle of his leg rapidly assumed a gangrenous type. His temperature and pulse became low. His strength continued to fall from the time of admission. He became delirious and speechless at times and died of gangrene on Thursday, November 25, 1880, at 2:40 p.m. He was only fifty-four years old. Reigart's body was taken to Philadelphia a few days later for final interment.

41.
POSTSCRIPT

———•◦•———

IT IS INTERESTING TO NOTE WHAT HAPPENED TO NAVAL PRO-
motions in the years directly following the period covered in this book.

Promotions continued to come in the order of the "list" for the fore-
seeable future. James Jouett, who was a focus of this book, was promoted
to commodore on January 11, 1883. He commanded the North Atlantic
Squadron and conducted operations in Panama during this period. On
February 19, 1886, James Jouett was promoted to Rear Admiral and shortly
after that became President of the Board of Inspection and Survey until he
retired in 1890.

Had Reigart lived just a few more years, he likely would have become
a Rear Admiral as well. Every one of the seventeen captains highlighted in
this book became a commodore by 1883. Those who lived long enough, or
stayed in the Navy long enough, became Rear Admiral.

On a list of Flag Officers as of January 1, 1892, ten of the seventeen
captains featured in this book are listed in the retired list of Flag Officers.
Seven of them retired as Rear Admiral (Earl English, John Upshur, Francis
Roe, Samuel Franklin, Edward McCauley, Stephen Luce, and James Jouett).
James Jouett was the last to retire in February 1890.

Of the ten retired Flag Officers who are listed in 1892 as Commodore or Rear Admiral, their date of ranks show that they had all continued to be promoted in the same order as the seniority list of 1880 featured in this book. The seniority list in 1880 had a remarkable similarity to the rank in class at Annapolis in 1846 and 1847.

The coveted rank of Commodore itself has had an interesting history. The rank of Commodore was superseded in 1857 by the rank of Flag Officer. The rank of Commodore was restored in 1862, when the rank of Rear Admiral was also added. The rank of Commodore was abolished in 1899. It was restored in 1943 as a temporary grade for wartime only, and the rank of Commodore was lapsed in 1950. Since that time, the Navy has only used it as an honorary title, although the Coast Guard continues to use it.

42.
EPILOGUE — DD770, D-38

———•◐•———

DURING 1944, A DESTROYER WAS LAUNCHED WHICH WAS named after Reigart Bolivar Lowry. The USS *Lowry* (DD770) served for nearly thirty years in a way that would have made Reigart proud. Bethlehem Steel Company of San Pedro, California, built the *Lowry*. Her keel was laid August 1, 1943, and she was launched on February 6, 1944, under the sponsorship of Miss Ann Lowry (later Ann Lowry Brawner), great granddaughter of Commodore Lowry. The ship was placed in commission on July 23, 1944, under command of Commander Lawrence H. Martin.

The *Lowry* had a length of 376 feet, 6 inches and an extreme beam of 41 feet. Her trial displacement was 2,200 tons, and her design speed was thirty-four knots. Eleven officers and 325 enlisted men made up the full complement of the ship. The vessel had three five-inch twin guns, two 40 mm twin guns, two 40 mm quad guns, eleven 20 mm guns, and two twenty-one-inch quintuple torpedo tubes.

After a shakedown, the *Lowry* joined the Pacific Fleet for the remainder of World War II. She served in the Luzon Operation, the Iwo Jima Operation, the Okinawa Gunto operation, and the Third Fleet operations against Japan. Seeing a great deal of action, the *Lowry* and her crew performed with distinction, often fighting off suicide bombers. There were many near misses.

One time, a Japanese Kamikaze closed on the *Lowry's* port beam and dove directly for a point between the stacks. The *Lowry's* gunners sheared off the enemy's right wing at 100 yards, and he corkscrewed twenty-five feet above the *Lowry* and crashed twenty-five yards off her starboard. Another time, a plane made a sweeping dive on the starboard quarter of the *Lowry*, striking its wing against a five-inch gun mount, passing over the port beam, and exploding some fifty feet from the ship. The *Lowry* was showered with fragments from the exploding bombs of the plane. Two men were killed and twenty-three wounded. Not all ships were so lucky. In one battle, one of the Lowry's sister ships, the *Drexler* (DD741), was struck by a crashing enemy plane. The *Drexler* broke in two and sank in two minutes.

After World War II, the *Lowry* went on a couple of training missions and was decommissioned and placed on reserve June 30, 1947. The *Lowry* was recommissioned in December 1950. In 1952, she joined the Seventh Fleet in support of the Korean War. Again, the *Lowry* was active and performed with honor. Following the Korean War, the *Lowry* completed an around-the-world cruise stopping at many foreign ports along the way.

Two more training cruises and another around-the-world cruise took up the next two years. During these cruises, the *Lowry* participated in Marine Division Landing Exercises that included a simulated full-scale invasion of Iwo Jima. The next three years saw four training courses, a tour in the Mediterranean, and an overhaul.

The next several years were spent in fleet exercises all over the world, including NATO maneuvers. During this time, in 1959, the *Lowry* participated in fleet reviews in New York City for Vice President Richard M. Nixon in honor of the 350th anniversary of the discovery of The Hudson River. In 1963, while on a cruise for Midshipmen, the *Lowry* set a roundtrip speed record through the Panama Canal in thirty-two hours. Beginning in 1966, the *Lowry* resumed her role as a training ship, a role of which Reigart would have been proud. Both in training and in fleet operations, the *Lowry* and her crews proved to be effective at Anti-Submarine Warfare, her prime mission. In 1968, the *Lowry* arrived in Vietnam to prove her worth in wartime for the third time. Following the Vietnam War, the *Lowry* resumed her role as a training ship.

*   *   *   *   *

BETWEEN MAY 13-15, 1973, I HAD THE HONOR OF BEING A guest on board the USS *Lowry*. The *Lowry* was about to begin a reserve cruise and I was invited along for the first part of it. My diary from those three days best describes what I saw and felt during my visit.

May 13

I leave New York City on the Metroliner at 9:30 A.M. This is just the reverse of the trip Reigart took to get to his first assignment. I am excited. I wonder what the three days will be like.

I arrive in Philadelphia at 10:42. Lieutenant Sheldon Margolis meets me and takes me to the naval base. We twist and wind through the base until we finally come out to a dock. I see four or five destroyers.

They look like one expects—maybe a little smaller and lower in the water. One of the more impressive features is the elaborate radar equipment on top of the ship. I notice that the crew has set up a basketball net on the helicopter landing pad.

The name *Lowry* is everywhere—on the gangplank, on the lifeboat, on signs. I am taken into the wardroom. The first thing I notice is its attractive wood paneling. The paneling is quite a contrast to the metal everywhere else on the ship. Six or seven men are sitting at a ten-foot-long table eating brunch.

Commander Stanislaus G. Dyro, my host, says, "If this is Mr. McClintock, you must have broken some speed records. It's only 10:50 and you weren't supposed to pick him up until 10:42."

Commander Dyro introduces himself and then all the other officers in the room. The atmosphere seems very informal. I join everyone for brunch.

They have stewards who do everything for the officers—pack, unpack, make the beds, and serve food and coffee. They are like servants. The officers seem to lead a good life.

My room is right off the wardroom, across from the X. O. (Executive Officer, Lieutenant Commander Al Mason). Commander Dyro tells me I have a roommate. In a little safe measuring 1' x 1' x 1' are the ashes of a person for a burial at sea. A pleasant thought!

My room is small. There are two bunks with a porthole next to the upper. On the right, there is a steel chest of drawers. One large piece folds down into a desk. There is a chair and a sink. The room is about 8' by 10'.

The supply officer takes me around the ship. We go in all the nooks and crannies, except the engine rooms. Everywhere you go, you climb up and down steep metal ladders. Each one seems to get steeper. There is metal all over—the floors, the walls, and the ceilings. You can see why they call these ships "tin cans." We go into supply rooms, the reefers (refrigerators), and inside the big guns. It is even smaller inside the guns than you might imagine. Fourteen men man the guns. It must get unbearably hot and crowded in there in the heat of battle.

At 4:30 p.m., it is time to start. There is a tug tied to the port bow. I go up to the bridge. I meet a captain who is a pilot. The wind seems right to pull out from the pier. We start. Commander Dyro wants to pull out faster so that the aft part of the ship will not swing back and strike the pier. He orders full speed ahead. The pilot panics. He fears his tug will be turned over. Dyro orders the tug cut loose. The pilot leaves.

Dyro and others talk about the pilot. He is used to smaller vessels where full speed comes fast. From a stop, full speed moves a destroyer very slowly at first.

We start down the Delaware River. Before we began, Dyro was informal, jovial, and kidded around. Once the ship is under way, he is all business. He yells a lot, takes full command, and makes a big point over small matters.

But when he turns to me, he becomes friendly and points out the sights along the river. He knows all the channels, buoys, and landmarks.

Commander Dyro hates to waste time getting down the river. He gets the boat up to twenty-two knots. Most destroyers take six hours to get down the river. Dyro only takes four and one-half hours.

I have binoculars marked "admiral." I am wearing a "770" cap and an officer's jacket. I spend most of the time on the bridge until we reach Cape May. I enjoy watching the radar. It is red and looks like a contour map of the river. It shows buoys, boats, bridges, and anything else on the water.

While going twenty-two knots, I am taken down to the engine room. There are hot, steaming pipes all around.

I spend a lot of time on the bridge in a place that sticks out to the side. You can see the whole length of the ship from here, and it is a place where I can keep out of the way. Dyro sits in a big chair on the bridge. Various officers "take the conn." They call out directions in degrees, speed, and rudder direction. Men behind respond with the wheel and other apparatus. Men with earphones and speakers look out fore and aft, port and starboard. They take bearings and sightings.

I meet a guy named Meade. He is a Southerner but claims to be a descendent of Union General George Meade. He called the general the black sheep of the family. He takes me to the War Room where he shows me radar and sonar devices in action.

At about 9:30 p.m., when we are out on the open sea, I go to the wardroom to see a movie. After the movie, I go to bed. There is a very gentle roll that rocks me to sleep.

May 14

The steward wakes me at 7:00 a.m. I have breakfast. I go out. It is a beautiful day. There is a blue sky and a calm sea. We are off Block Island. Soon I hear someone shout, "Man overboard!" It turns out to be a drill. A dummy had been tossed into the sea, and we must go retrieve it. We make a good rescue.

At 10:50 a.m., we arrive in Newport, Rhode Island. Dyro decides to go in without a tug. We pull in beside the *Bowan*, a destroyer escort circa 1970. We tie up safely without ever touching her. I spend most of the afternoon in the wardroom, talking with the officers.

I see a lot of other destroyers. None seem to be in as good condition as the *Lowry*, though. She is about the oldest still in active service. The men are proud of her and let it be known. She can still make the top speed she was designed for thirty years ago. Commander Dyro is proud of his ship, and I suspect that his pride has filtered down through his crew.

In the evening, I play a few hands of bridge with the officers and go into town with them. We must go through the *Bowan* to get on shore.

May 15

In the morning, I go on the *Bowan* for a tour with some of the officers. It carries rockets. It is much bigger. It has hallways and stairs instead of passageways and ladders. The War Room and the Bridge have scads of room unlike the *Lowry*.

Dyro is having a party for the officers tonight. I really want to go but must get home for other commitments. I catch a bus at 4:30 p.m. and return home by 9:30. These past three days have been exciting and memorable.

* * * * * * *

I MADE A SECOND VISIT TO THE *LOWRY* ON OCTOBER 29, 1973. I was hoping that this second visit would not come so soon. The occasion was the decommissioning of the *Lowry*.

I arrived with Ann Lowry Brawner at about 1:30 p.m. after having traveled two hours from New York in a driving rainstorm. We were piped aboard. As we boarded, we walked between two lines of saluting officers in their dress blues, swords hanging at their sides. Lieutenant Commander Al Mason pulled me aside. He was now Commander of the Lowry because Commander Dyro has had an operation. He told me that he was planning to present Mrs. Brawner with the "decommissioning pennant." I decided not to tell her so that it would come as a surprise.

Because of the rain, the ceremonies were held inside the ship on the mess deck. The stewards took our coats, and we were directed to the room where the ceremonies were to be held. Mrs. Brawner and I were seated in the front row alongside the commander's family.

Besides decommissioning, there was to be a transfer ceremony. The United States was giving the *Lowry* to the Brazilian Navy. The room began to fill up. It was not a large room, but there were probably a hundred people in it by the time the ceremonies began. Destroyers are not roomy ships. The ceiling of the mess deck was just barely six feet high. Since a few of the speakers were quite tall, a plate had been removed from the ceiling above the speaker's stand.

The official party arrived, and Lieutenant Commander Thomas F. Johnson delivered the invocation. Captain S. C. Gamache, USNR, Commander, Destroyer Squadron Thirty, gave a few remarks and then introduced Lieutenant Commander Albert T. Mason. Lieutenant Commander Mason is 6 feet, 4 inches tall. It was a good thing that the plate in the ceiling had been removed because his head was four full inches above the ceiling. It was rather humorous.

Mason was proud of the *Lowry*. You could tell that he hated to give her up. While he had only commanded her for a few months, he had served on her for twenty-seven months. The *Lowry's* inspections and her record compared favorably with any other destroyer. Mason's orders compelled him to declare the *Lowry* ready for decommissioning, but he found this difficult to do. Fortunately, the *Lowry* would not be sold for scrap. Instead, she was to become an active part of the Brazilian Navy.

Rear Admiral J. L. Coleman, USN, Commandant, Fourth Naval District, concluded the remarks for the United States and handed the ship over to Rear Admiral Ramon G. L. Labarthe, Brazilian Naval Attaché. Rear Admiral Labarthe delivered speeches in both English and Portuguese. There were a good number of wives and children who had come up from Brazil in the audience. The now former *Lowry* was then commissioned into the Brazilian Navy as the *Ct Espirito Santo* (D-38). The new commander of the *Ct Espirito Santo*, Commander Roberto Gomes Pereira, delivered a few remarks. Representatives from both countries then signed the legal papers and the ceremonies were over. In thirty minutes, the *Lowry* had been decommissioned, transferred, and recommissioned as the *Ct Espirito Santo*.

Everyone adjourned to the wardroom for a reception given by the Brazilians. About one hundred people crammed into a room that normally would hold about fifteen people comfortably. Even though it was so crowded, the reception went very well. Hors d'oeuvres, bourbon, scotch, and orange juice were served. At one point, Lieutenant Commander Mason presented Mrs. Brawner with the "decommissioning pennant," a picture of Commodore Reigart B. Lowry, and a picture of herself christening the *Lowry* nearly thirty years ago.

It was a sad day for many. Not only was the *Lowry* no longer a United States ship but also her crew had to be reassigned. Many of these men had served with each other for a couple of years. Now they may never see each other again.

A part of the decommissioning and transfer ceremonies was the lowering of the United States flag and the raising of the Brazilian flag. We could not see these events because of the rain, and it was a little bit of a shock to come outside and see a Brazilian flag flying over the ship. Wherever the name *Lowry* had appeared before, the name *Espirito Santo* appeared now. We said goodbye to Commanders Mason and Pereira. As I was leaving, I wished Commander Pereira good luck with the ship. I commented to him that it was nice that the ship was going to South America since that was where Reigart Lowry had been born. Commander Pereira responded, "Yes. He was born in La Guayra, Venezuela. I know a lot about your Commodore Lowry."

The *Ct Espirito Santo* served well in the Brazilian Navy. The former *Lowry* remained in Brazilian service until she was struck from service on February 2, 1996, used as target practice, and ultimately sunk in 1998.

REFERENCES

———•◦•———

WHILE THERE ARE NO SPECIFIC FOOTNOTE REFERENCES IN the body of this book, the following represents a chapter-by-chapter list of references consulted. In some cases, specific page numbers are also listed.

Chapter 1

> R.B. Lowry, Letters in my personal collection (hereafter referred to as Lowry Letters).

Chapter 2

> Lowry Letters

Chapter 3

> Lowry Letters

Chapter 4

> Lowry Letters

> National Archives. Letter of Acceptance as Midshipmen by Reigart B. Lowry.

Chapter 5

> Alexander Howard, Cruise of the Sabine (hereafter Howard), p. 29.

Lowry Letters

"Navy Yard, Brooklyn," in National, pp. 459-460.

Captain William Harwar Parker, Recollections of a Naval Officer 1841-1865, (hereafter Parker), pp. 2, 4-7.

Chapter 6

Dudley W. Knox, A History of the United States Navy, pp. 159-161.

Lowry Letters.

National Archives, Letters to the Secretaries of Navy from Officers.

National Archives, Reigart B. Lowry's Civil War Pension File (hereafter NAPF).

Division of Naval History — Navy Department, ZB File, Reigart B. Lowry (hereafter NDZB).

Charles Oscar Paullin, Diplomatic Negotiations of American Naval Officers 1778-1883 (Hereafter Paullin — Diplomatic), pp. 190-194, 204.

Chapter 7

Samuel John Bayard, A Sketch of the Life of Robert F. Stockton, pp. 81-93.

Division of Naval History — Navy Department, Ship's File (hereafter NDSF — name of ship), Princeton.

Lowry Letters.

National Archives, Logs (hereafter Logs — name of ship), Princeton.

Chapter 8

Samuel John Bayard, A Sketch of the Life of Robert F. Stockton, pp. 81-93.

R.M. Devens, "Awful Explosion on the USS Princeton in 1844, "from Our First Century, pp. 441-442, 446.

Lowry Letters.

Log — <u>Princeton</u>.

Chapter 9

Park Benjamin, The United States Naval Academy, chapter 10 and 11.

Lowry Letters.

Edward Chauncey Marshall, History of the <u>U.S.</u> Naval Academy.

Parker, pp. 118-119.

Fletcher Pratt, A Compact History of the <u>United States</u>, p. 112.

Franklin Delano Roosevelt Library, Hyde Park, MSS Collection, U.S. Naval Academy.

Professor James Russell Soley, USN, Historical Sketch of the <u>U.S.</u> Naval Academy, pp. 63-65, 67-82.

Chapter 10

Nathan C. Brooks, A Complete History of the Mexican War, pp. 468-474.

P.S.P. Conner, The Home Squadron. pp. 3, 14-15.

Log — Spitfire.

Lowry Letters.

Parker, p. 68.

Raphael Semmes, Service Afloat an Ashore During the Mexican War, p. 206.

SEE ALSO:

George Fox Emmons, The Navy of the <u>United States</u>.

K. Jack Bauer, Surfboats and Horse Marines.

Lucius W. Johnson, "Yellow Jack, Master of Strategy,"

United States Naval Institute Proceedings, LXXVI, 1950.

Charles J. Peterson, The American Navy.

Chapter 11

Lowry Letters.

Log — Allegheny.

NDSF — Allegheny.

NAPF.

Chapter 12

Frank M. Bennett, The Steam Navy of the <u>United States</u>, pp. 128, 129, 130, 133.

William Elliot Griffis, Matthew Calbraith Perry, pp. 285-290.

Francis L. Hawks, ed., Narrative of an Expedition of an American Squadron to the China Seas and Japan, pp. 75, 77, 80, 114, 133, 252-256, 280, 332, 346, 375.

Howard, p. 29

Logs — <u>Plymouth</u>, Powhatan, <u>Saratoga</u>, Susquehanna.

Lowry Letters.

Samuel Eliot Morison, "Old Bruin," Commodore Matthew Calbraith Perry, pp. 269 and ff.

NAPF.

Paullin — Diplomatic, pp. 246-248.

John S. Sewall, "Our Typhoon," New Englander, Article III, December 1890.

SEE ALSO:

Roger Pineau, ed., The Japan Expedition.

Chapter 13

Frank M. Bennett, The Steam Navy of the United States, pp. 174-175.

Howard, pp. 14-19.

Log — Preble.

Lowry Letters.

Parker.

Chapter 14

Lowry Letters.

Jessie Ault Marshall, ed., Private and Official Correspondence of General Benjamin F. Butler (hereafter Butler Correspondence).

Albert Mordell, ed., Civil War and Reconstruction, Selected Essays by Gideon Welles.

SEE ALSO (for Civil War general):

Bern Anderson, By Sea and by River.

Captain Daniel J. Carrison, USN, The Navy from Wood to Steel.

Division of Naval History — Navy Department, Civil War Chronology.

Harry Hensen, The Civil War.

William Howard Russell, My Diary North and South.

Philip Van Doren Stern, The Confederate Navy.

W.J. Tenney, The Military and Naval History of the Rebellion in the United States.

Gideon Welles, Diary.

Richard S. West, Jr., Mr. Lincoln's Navy.

Chapter 15

Charles B. Boynton, History of the Navy During the Rebellion, (hereafter Boynton), Vol. I, pp. 320-321.

Virgil Carrington Jones, The Civil War at Sea (hereafter Jones), Vol. I, p. 118.

Lowry Letters.

Official Records of the <u>Union</u> and Confederate Navies in the War of the Rebellion (hereafter ORN, all assumed to be Series I unless otherwise identified). IV: 478-481, 520, 522-523, 545-546, 564-565, 572-573 V: 785.

SEE ALSO:

Margaret Leech, Reveille in <u>Washington</u>.

Chapter 16

Boynton, Vol. I, pp 335-345.

Lowry Letters.

Butler Correspondence, Vol. I. Pp. 213, 226-228.

ORN, V: 689-690, VI: 7, 12, 50, 78-79, 121, 140-141, 173-174.

Robert Means Thompson and Richard Wainwright, eds., Confidential Correspondence of Gustavus Vasa Fox, Vol. I, pp. 367-368.

SEE ALSO;

Robert S. Holzman, Stormy Ben Butler.

Richard S. West, Jr., <u>Lincoln</u>'s Scapegoat General, A Life of Benjamin F. Butler.

Chapter 17

Boynton, Vol. I, pp. 335-345.

Butler Correspondence, Vol. I, pp. 234-235.

Lowry Letters.

Official Records of the Union and Confederate Armies in the War of the Rebellion (hereafter ORA), IV: 586.

ORN, V: 689-670 VI: 120-122, 124, 128, 131, 133, 140-142, 158, 160, 173-174.

SEE ALSO:

Daniel Ammen, The Atlantic Coast.

Chapter 18

Annual Reports of the Secretary of Navy, 1861-1865.

Captain Charles H. Davis, Life of Charles Henry Davis, p. 199.

Jones, Vol. I, p. 325.

Lowry Letters.

ORN VI: 162, 175, 186, 206, 217, 233, 234, 252, 253, 257, 267, 279, 280, 290, 307, 309, 316, 344, 345, 377, 378, 410, 429.

Chapter 19

Lowry Letters.

NDSF — Underwriter.

ORN, VI: 398-399, 400-405.

Chapter 20

George H. Baker, Poems of the War.

Battles and Leaders of the Civil War, II: 63.

Boynton, Vol, II, pp. 141-166, 175-176, 196.

Lowry Letters.

Admiral David D. Porter, Naval History of the Civil War, 189 and ff.

SEE ALSO:

J.T. Headley, Farragut and our Naval Commanders.

Loyall Farragut, Life and Letters of D.G. Farragut.

Captain A. T. Mahan, Admiral Farragut.

W. Adolphe Roberts and Lowell Brentano, eds., The Book of the Navy.

Chapter 21

Lowry Letters.

ORN, XVII: 125-127 XVIII: 529-531, 556-567.

SEE ALSO:

Jefferson Davis Bragg, Louisiana in the Confederacy.

Chapter 22

Boynton, Vol. I pp. 188-196, 214-216, 222-224.

Lowry Letters.

Chapter 23

Boynton, Vol. I, pp. 223-224.

Francis Vinton, Greene, Campaigns of the Civil War-The Mississippi, pp. 23.

ORN, XVIII: 577-578, 582, 585, 588, 600, 602-603, 605-608, 716.

Lowry Letters.

Chapter 24

Francis Vinton Greene, Campaigns of the Civil War-The Mississippi, pp. 23-24.

Lowry Letters.

ORN, XVIII: 589-593, 595 XIX: 5-7, 23, 115.

Admiral David D. Porter, Naval History of the Civil War, pp. 262-262.

SEE ALSO:

John D. Milligan, From the Fresh Water Navy.

John D. Milligan, Gunboats Down the <u>Mississippi</u>.

Chapter 25

Boynton, Vol. II, pp. 270-271.

Butler Correspondence.

Lowry Letters.

ORA, XV: 167, 568-569.

ORN, XIX: 138, 183, 188-189, 192, 247-249.

Chapter 26

James Morris Morgan, "Jim Jouett," in Price and Boatswain.

Lowry Letters.

Chapter 27

Lowry Letters.

ORN, XIX : 446-450, 504, 735-736.

Chapter 28

Lowry Letters

ORN, XIX: 739 Series 2: II: 18-20, 451-452, 506-508.

SEE ALSO:

Raphael A. Semmes, The Confederate Raider <u>Alabama</u>.

Chapter 29

Thomas A. Bland, Life of Benjamin F. Butler, p. 96.

Benjamin F. Butler, Butler's Book, pp. 543, 637-657.

Lowry Letters.

ORN, XXVII: 499-500.

Chapter 30

Lowry Letters.

NDSF — Sabine.

Chapter 32

Charles Oscar Paullin, Paullin's History of Naval Administration (hereafter Paullin-Administration), pp. 250, 277-279, 321-334, 341.

Franklin Delano Roosevelt Library, Hyde Park, MSS Collection, Reigart B. Lowry Letter.

SEE ALSO:

E.H. Hart, U.S. Naval Training System.

Chapter 31

Lowry Letters.

Chapter 32

Lowry Letters.

National Archives, Microfilm of Reigart B. Lowry's Promotion Record.

NDZB.

Chapter 33

Samuel Flagg Bemis, ed., The American Secretaries of State and Their Diplomacy, p. 182.

F.E. Chadwick, The Relations of the United States and Spain: Diplomacy. (hereafter Chadwick), pp. 317, 319, 339.

Rudolph de Cordova, "The Virginius Incident and Cuba," 19th Century, (hereafter de Cordova), LX, December 1906, pp. 253, 980, 984.

S.G. Lapham, "Commander Cushing and the Virginius," Americana, Vol. 10, October 1915, p. 904.

Lowry Letters.

Stephen Bleecker Luce, Seamanship.

Allan Nevins, Hamilton Fish, pp. 670-671.

Pamphlets on the Virginius Affair (hereafter pamphlets).

Charles W. Stewart, "William Barker Cushing," United States Naval Institute Proceedings, XXXVIII, September 1912, pp. 914-915.

Commodore E.B. Underwood, "An International Incident," United States Naval Institute Proceedings, LII, January 1925, p. 84.

U.S. State Department, Message from the President Transmitting Correspondence Between the United States and Spain in Relation to the Island of Cuba, 44th Cong; 1st Sess: March 15, 1875, (hereafter U.S. State Dept. — 44th Cong.), pp. 40-42.

U.S. State Department, Steamer Virginius, 43rd Cong., 1st Sess: House Exec. Doc. No. 30. (hereafter U.S. State Dept.-43rd Cong.) pp. 15, 29, 38, 41, 72, 157.

Jeannie Mort Walker, Life of Capt. Joseph Fry, (hereafter Walker), pp. 215-219, 224, 229, 234-239, 261-262, 269-270, 278-281.

Theodore Dwight Woolsey, Introduction to the Study of International Law, (hereafter Woolsey), p. 367.

Chapter 34

Chadwick, pp. 318-319, 327fn, 342, 350.

George Ticknor Curtis, The Case of the Virginius, Considered with Reference to the Law of Self-Defense,

De Cordova, p. 980.

William B. Hesseltine, Ulysses B. Grant, p. 302

Charles Cheny Hyde, International Law, pp. 115-116, 420-421.

Lowry Letters.

John Bassett Moore, A Digest of International Law, pp. 962-968.

Nevins, pp. 671, 675, 677-678, 680, 684.

New York Herald.

Pamphlets, pp. 1, 5, 9, 10-12, 14-16, 21, 24, 33, 40, 50, 52, 48, 57, 60, 62, 63, 37, 73, 75-77, 90, 108, 132.

U.S. State Dept. — 43rd Cong. Pp. 39, 43, 21, 57, 77-78, 148.

U.S. State Dept. — 44thCong., pp. 42-44.

U.S. State Department, Message from the President Relating to Indemnity, Special Session: Sen: Exec B: March 15, 1875 (hereafter U.S. State Dept .— Spec Sess.), pp. 7, 83, 108-111.

Walker, pp. 293-297, 303-304, 234, 318-319, 322-324.

Woolsey, p. 366.

Chapter 35

Chadwick, pp. 329-345.

De Cordova, pp. 977-978.

Lowry Letters.

Nevins, pp. 673-686.

New York Herald.

Pamphlets, p. 49.

Commodore E.B. Underwood, "An International Incident," United States Naval Institute Proceedings, XXXVIII, September 1912, pp. 86-89.

U.S. State Dept. —43rd Cong., pp. 2, 66-69.

U.S. State Dept. —Spec. Sess., pp. 11-14, 83.

Walker, pp. 230, 244, 325, 327, 330-340, 345.

Chapter 36

Lowry Letters.

Nevins, pp. 675, 680-681.

New York Herald.

Pamphlets, pp. 5, 30, 23, 72, 182.

U.S. State Dept.-43rd Cong., pp. 145, 150, 174, 176, 210.

U.S. State Dept.-44th Cong., pp. 56-63, 65-81.

U.S. State Dept.,Spec. Sess., pp. 5-10, 20-25, 95-97, 102-116.

Walker, pp. 215, 218, 271, 290, 312.

Chapter 37

Log — Canandaigua.

Lowry Letters.

New York Times, December 31, 1874, p. 1.

Chapter 38

Lowry Letters.

New Orleans Daily Picayune, 9/30/1874, 10/14/1874, 12/12/1874.

Paullin-Administration, pp. 347-351.

Chapter 39

Lowry Letters.

Chapter 40

Lowry Letters.

NAPF.

NDZB.

Philadelphia Evening Bulletin, 11/26/1880.

W.G. Shanks, "The Brooklyn Navy Yard," Harper's Monthly, December 1870, pp. 11-12.

Chapter 41

Navy Department — History of the USS Lowry.

BIBLIOGRAPHY

———•○•———

General Historical References

Willis J. Abbot, The Naval History of the United States (2 vols.), New York, 1886.

Daniel Ammen, The <u>Atlantic Coast</u>, (Reprint), New York, 1960.

Bern Anderson, By Sea and By River, New York, 1962.

Thomas A. Bailey, A Diplomatic History of the American People, New York, 1946.

George H. Baker, Poems of the War, Boston 1864.

K. Jack Bauer, Surfboats and Horse Marines, Annapolis, 1969.

Samuel Flagg Bemis, ed., The American Secretaries of State and Their Diplomacy, New York, 1909.

Park Benjamin, The <u>United States</u> Naval Academy, New York, 1900.

Frank. M. Bennett, The Steam Navy of the <u>United States</u>, Pittsburgh, 1896.

Charles B. Boynton, History of the Navy During the Rebellion, (2 vols.), New York, 1867.

Jefferson Davis Bragg, <u>Louisiana</u> in the Confederacy, Baton Rouge, 1941.

Nathan C. Brooks, A Complete History of the Mexican War, Philadelphia, 1849.

Battles and Leaders of the Civil War, (4 vols.), New York, 1884-1888.

Captain Daniel J. Carrison, USN, The Navy From Wood to Steel, New York, 1965.

F.E. Chadwick, The Relations of the United States and Spain: Diplomacy, New York, 1909.

Howard I. Chapelle, The History of the American Sailing Navy, New York, 1949.

P.S.P. Conner, The Home Squadron, (n.p.), 1896.

James Fenimore Cooper, History of the Navy of the United States of America, New York, 1854.

George Ticknor Curtis, The Case of the Virginius, Considered with Reference to the Law of Self-Defense, New York, 1874.

Rudolph de Cordova, "The Virginius Incident and Cuba," 19th Century, LX, December 1906.

R.M. Devens, "Awful Explosion on the USS Princeton in 1844," from Our First Century, Springfield, Mass., 1881.

George Fox Emmons, The Navy of the United States, Washington, 1853.

Francis Vinton Greeene, Campaigns of the Civil War-The Mississippi, New York, 1882.

Harry Hansen, The Civil War, New York, 1961.

E.H. Hart, U.S. Naval Training System, New York, 1889.

William B. Hesseltine, Ulusses B. Grant, New York, 1935.

Alexander Howard, Cruise of the Sabine, Portsmouth, 1861.

Charles Cheny Hyde, International Law, Boston 1922.

Lucius W. Johnson, "Yellow Jack, Master of Strategy," United States Naval Institute Proceedings, LXXVI, 1950.

Virgil Carrington Jones, The Civil War at Sea, (3 vols.), New York, 1960.

Dudley W. Knox, A History of the United States Navy, New York, 1936.

S.G. Lapham, Commander Cushing and the Virginius," <u>Americana</u>, vol. 10, October 1915.

Margaret Leech, Reveille in <u>Washington</u>, New York, 1941.

Stephen Bleecker Luce, Seamanship, New York, 1863.

Edward Chauncey Marshall, History of the <u>U.S.</u> Naval Academy, New York, 1862.

John D. Milligan, Gunboats Down the <u>Mississippi</u>, Annapolis, 1965.

John Bassett Moore, A Digest of International Law, Washington, 1906.

Albert Mordell, ed., Civil War and Reconstruction, Selected Essays by Gideon Welles, New York, 1959.

Robert Weldon Neeser, A Statistical and Chronological History of the <u>United States</u> Navy, New York, 1909.

Charles Oscar Paullin, American Voyages to the Orient 1690-1865, Annapolis, 1965.

Diplomatic Negotiations of American Naval Officers 1778-1883, Baltimore, 1912.

Paullin's History of Naval Administration, Annapolis, 1968.

Charles J. Peterson, The American Navy, Philadelphia, 1848.

Admiral David D. Porter, Naval History of the Civil War, New York, 1886.

Fletcher Pratt, The Compact History of the <u>United States</u>, New York, 1957.

W. Adolphe Roberts and Lowell Brentano, eds., The Book of the Navy, New York, 1944.

Admiral Raphael Semmes, CSN, The Confederate Raider <u>Alabama</u>, (Reprint), Greenwich, Conn., 1962.

Service Afloat and Ashore During the Mexican War, Cincinnati, 1851.

John S. Sewall, "Our Typhoon," New Englander, Article III, December, 1890.

W.G. Shanks, "The Brooklyn Navy Yard," Harper's Monthly, December, 1870.

Professor James Russell Soley, USN, Historical Sketch of the U.S. Naval Academy, Washington, 1876.

Harold and Margaret Sprout, The Rise of American Naval Power, 1776-1918, Princeton, 1939.

Philip Van Doren Stern, The Confederate Navy, New York, 1962.

Charles W. Stewart, "William Barker Cushing," United States Naval Institute Proceedings, XXXVIII, September, 1912.

W.J. Tenney, The Military and Naval History of the Rebellion in the United States, New York, 1865.

James C. Tily, The Uniforms of the United States Navy, New York, 1964.

Commodore E.B. Underwood, "An International Incident," United States Naval Institute Proceedings, LII, January, 1925.

Richard S. West, Jr., Mr. Lincoln's Navy, New York, 1957.

Theodore Dwight Woolsey, Introduction to the Study of International Law, New York, 1895.

Diaries, Biographies, and Letters

Samuel John Bayard, A Sketch of the Life of Robert F. Stockton, New York, 1856.

Thomas A. Bland, Life of Benjamin F. Butler, New York, 1879.

Benjamin F. Butler, Butler's Book, Boston, 1892.

Captain Charles H. Davis, Life of Charles Henry Davis, New York, 1899.

Loyall Farragut, Life and Letters of D.G. Farragut, New York, 1879.

William Elliot Griffis, Matthew Calbraith Perry, Boston, 1887.

J.T. Headley, Farragut and Our Naval Commanders, New York, 1867.

Robert S. Holzman, Stormy Ben Butler, New York, 1954.

Reigart B. Lowry, Letters in my personal collection.

Captain A.T. Mahan, Admiral Farragut, New York, 1892.

Jessie Ault Marshall, ed., Private and Official Correspondence of General Benjamin F. Butler, (5 vols.), Massachusetts, 1917.

John D. Milligan, ed., From the Fresh Water Navy, Annapolis, 1970.

James Morris Morgan, "Jim Jouett," in Prince and Boatswain, New York, 1906.

Samuel Eliot Morison, "Old Bruin," Commodore Matthew Calbraith Perry, Boston, 1967.

Allan Nevins, Hamilton Fish, New York, 1936.

Captain William Harwar Parker, Recollections of a Naval Officer 1841-1865, New York, 1883.

Roger Pineau, ed., The Japan Expedition, Washington, 1968.

William Howard Russell, My Diary North and South, Boston, 1863.

Karl Schuon, U.S. Navy Biographical Dictionary, New York, 1964.

Robert Means Thompson and Richard Wainwright, eds., Confidential Correspondence of Gustavus Vasa Fox, (2 vols.), New York, 1920.

Peter Wager, Defense Against Forced Retirement, Philadelphia, 1858.

Jeannie Mort Walker, Life of Capt. Joseph Fry, Hartford, 1874.

Gideon Welles, Diary, Boston, 1911.

Richard S. West, Jr., Lincoln's Scapegoat General, A Life of Benjamin F. Butler, New York, 1965.

Primary Government Sources

Annual Reports of the Secretary of the Navy, 1861, 1862, 1863, 1864, 1865, Washington.

American Naval Fighting Ships, (A-Q), (5 vols.), Division of Naval History, Navy Department, Washington, 1959-1970.

Division of Naval History — Navy Department, Civil War Chronology, (6 vols.), Washington, 1961-1966.

Ship's File: Allegheny, <u>Princeton</u>, Sabine, Underwriter, and others.

ZB File, Reigart B. Lowry.

Foreign Relations, Washington, 1872, 1873, 1874, 1875.

Francis L. Hawks, ed., Narrative of an Expedition of an American Squadron to the <u>China Seas</u> and <u>Japan</u>, Washington, 1856.

National Archives, Archives Record Group 45, Entry 22, Letters to the Secretaries of Navy from Officers, 1840-1880.

Archives Record Group 45, Entry 24, Logs of the Following Ships: Allegheny, <u>Brooklyn</u>, <u>Canandaigua</u>, <u>Michigan</u>, <u>Mississippi</u>, Pawnee, <u>Plymouth</u>, Powhatan, Preble, <u>Princeton</u>, Sabine, <u>Saratoga</u>, Sciota, <u>Severn</u>, Spitfire, Susquehanna, and others.

Letter of Acceptance as Midshipman by Reigart B. Lowry.

Microfilm of Reigart B. Lowry's Promotion Record.

Reigart B. Lowry's Civil War Pension File.

Official Records of the Union and Confederate Armies during the War of the Rebellion, (130 vols.), Washington, 1880-1901.

Official Records of the Union and Confederate Navies in the War of the Rebellion, (30 vols.), Washington, 1894.

Franklin Delano Roosevelt Library, Hyde Park, MSS Collection, Reigart B. Lowry — letter.

MSS Collection, U.S. Naval Academy.

U.S. State Department, Message from the President Relating to Indemnity, Special Session: Sen: Exec B: March 15, 1875.

Message from the President Transmitting Correspondence Between the United States and Spain in Relation to the Island of Cuba, 44th Cong: 1st Sess: House Exec. Doc. No. ? (torn).

_____, Steamer Virginius, 43rd Cong., 1st Sess: House Exec. Doc. No. 30.

Newspapers, Periodicals, and Pamphlets

Americana

Harper's Monthly

National

New Englander

New Orleans Daily Picayune

New York Herald

New York Times

19th Century Pamphlets on the Virginius Affair, a scrapbook of newspaper articles on the Virginius Affair in the New York Public Library Annex.

Philadelphia Evening Bulletin

United States Naval Institute Proceedings